elephant

This is not the book I expected you to be reading. Nor is it the book I expected to be writing. Nor, indeed, is it the book my publisher expected to be publishing.

Gillian Shirreffs

elephant

Gillian Shirreffs

into books

Elephant is about Shirreffs waiting — to be seen, to be told, to be treated, to be scared, to be relieved, to be healed, to be again. Her contemporary notes share the twin burdens of illness and treatment, but also care as communion. A masterpiece.

Victor Montori M.D.
Professor of Medicine at Mayo Clinic, Rochester

Written entirely in the media of our time - emails, text messages, social media posts - this book is a rare and wonderful thing. Using her own body as the canvas, and tracing the scars etched upon it by multiple medical interventions, Gillian Shirreffs has laid bare the physical and emotional impact of a life-threatening diagnosis. But she has done so with such humanity and hope that we are left in no doubt about the strength of the human spirit and our will to survive.

Elissa Soave
Author of Ginger and Me, Graffiti Girls

A heartfelt, intimate story. The author's ability to show us under the skin of her journey is compelling. A must-read.

Sandra Ireland
Author of Beneath the Skin, Sight Unseen, The Unmaking of Ellie Rook

This honest and very personal account of Gillian's experience will resonate with many readers. The book addresses fundamental life issues in such an accessible and relatable way. I have no doubt it will bring inspiration to readers.

Gillian Hailstones
CEO, Beatson Cancer Charity

Elephant is a smart and witty verbatim record of illness that allows us to name the undercurrents we often try to gloss over. We delve into each page and know: this is strength; this is terror; this is putting one foot in front of another, one word after another; this is how we might record a time when our relationship to all words, to all things, is in movement. Gillian is a funny, forthright guide and *Elephant* is an assertive, bright and tender beast of a book.

Dr Elizabeth Reeder
Senior lecturer in Creative Writing at University of Glasgow; author of An Archive of Happiness, Ramshackle, Fremont

Moving, witty and inspiring.

Olga Wojtas

Writer, journalist and former Scottish editor of the Times Higher Education Supplement; author of the Miss Blaine's Prefect Series

A moving, heartbreaking yet funny and frank look at a terrifying time, told through shared moments with friends and family. A real insight into Gillian's life but one which will resonate with so many. I'm also in love with her parents and I don't even know them!

Laura Boyd
Entertainment reporter at STV News; co-host of What's On Scotland

Elephant is such an important book — sharp, modern, moving and unflinchingly honest. It is also brave, bold and brilliant. Just like the talent that is Dr Gillian Shirreffs.

Heather Suttie
TV and radio presenter; newspaper columnist

Elephant by Gillian Shirreffs

First published in the United Kingdom in 2025 by Into Books
an imprint of Into Creative

ISBN 978-1-7385149-0-8

A CIP catalogue record for this book is available
from the British Library.

Cover and page design by Stephen Cameron.

Typeset in Garamond.

Printed and bound by
J Thomson Colour Printers Ltd. Glasgow G5 8PB

MIX
Paper | Supporting
responsible forestry
FSC® C023105

For sales and distribution, please contact:
stephen@intocreative.co.uk

To Mum and Dad.
Nurses. Runners. Gardeners. Adventurers.
Thank you for everything.

In loving memory of Joseph Cameron Shirreffs.

King Leek. Joe Cool. Dad.
5 June 1937 - 8 March 2025

Preface

Elephant is a book that found me. I'm glad that you have now found it.

It's a book about connections and I'm grateful to be connected to you.

I have to confess this is not the book I expected you to be reading. Nor is it the book I expected to be writing. Nor, indeed, is it the book my publisher, the brilliant Stephen Cameron of Into Creative, expected to be publishing.

The book I was writing is called *The Accidental Immortals*. It's about three women who, in the Scotland of the 1600s, become accidentally immortal.

That was a book about immortality.

The book that found me is about mortality.

My own mortality.

Elephant is the story of a writer diagnosed with breast cancer.

I've been writing about illness for the last 18 years. At first, I didn't have an option. I'd just been diagnosed with multiple sclerosis and was on bedrest, having lost the feeling from my toes to my chest. I was on my own for long periods and I was bored. I was also finding it difficult to sleep due to the nerve pain that accompanied the numbness.

I would wake in the wee small hours with words rattling around my head. During long days of bed rest, I would try to make sense of them. As I did, the words seemed to arrange themselves into long thin poems, which was a surprise, because I'm no poet.

These long thin poems told the story of those initial weeks and all the strangeness that accompanied the sudden onset of serious illness.

After months – and twelve poem-shaped slivers of memory – words stopped waking me up. By this time, though, I was hooked. I'd discovered that when I was fighting with word after word and line after line, I was not aware of the invisible shards of glass sticking into my skin. When I stopped writing, the neuropathic pain would return.

As I ventured back out into the world, the feeling having returned to my body,

I made an unwelcome discovery. People were no longer at ease around me.

I seemed to make them uncomfortable.

I didn't even need to speak to do so. My mere presence was all that was required.

My initial reaction was to feel shame, which I couldn't understand.

I'd done nothing wrong, so it didn't make sense to feel this way.

But I did.

My next reaction was to write.

I wrote stories in which I would give a character a neurological illness to see what would happen to them and the people around them; a sort of working out. It was also my way of trying to connect. To normalise illness. To cry out into the void that it can happen to any of us.

At any time.

It's therefore not surprising that fourteen years later when I found a lump and was told there was 'something' in my right breast that shouldn't be there, my response, once again, was to write.

I wrote my way through diagnosis, treatment and the aftermath of treatment. Sometimes longer pieces trying to make sense of the situation, but most often just short bursts of words. Reaching out to friends, family, clinicians, and to anyone who might notice me waving as I bobbed along on the sea of social media.

If emails, text messages and tweets are the letters of today, then it might not be too grand to call *Elephant* an epistolary for our times.

As I wrote the emails, text messages and tweets that appear in *Elephant*, I didn't expect they would one day form the book you now hold in your hands, but no matter how hard I tried to apply my mind to fiction, the story that is *Elephant* refused to leave me alone. It demanded my attention until I finally succumbed.

It's the craft of the writer to curate and that is the work I found myself doing. I uncovered almost 200,000 words I'd written from July 2021 until September 2023, and I had to decide where, within them, the story lay.

Then there was the problem of what to call this unusual creation of mine. I struggled with words and phrases. At some point I realised that this book is what I keep doing. It's an attempt to normalise illness. To make friends with the elephant in the room.

It reminded me of something.

Years ago, I bumped into a friend of a friend in the street.

She smiled and asked, 'How are you?'

I was struggling with nerve pain and, unusually for me, I deviated from the standard reply.

I didn't say, 'Good. How are you?'

Instead, I said something along the lines of, 'Not brilliant, actually.'

She broke eye contact, muttered about somewhere she needed to be, and was gone.

I went home and, in a matter of minutes, wrote the untitled poem that begins this book.

A book that is not just about illness and my desire to bring the experience of it out into the light but, just as importantly, one that is about friendship and kindness.

On the 24th of May 2022, I wrote the following words:

"In the last 250 days I've had eight cycles of pre-surgical chemo, two surgeries, fifteen sessions of radiotherapy and am now in cycle three (of fourteen) of TDM1 treatment.

I lost my hair, my eyebrows, my eyelashes, my sense of safety, my sense of dignity (did I mention the campylobacter infection that accompanied the sepsis…?), but not my terrible sense of humour.

I couldn't have managed it without each and every person who wrote me an email, sent me a text, posted me a letter, hand-drew me a card, knitted me a hat, gave me a scarf, bought me thick woolly socks, sent me flowers, went for a walk with me, made me banana bread, supplied me with Pan Drops, sent pyjamas across the Atlantic, carefully chose a book for me, dropped off a care package at the door, said a prayer for me, or took a moment to wish me well.

Getting to day 250 takes a village.

I'm very grateful for mine."

They say it takes a village to raise a child. I believe it takes a village to get someone through serious illness.

Some members of my village appear in *Elephant*. Others do not.

This book tells the story of 800 days by carving a path through tens of thousands of words I wrote during that period. The names that appear also represent those that don't.

The people who are mentioned in *Elephant* are real. They are family members, friends, neighbours, colleagues and clinicians. However, some names have been pseudonymised.

For instance, I've renamed my breast cancer team because it feels appropriate to do so. As they all deserve an A star, I've chosen to give them names that begin with the letter A.

Let me introduce you to my village in the order they appear.

Stephanie is a friend from our time living in Wisconsin. She's also a great supporter of my writing.

Clair is my best friend from school. We get up to all sorts of silliness, so luckily for me she lives just around the corner.

Susan is a neighbour and friend. Not to be confused with Susan the Bird who is a local blackbird.

Molly Jo is my brilliant Pilates instructor. I have a class with her every Tuesday and Friday. She taught me when we lived in Wisconsin and now does so online.

Michelle is a doctor in California. I met her through an incredible organisation called The Patient Revolution; in March 2021 we began a shared writing space called love, time, space, and beyond.

Misti is a writer friend who lives in the US. We met 15 years ago when we were both living in Vienna.

Ronnie is my husband and my rock. In September we'll have been married 25 years.

Karen is my one and only sibling, my big sister; she's always there to catch me when I fall.

Maggie is the brilliant Program Director of The Patient Revolution.

Victor founded The Patient Revolution; he is an amazing doctor and the author of Why We Revolt.

Maureen is the lovely HR person at the company I was doing consultancy work for when I was diagnosed.

Diana is my hairdresser of 18 years and my friend.

Karen Scobie is a friend who, very helpfully, is also a naturopathic nutritionist.

Dr Alasdair Kerr is a medical oncologist. I have been known to declare, 'I love Dr Kerr.' Sorry, Ronnie.

Father Jim is the parish priest at the Immaculate Conception in Maryhill.

Elizabeth and Kate were my wise and wonderful doctoral supervisors, now friends. We communicate via a joint WhatsApp group called No Corrections… because at my Viva, I got no corrections.

Jenny was my university roommate; we became fast friends whilst living in Maclay Halls (1988-90).

Dr Fred Spence was Editor of The Polyphony, a medical humanities journal.

Sally is a writer and friend; we met whilst doing our doctorates.

Anna Woods is a clinical nurse specialist; she was there from the outset of my journey, offering wisdom and care.

Mr Andrew Walker is a consultant breast surgeon to whom I will be forever grateful.

Georgi is a writer friend and the best possible lockdown pen pal with whom I wrote a madcap novel.

Kate is Dr Kate Reid of Elizabeth and Kate.

Sam is a vet, a reader, a writer and my friend.

Michael is the co-ordinator of the readers' rota at the Immaculate Conception.

Katie is a friend I met when I facilitated writing workshops for Glasgow Women's Library.

Elizabeth is Dr Elizabeth Reeder of Elizabeth and Kate.

Johanna is a neighbour, a doctor and my friend.

S,C,W&J is an abbreviation for Stephanie, Cindy, Wendy and Jen who are Wisconsin friends.

Ruth is a friend from our time living in Wisconsin.

Alan is a writing teacher and the editor of the fantastic publications produced by thi wurd; if I write any good sentences, the credit goes to him.

Hilary is my friend; we met whilst living in Maclay Halls.

Yvonne is my friend; we also met whilst living in Maclay Halls.

Alison Forest is clinical nurse specialist who showed me kindness and care, which included indulging my terrible sense of humour and excessive use of email.

Cousins refers to a WhatsApp group where I communicate with 'The Shirreffs Girls' a.k.a. Marie, Suzanne, Jacqueline, Karen and Caroline.

Sandra Ireland is an author and a teacher; she ran the Writing Just For You online course I attended during chemo.

Kirsten is a writer and my friend; we met through thi wurd.

Isobel is a friend of my parents and a neighbour from my childhood village.

Gitte is a Danish friend I first met in Edinburgh; she also lived in Wisconsin at the same time as me.

Laura is a friend from our time living in Florida; she's a ray of sunshine in any situation.

Olga Wojtas is the author of, amongst other books, the Bunburry Series; these brilliant audiobooks kept me company through the sleepless nights of chemo.

Sarah was my literary agent from December 2020 until June 2023.

Libbe and her lovely family were our next-door neighbours when we lived in Wisconsin.

Zoe is a writer, a teacher and the Professor of Creative and Interdisciplinary Practice and the Dean of International and External Partnerships at the University of Glasgow.

Jen is a friend from our time living in Wisconsin.

Linsey was the Beatson Cancer Charity's PR & Communications Officer.

EK (Evelyn Kate) is the fabulous daughter of our Wisconsin friends Ruth and Josh.

Jacqui is a teacher, a reader, a writer and my friend.

Alyssa is a writer friend who was the organiser of Connect Fest.

Angela Meadows is a clinical nurse specialist who showed me kindness and care whilst getting me through the latter part of my treatment.

Lynsey is Ronnie's cousin and my friend.

Annabel One is the lovely chemo nurse I saw most often during my 22 infusions; she distracted me with chat about dogs and books.

Annabel Two is another very nice chemo nurse whom I saw less often.

Alice Brooke is a fabulous oncology pharmacist; I loved our pre-chemo chats; she outsmarted each new chemo symptom that came along.

Paul is a superstar; he also manages the Beatson Cancer Charity Telephone Befriender Service.

Lauren was my lovely telephone befriender.

Morgan is a friend from our time living in Wisconsin.

Tony is a writer friend I met whilst doing my MLitt in Creative Writing.

Stephen Cameron is the founder of Into Creative and my brilliant publisher.

Andy is my friend Stephanie's husband.

Heather Suttie is a book loving force of nature; she's also journalist, TV and radio presenter and the founder of the fabulous BookFace community.

Janice Forsyth is a legend of Scottish radio.

Charlene is the amazing Regional Fundraising Manager for Beatson Cancer Charity.

Bella is the brilliant daughter or our Wisconsin friends Jen and Angelo.

Clare English is a journalist, presenter, events host extraordinaire and my friend with whom I share many a coffee and 'tear-ee' bun (as in a bun you can tear).

In addition to the people in my village, there are two organisations that appear in the pages of *Elephant*. Each one offers much needed support to those affected by cancer from the point of diagnosis, through treatment and beyond.

Firstly, **Beatson Cancer Charity**. An organisation I can never thank enough. I used many of their vital services and received amazing support from staff and volunteers alike.

Secondly, **Maggie's Glasgow**, a beautiful haven of kindness and care where I attended the Look Good Feel Better course and made great friends in the aftermath of treatment.

These organisations do incredible work ensuring that no one has to go through the experience of cancer alone.

Icons used in *Elephant*

WhatsApp   Twitter   Email   Google Doc   Phone Text

you are huge
granite grey
yet unspoken
as you sit
sipping
peppermint tea
on the Laura
Ashley chaise
longue opposite

I see brows knit
faces turn flint
if I even hint
at you –
how rude
to allude
to the recumbent
gargantua
in the room

others dance
around you
romance you –
infer
if you were
there
how benign
you would be
how mannerly

you wink
as you sit
unsaid
patiently
sipping
herbal tea
on that chic
pink chaise
by Laura Ashley

July 2021

📞 **Thursday, 8th of July**

To Stephanie

There are no proper graduations this year, but I got sent the gown for a week to take private photos. Can you imagine the nonsense I've been getting up to?!

📞 **Saturday, 10th of July**

To Clair

From Susan the neighbour (not Susan the bird). xx

To Clair

Speaking of! We met Susan the bird on our way back. She was hanging out across from ours.

EXAM SUCCESS

GILLIAN ELAINE SHIRREFFS

Congratulations to our daughter Gillian, former pupil of St Nininans High School, on her graduation from Glasgow University on June 29, 2021, with Doctor of Fine Arts degree D.F.A in creative writing.
Love Mum and Dad xx.

🐦 **Monday, 19th of July**

So, my parents did a thing (they're in their 80s). I'm equal parts mortified and touched. The only other time I was in the Kirky Herald was when I won the Strathkelvin Essay Competition in 1982. I was twelve. About the age I felt when I saw this.

💬 **Thursday, 22nd of July**

To Molly Jo

I'm going to have to cancel my class tomorrow unfortunately. I noticed a lump in my right breast on Tuesday and have a doctor's appointment at 3.05pm tomorrow. Sorry.

Sunday, 25th of July

To Michelle

I'm sorry to have been so absent. It isn't like me.

I noticed a lump in my right breast and have been distracted as a result. It happened a couple of days before the scheduled telephone doctor's appointment for my sore eyes, so it seemed sensible to just tell the doctor about it then, instead of trying to obtain a different appointment.

I did so and she made an appointment for me to go to the surgery to see one of her colleagues. By the time I left the GP surgery I had a prescription for preservative free eye drops, an appointment on Tuesday morning to have bloods done, and an urgent referral to the breast clinic. I'd also heard the words: I'm not going to lie to you, it could be breast cancer. [pause] But it might not be.

I'm currently working hard to employ my usual strategy of folding a difficult thing into the smallest of small squares and slotting it into its very own miniscule box in my brain. I'll open it up when I get a letter inviting me to attend the breast clinic (I should be seen within two weeks). But the frantic tiny wings that had for days been fluttering in the dark corners of my mind made it difficult for me to give my full attention to anything else. Including this lovely document and the important work of the Patient Revolution. And for that I'm sorry. Partly because as distractions go, this seems like a very helpful one.

I hope you're having a great weekend and that the week ahead is a good one.

Very best,

Gillian x

✉ **Sunday, 25th of July**

To Misti

Hi Misti,

It was so good to speak to you the other week. I'm sorry I haven't been in touch since.

I've been a bit distracted because I noticed a lump on my right breast. I've had a phone conversation with a doctor in my GP practice and as a result have an appointment with a different doctor in my practice this afternoon, so that she can do an exam with the intention of then referring me to the hospital. There's a family history of breast cancer on my dad's side, which meant that until I was 50, I was part of a family history clinic, but was discharged last year as my risk was deemed lower over 50.

The previous part of my email was written on Friday. It's now Sunday.

When I left the GP surgery I had a prescription for preservative free eye drops, an appointment on Tuesday morning to have bloods done, a bowel screening kit, a prescription for a four-week course of omeprazole, and an urgent referral to the breast clinic. I'd also heard the words: I'm not going to lie to you, it could be breast cancer. [pause] But it might not be.

The other items on the list refer to ongoing "issues" that haven't been dealt with by a doctor as yet (including a GI bug I had in November that just won't properly go away).

I hope things have been going well with you and that you've done some writing since we last spoke. I was wondering if you want to have another Tuesday Chat (see what I'm doing there, although you might need my thick Scottish accent to hear it) at 9am your time on August 3rd...?

I hope you have a lovely Sunday (as I switch from alliteration to assonance).

Gillian x

---

thi wurd

CALL FOR SUBMISSIONS

thi ... @. · Jul 31, 2021
CALL FOR SUBMISSIONS: Writers, we are putting together a new anthology. Send us your fiction by Monday 16th August. ...

🐦 **Saturday, 31st of July**

A game of darts turns nasty. Inspiration whether you submit or not (but do). Brilliant.

August 2022

Tuesday, 10th of August

To Ronnie

I've seen a doctor and she said it's a lump that needs to be investigated. I'm waiting for a mammogram then I'll have an ultrasound. If it's solid material, they'll do a biopsy. If it's fluid, they'll drain it. She was both serious and efficient.

To Karen

Had the mammogram. The woman was very nice but did say: even if it's the worst outcome, the staff here are very good. x

To Ronnie

Had the mammogram and now waiting for the ultrasound.

To Karen

I've had three biopsies and been told there's something in the breast that shouldn't be there. There's also a lymph node involved. I've had a second mammogram because they inserted a clip in each site and needed to check their placement. I'm waiting to be spoken to again. I'm sorry it's not good news. x

To Ronnie

Can you pick me up?

To Clair

It is the worst. Sorry. They don't have the pathology yet to know what exactly it is. I have an appointment with the consultant next Thursday to discuss the treatment plan. Sorry. xx

To Karen

I was thinking I might drive over to you in a bit and sit in the garden. Would that work? I'm going to walk the dogs just now. X

To Clair

Thanks. I know. I was a very brave girl with those biopsies. It took a long time. But I was warned. xx

To Maggie and Victor of
The Patient Revolution

Dear Maggie and Victor,

I hope this find you both well.

I have some news that isn't great. I had three biopsies today as there are changes in my right breast and in the adjacent area under my arm. I have an appointment with a consultant next Thursday to discuss my treatment plan as he'll have the pathology results by then.

I found a lump and was given an urgent referral. Today's news wasn't what I wanted, but I'm okay (I might be on autopilot right now). I've suggested to the company I'm doing HR consultancy for that they should get a different consultant because unfortunately I won't be able to give the project the appropriate focus.

I do intend to keep writing, though. It's been good medicine for me in the past and I'm quite sure it will continue to be so. I started a piece for the Patient Revolution that I intend to work on this week.

I did write a short story over the last couple of days as a distraction (and because a publisher I like a lot put out a call for short fiction). I've attached it as an antidote to the news I've just given you as I hope you'll find some humour in it. It's not about illness; it's about the soft but dark underbelly of Scottish rural life. (I'm not sure if the title will translate... to give someone daggers is to give them an evil stare.)

Very best,

Gillian x

Daggers

I ruined it for everyone.

That's what May Canning said.

She wasn't wrong either.

The annual whist competition was a highlight in the village calendar. The competition was held in the hall on the first Saturday of the Glasgow Fair. Or, to give it its full name, The Village Hall. Back then this was a recent development, a large sign having appeared on the door in the dead of night.

The sign was the main topic of conversation for weeks. No one admitted to it. Old Davie Lafferty was the prime suspect. He was known to be very handy and had amassed all manner of tools over the years. People said he had a workbench the full length of his garden hut.

To soothe village nerves, May Canning told anybody who would listen that she had it on good authority the council were happy to turn a blind eye. A story a surprising number chose to swallow, including my own parents. Apparently, May's cousin cleaned the house of some high heid yin on the estates and planning committee.

I was ignorant of the extent of the sign ruckus until I overheard a couple of old biddies in Hendry's paper shop. Being a nice big sister, I'd cycled the three miles to pick up Calum's comics and could hardly get served thanks to the two of them going at it hammer and tongs.

'You need to be an actual village to have a village hall. Wouldn't you say?'

'I would, Kathleen. A wee row of houses facing the main road just doesn't qualify.'

'If you ask me, it's not even a hamlet.'

This latest controversy came hard on the heels of the debacle known as The Piggery Incident: a game of dominoes gone wrong. The prevailing wisdom was that even the worst of the resulting violence was entirely justified because if there was one thing the folk in our village couldn't abide, it was cheating, which brings me to the annual whist competition.

Those first two years I was only laying the groundwork. I'd been paired with Fiona Houston who was by nature uncompetitive. She also knew the kids were just there to make up the numbers and wasn't about to make waves; what with the Garibaldi biscuits and the diluting juice. I, on the other hand, wanted my name on that trophy.

The rule was you had to be ten. Any younger and you'd slow things down, people said. This meant my first two competitions were all about watching and learning, biding my time until Calum was old enough. He's an August birthday, so we had to wait until he was almost eleven. We didn't mess about though; we made good use of the intervening holidays in Ballybofey.

My dad used to say Donegal would be great if it had a roof. But we were quite happy. Day and night stuck inside playing gin rummy and whist with my mum's old uncles, card sharks to a man. And they were happy to oblige so long as we kept their glasses topped up.

It was raining the day of the competition, too. I was nonchalant as I signed us up.

'Aw, that's lovely. You and your wee brother,' Helen Fordyce said as she took the two fifty pence pieces out of my hand. 'You're a good girl. I've always said that.'

The Village Hall had been set up the night before. The same women did it every year. Bunting hung from the windows. The ten square tables, in yellow Formica, arranged in a rectangle around the room. Four blue plastic chairs pushed in all the way at each one.

It would be noon before the refreshments came out of the kitchen, so all that was on the long table at the front was the trophy. A big silver cup engraved with the surnames of the winning pair. Canning & Fordyce scratched into the metal over and over.

I made my way to the edge of the crowd, tucking the pencil I'd been given behind my ear and slotting the carefully folded scoring sheet into my trouser pocket. People milled about exchanging pleasantries in their finery, eyeing each other up and down. At twelve and a half, I was virtually invisible.

Charlie Fleming, a widower of some standing, had long ago been given the task of collating the scores after each round. A beanpole of a man, he would lick the tip of his pencil before entering each score into his leather-bound notebook. It was said he neglected himself terribly since his Etta passed, which is why there was a constant stream of women at his door offering soup and solace. Despite this, he was known to be a stickler for propriety, hence his early elevation to such an important position.

Charlie would scan the hall during rounds, taking full advantage of his height as he patrolled. He was wise to all the tricks: a surreptitious wink; a swift kick; a scratch of the nose; someone clearing their throat. None of it was tolerated. He also told you where to sit.

With five minutes to go, he directed me and Calum to the table nearest the gents. Our first opponents were to be Celia Campbell and Alice Dunne. Ordinarily they didn't get on, but it seemed they'd realised that in the game of competitive cards, you keep your enemies close.

Celia and Alice didn't see it coming. They were rarely beaten, never mind by two kids. At the start Alice was making out they were going easy on us. If they were, they regretted it because they left themselves with a mountain to climb and no time to do it. I think they would have been properly angry if it hadn't been for Calum and that big smile of his.

We made our way around the hall in similar fashion: table after table; pair after pair. Each time winning by only a couple of points, so that we didn't arouse too much suspicion. We knew the grown-ups would never believe it was all down to skill.

Soon enough Charlie Fleming was watching our every move.

By the time we sat down at the table with May Canning and Helen Fordyce, I knew word must have gotten round that we were the pair to beat. But those two didn't crack a light.

I'd had my suspicions about Helen Fordyce since Fiona and I played them that first year. Outside of the whist she was never syrupy sweet, and her eye contact was a bit too intense. May Canning was, however, her normal nippy self. They'd hammered us, as though they weren't even trying.

The second year I was alert to it, which is why by the third year I knew Helen Fordyce was in the habit of keeping extra cards in her waistband. I also knew that with Charlie hovering, she'd have to play us fair and square. Her face was a picture.

As Charlie totted up the final score, I felt the long nails of May Canning on my neck, her breath hot in my ear as she hissed that I should be a good girl and admit what we'd done.

'Admit we've been practicing for years, you mean,' I said, smiling, as I turned round to face her. 'Or admit I know what's hidden in Helen's skirt.'

My parents weren't happy about it, but I insisted they put the trophy right smack in the middle of the mantelpiece. Our surname etched into the silver: Wylie & Wylie.

It was said people lost their appetite for cards. The next summer the inaugural Village Flower Show was held in The Village Hall on the first Saturday of the Glasgow Fair. May Canning won the Grand Prize for her Abyssinian Sword Lilies and Helen Fordyce came a close second with her Good As Gold Roses.

It was another four years before I got out. Four years of daggers.

Every time I walked the length of the village to catch the school bus or get the 75 into town. Daggers.

THE END

📧

To Maureen

Thanks, Maureen. I'm just going to try to get through the next eight days on autopilot (with occasional sobbing). I have an appointment with the consultant next Thursday to talk about my treatment plan; he'll have the pathology results by then. In the meantime, I'm going to try to write as that's usually the best distraction for me.

I appreciate your kindness.

Gillian

📧

To Diana

Thanks for making that appointment for me, Diana. I appreciate it.

I'm sorry Ronnie gave you so much detail. I hope he didn't upset you. I'm doing okay, just on autopilot right now I think, and I'm a bit sore after the biopsies. We won't know the full details of exactly what it is or of the treatment plan until next Thursday, so I'm just trying to get through until then.

Thanks again,

Gillian x

📱

To Molly Jo

I'm really sorry to give you this news. Things didn't go well at the hospital. They did biopsies because I have two areas of abnormality in my right breast and one site under my arm. I have an appointment with a consultant breast surgeon next Thursday so that he can discuss my treatment plan; he'll have the pathology results by then. I'd still like to do our class tomorrow but won't be able to do anything lying on my front. I'm sorry to tell you over text but I'm struggling a little and it's easier to write the words than say them.

📱 **Friday, 13th of August**

To Susan

I was the mad woman waving at you from the blue car this morning. I was off to Mass as I'm such a foul weather Catholic. I was at the hospital on Tuesday and got bad news. I have an appointment next Thursday with a consultant to talk through a treatment plan; he'll have the pathology results by then. I realise this is over-sharing (it's not my plan to do this, in general), but it feels like I can over-share with you. I'm a bit all over the place, so that's my excuse if it's inappropriate. x

🐦 **Saturday, 14th of August**

**Saturday night dog walk.
#SummerinScotland #dogsoftwitter**

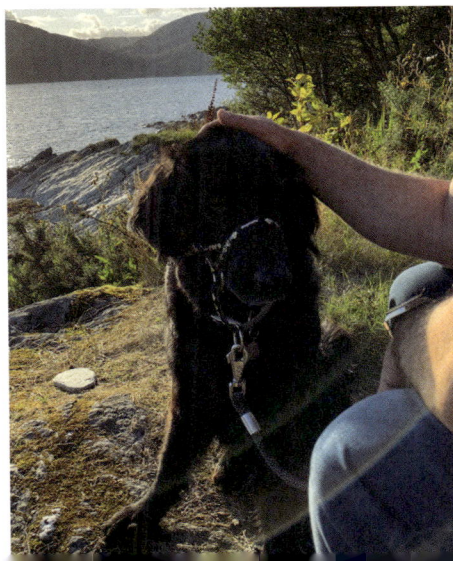

Monday, 16th of August

To Karen Scobie

Hi Karen,

I hope everything is good with you and with the family.

I'm sorry to write to you under these circumstances. I noticed a lump in my breast and was referred to the breast clinic at Gartnavel General. I had biopsies last Tuesday as there are changes in my right breast and in the adjacent area under my arm (they used words like abnormal and diffuse). I have an appointment with a consultant on Thursday to discuss a treatment plan; he'll have the pathology results by then.

I wondered if there was anything specific that you'd recommend in terms of nutrition...?

Gillian x

Thursday, 19th of August

To Karen

I've seen the consultant and am waiting for a chest x-ray. It's hormone negative, HER2 positive. The positive news is that it is very treatable. The first stage is chemotherapy, which should be over four months, and then surgery. I have an appointment with oncologist Dr Alasdair Kerr next Wednesday. X

To Father Jim

The positive news is that it's very treatable. It's hormone negative, HER2 positive, which means that the initial treatment is chemotherapy at the Beatson for four months and then surgery. Thank you for the time you spent with me on Tuesday. It really did help. I took the Child of Prague in my bag today.

Elizabeth and Kate

The positive news is that it's very treatable. It's hormone negative, HER2 positive, which means I'll start with chemotherapy (four months: six cycles at three weekly intervals at the Beatson) then surgery. It's much better news than it could have been, so I'm using that as a galvanising force. And I spent so many years stateside, which I think helps with the positive thinking. Definitely yes to meeting soon. If we could do it before I begin chemo that would be brilliant. I have an appointment with an oncologist next Wednesday to understand his plan for my treatment, but I'm not sure when it will start. Thanks to both of you for your friendship and support.

Friday, 20th of August

To Jenny

Thanks for letting the others know. I'm sorry you had to do that. And thanks for how good you were with me today. I appreciate it. You dealt with it like a star and were really helpful. xx

Tuesday, 24th of August

Direct Message to Dr Fred Spence

Hi Fred, I hope this finds you well. I've written a piece and I'm wondering if you would be interested in it for the Polyphony. If I'm honest, I'm not sure about it myself. It chronicles the nine days between having biopsies for suspected cancer until the day before I met with the consultant to get the pathology results. It stops just short of that meeting because the purpose of the writing was to explore that waiting room of days. When I met him, I was diagnosed with breast cancer (hormone negative, HER2 positive) and will have six cycles of chemo then surgery (then possibly more chemo). Due to the subject matter, I didn't want to send it unsolicited without checking first.

Wednesday, 25th of August

To Misti

I'm so sorry, Misti! I thought I had written to you (how did that happen?!).

It's hormone negative, HER2 positive. The cells are cancerous in the lump I found in my breast, precancerous in the other lump (which is close to the original one) and the biopsy from the lymph node came back as cancerous, too. The treatment is six cycles of chemo at three-weekly intervals then surgery (then more chemo if necessary). The consultant I met with on Thursday is a breast surgeon, so I meet with an oncologist at 10am this morning. He'll give more information about the chemotherapy/timescales.

Again, sorry! I had intended to email on Thursday afternoon. I had a few people to update (family and a couple of friends) and did it on autopilot. I'm so sorry I didn't let you know. That wasn't my intention.

I'll let you know how I get on this morning and please get in touch any time. I'm always happy to tell you what's going on.

G x

To Diana

Hi Diana,

I had my oncology appointment this morning and I'm due to start chemo the week of the 6th of September. The oncologist said this is a treatment where the hair falls out and it happens quickly, so I'm wondering when we should cut my hair. I have an appointment tomorrow, so could do it then or an evening next week if you were able to do that…?

Thanks for your help with this.

Gillian x

Thursday, 26th of August

To Susan

I'm getting my hair cut off today. I had the appointment booked (not for this) and think there's no point waiting until next week. I'm starting chemo on 9/9 (our 21st wedding anniversary) and it seems the advice is the less hair you have the less traumatic it is when it falls out. I've been told it's a certainty with this chemo. So, I may need scarf support in the near future… I have plenty, it's just the styling I'm lacking.

Friday, 27th of August

To Father Jim

Just a wee update. I start chemo on 9/9. It'll be followed by surgery then radiotherapy. I've had my hair chopped (to give you fair warning) because hair loss is a virtual certainty with this particular chemo and the advice is that it's less distressing if it's already short. Thanks again for your prayers. They're much appreciated.

To Sally

It's good to hear from you. My head is a bit jumbled with everything. There's a plan for the chemo now. I start on 9/9. Hair loss is a virtual certainty, so I had my hair chopped yesterday (the advice is to go short in advance so that it's less traumatic when it's coming out). I did some editing on the Patient Record piece and sent it to Fred Spence at The Polyphony. It goes out on Monday. It gives me a way to be open about my new reality without having to talk about it, which is what appeals.

To Victor

I'm doing okay. I do feel a lot calmer since my meeting with the consultant. I know what it is now and that there's treatment for it. I had an appointment with an oncologist on Wednesday. In the time we spoke (75 minutes) he changed his mind about my treatment plan twice, which speaks to the fact he wants it to be the right plan for me. His original plan involved a drug that would very likely have caused nerve damage and as I already have nerve damage, he's not comfortable using it. He ended up with a plan where he reverses the order of the drugs, which will give the option of earlier surgery and the possibility I won't need to have that drug combo (in line with a clinical trial that's about to start in the UK). Depending on how the cancer reacts to the initial drug I may only need it, then surgery, radiotherapy, and a further drug regime. (only!)

I liked that he was adapting his thoughts on my treatment plan as he was getting to know me. It did feel like careful and kind care. He didn't seem to like my terrible sense of humour though. But I suppose I can't have everything.

Thanks for checking in with me. It's much appreciated.

Gillian x

Monday, 30th of August

As in the past, I've found writing to be a helpful way both to distract myself and to process a situation that I don't feel comfortable talking about, as yet.

The Polyphony,
30th August 2021

Gillian Shirreffs has a Doctor of Fine Arts degree in Creative Writing. In it, she explored the relationship between object and illness, with specific reference to multiple sclerosis. In her creative practice, she uses fiction to navigate the world of illness and the essay form to examine hidden medical places and spaces. In this most recent piece, which has been pseudonymised, she uses narrative nonfiction to better understand the new medical situation in which she finds herself.

A Patient Record

TUESDAY 10th AUGUST 2021

The hospital didn't go well. It seemed that everyone from the first doctor who examined me already knew, instinctively. Although that can't really be true.

Perhaps I've been part of the family history clinic for so long that a detailed map of my breasts is part of our collective history, so the difference in my right one was immediately apparent.

The area was outlined in black pen, and I was sent to radiography.

The doctor – I only remember her first name, which was Valerie – walked me out of her office and partway down the next corridor until we reached a point from which it was easy to instruct me the rest of the way.

The radiographer was lovely, and I knew she knew. At least, I thought she knew something that was beginning to dawn on me.

I was then sent for an ultrasound. This doctor was also very nice, but she was in quite a lot of PPE, which was disconcerting. She told me her name, but I wasn't listening. More accurately, I couldn't hear. I was distracted by the room. By what I knew might happen there. I wish I had heard because I'd like her to have a name rather than just a job title as I write about our time together.

The doctor took a long time going over and over the area marked in pen, then the rest of my breast, then the adjacent area under my arm. I stared at the wall, pretty sure of what was coming. But it was still a shock. She explained that there were three abnormal areas: two in the breast and that a lymph node under my arm was also involved. She would have to biopsy all three sites. It would be a lengthy process. I felt immediately sick and asked if I could sit up.

Of course.

Of course, I could.

The atmosphere in the room changed. I had become human, and both the doctor and the nurse followed suit.

They told me it was normal to feel this way. They said other stuff I can't remember. But it was all human stuff.

When I was ready, which was only a couple of minutes, the doctor returned to clinical focus, as was appropriate. She wanted to do her best job. I knew this.

She talked me through each process: the local anaesthetic; the loud noise of the instrument she would use (it sounded like an industrial stapler); the metal clip she would need to insert afterwards to mark the areas she had biopsied.

The nurse readied the instruments as I got my body into exactly the shape she needed. If I was to do two stars and a wish... my wish would be that the doctor had code names for scalpel, blue needle, and long green needle. I'm thinking... jam sandwich, sausage roll, and broccoli quiche.

'I'll have a jam sandwich, thanks, Diane.'

'I think I'm ready for a sausage roll.'

'Not the mini broccoli quiche, Diane. I'll have a family-sized one instead.'

 But. We did it.

I'm guessing twenty-minutes per biopsy. So, an hour altogether. Diane holding my hand and telling me when to take nice long breaths. The doctor (whose name I never caught) explaining, warning me of each sharp sting and loud stapler noise. Me, talking about what I do, my project, Brodie, places I've lived. Whatever they asked, I obliged, slowly shifting from terse answers to stories intended to entertain as I became an old hand at it (Diane's words). It did become harder at the end. It's more awkward to have an area of your armpit biopsied, and more tender. Diane said a couple of times: I think you're getting tired. Are you getting tired?

And then it was over.

I had to go for a second mammogram to ensure there was a record of where the clips were, for the surgeon, or in case someone needed to take more tissue.

After that it was back to the original doctor. Dr Valerie Something. I'm annoyed that I can't remember her surname. She explained that it was not what she'd wanted to tell me. She used words like abnormal and diffuse. She told me cancer treatment wasn't the same as it had been in the 1950s or even ten years ago, or five.

There was a knock at the door. A clinical nurse specialist came in. Anna, I think. Valerie explained Anna had a room next door and I would go in there next so that I could speak to her. Once we'd finished. Valerie told me about Mr Andrew Walker. Anna would set up an appointment with him for next week. He would have the pathology results by then. He would be able to talk me through my treatment plan. I started to cry, and Valerie handed me a fistful of hankies.

I was in the right place. Things have progressed so much. Andrew Walker is excellent. I should take someone with me. This is very important. Did I have any questions? Understandable that I don't. I should go with Anna.

And then I was in Anna's room (Anna? I think she was Anna). Did I want water?

Yes.

More than water. I wanted Anna to go and get the water. I wanted a minute. To process. To breathe.

While she was out, she made the appointment for me, too. Did I have questions? Did I want to talk?

I told her I was worried about how to tell my parents. They're in their eighties. My dad lost his mum to this when he was thirteen.

I should keep it simple. I have something in my breast that shouldn't be there. I've had biopsies. I'll meet a consultant next week who'll talk to me about my treatment plan.

I didn't tell Anna that my parents are nurses (retired nurses, but still nurses) who probably need something other than: I have something in my breast that shouldn't be there. (Me: A toy car? A teeny-tiny teapot?)

I got tired again. Anna continued to speak, but my mind had left the room already.

Anna told me I didn't need to go back through the waiting room, which meant, like one of the wise men, I went back by another way.

FRIDAY 13th AUGUST 2021

It's been a few days since the day in the hospital that didn't go well. Other memories have floated to the surface. I suppose these are the ones that have less light, less heat.

One of the things I've remembered would have added a nice comic touch to my initial record, but it feels more truthful to write it here.

When I was in that first room with that first doctor at the beginning of that time that has stretched in length and breadth, like putty in my mind, but was in fact around two and a half hours, I was asked to take everything off from the waist up.

I did as I was directed.

There was now a curtain between us to spare my modesty, which might be a thought for another time. [Is the act of undressing more personal than the act of lying on a medical plinth wearing nothing from the waist up? Maybe so.]

The curtain was pulled back and there was a pause.

I could feel the pause.

I looked up into the face of the doctor whose surname I had failed to catch.

She looked confused.

I followed her gaze to my chest.

Unbeknownst to me, I had, in fact, failed to follow her instruction.

My chest was not naked. Instead, it was sporting a very comfortable bra.

I spluttered a laugh at the ridiculousness of it. A laugh that came from an area in my gut adjacent to where I'd later experience the desire to vomit.

I apologised. Leapt off the plinth. Took off the bra in full view of Dr Valerie Something and lay back down, excusing my error as nerves and explaining I'd chosen to wear comfy clothing. A bit too comfy, I quipped.

Dr Valerie Something just looked nervous.

Another memory I've been playing, and replaying, is the point at which the very nice doctor (whose entire name I didn't catch), stopped rolling the ultrasound wand and started to tell me what she now knew, because of the time she'd spent going over and over my breast and underneath my arm.

As I watch this happen, I notice that I am still lying on my left side, facing the wall. She tells me that thing she told me. The thing that made me feel sick. And I wonder if the memory has stopped being true. Had I, in fact, rolled back onto my back? It seems I must have. But in the memory as it has become encased in the amber of my mind, I'm lying on my side.

Is it that time stopped in the second before she said those words, leaving me trapped on my left side? Perhaps time split in two. One track follows her as she speaks, the other stays with me as I lie frozen on my side.

Or is it that I was still lying on my side as she began to speak? Was I facing the wall as she told me that there was something in my breast that shouldn't be there?

I don't remember being on my back.

In my memory, as I tell her I feel sick and ask to sit up, I'm lying on my left side.

Can this be true? And if it is, why would it be so?

And even if I was on my back (I must have been) why wasn't I sitting up as she told me?

Is there an issue of time?

A lack of time?

Too little to stop partway through the ultrasound / biopsy continuum to have the person sit up?

To look them full in the face. [Your eyes meeting mine.]

To deliver bad news in a way that is less efficient.

To deliver bad news in a way that embodies care that is careful and kind.

MONDAY 16th AUGUST 2021

Six days after I was told there was something in my breast that shouldn't be there, I got a phone call from Lesley at my GP surgery. She said that Dr Reilly, the doctor who saw me two days after I discovered the thing that shouldn't be there, knew that I'd been to the breast clinic and wondered if I'd like to make an appointment to see her.

I said something similar, if not identical, to, 'Yes. Thank you. That's good of her. I would.'

Lesley said she would check for Dr Reilly's next appointment. After a moment she asked if I could do the 10th of September.

I admit to being confused. I said something along the lines of, 'I can't see her until then? How long away is that?'

Oh. No. Lesley had got it wrong. That wasn't the soonest appointment. Dr Reilly could actually see me on the 6th of September at 2pm. Would that be okay?

I said something along the lines of, 'I don't know. Is that appropriate? I'm going to find out on Thursday I have breast cancer. Is that the appropriate level of support from my GP surgery? I genuinely don't know. I've never been in this situation before.'

Lesley didn't engage with my question. Instead, she said she would pass my comments on to Dr Reilly. She also suggested she go ahead and make the appointment for the 6th of September.

'Sure,' I said. 'That's fine.'

TUESDAY 17th AUGUST 2021

One day after Lesley called, one week after I was told there was something in my breast that shouldn't be there, I received a call from a Glasgow number. I wasn't sure but I thought it might be the number of my GP surgery.

I answered and a female voice told me she was calling from the surgery. She then verified my name.

She didn't tell me her name, but she did tell me she was a colleague of Lesley, who was off. Lesley had left a message for someone else to call me to tell me that she had spoken to Dr Reilly, who wondered if I would be available for a telephone appointment on Friday.

Yes. Yes, I would. Thank you.

This second phone call took place on the day I'm writing about it. All my other words have had a greater time lag.

I don't know what to think or how to feel about this episode. It reminds me that in three days when I speak to Dr Reilly, I'll have been told what is in my breast and in the lymph node that was biopsied.

I'll know that thing that I don't yet know.

I desperately want our conversation to be about the fact that this is something that can be treated; can be fixed. I desperately don't want it to be about anything else and as I type these words, I have tightness in my chest and nausea in my gut.

WEDNESDAY 18th AUGUST 2021

Lesley phoned back.

Poor Lesley. Imagine having to make the call. Drinking a coffee first to stall, to galvanise. That's what I would do.

Hi. It's Lesley from Abercorn. I spoke to Dr Reilly and she's able to fit you in on Friday.

I'm a little confused at this point because Lesley's colleague had already covered this ground.

She's not sure exactly when but she'll try to do it before her clinic starts (did she say clinic?) unless something comes up. So about ten thirty. Or maybe eleven. Just depending.

I'm not sure of Lesley's exact words, but this is the information they conveyed. And she sounded nervous. In that way when you're forcing yourself not to sound nervous.

She ended our conversation with, 'Take care.'

A WAITING ROOM OF DAYS

It's eight days since I was told there was something in my breast that shouldn't be there.

During this in-between time, I've experienced something that might best be described as fear. I've previously only known this feeling in very short bursts, like when one of the engines stopped working in the plane that I was travelling in from Dallas to Boise at some point in the early 2000s. We were over the Sawtooth Mountains when the pilot made the announcement. We practiced the brace position for the last half hour of the flight and landed at an adjacent airfield; the main airport being deemed too risky. A livestream of our descent and the ambulances and fire engines chasing us round and round until we came to a final stop was aired on the local channels, interrupting normal programming. If this feeling is indeed fear, it has an added quality this time around; it eddies and billows; unannounced it catches you in the gut, the throat.

When I was told that there was something in my breast that shouldn't be there, I was also told this would be the most difficult time. Waiting. I was told that when I speak to Mr Andrew Walker he will have a treatment plan, which will be better than this not knowing.

Maybe that's true. Maybe the intrusive thoughts are worse than the knowledge to come. I'll know tomorrow.

He almost had to break my ribs to get images that would pass muster (I think there's still a slight question mark on that.) I'd say I'll be pretty bruised. It was fine though. And he (Adam) was very nice.

To Maggie

Thank you, Maggie. I really appreciate your kind wishes. It makes me happy that my writing might be of use (and hopefully gives some pleasure in the reading of it, even if the subject matter is difficult).

I start chemo on the 16th and will be in the cancer centre for a full day each time, so my plan is to take both my laptop and a book with the hope I'll be able to read or write. Better still, both.

I hope everything is well with you. Thank you for reaching out. It's much appreciated.

Gillian x

Tuesday, 7th of September

To Katie

Thank you, Katie. I really appreciate you reaching out. I'm doing much better now (it's amazing how quickly things become normalised). There's a treatment plan involving chemo, surgery, (maybe more chemo), and radiotherapy, which whilst it sounds awful is a treatment plan that they're very positive about, so I'm just going to take it one day at a time and focus on doing the best I can that day (in terms of keeping myself as healthy and well as I can through the process). I've no doubt there will be days that are more difficult than others, but that's what Team Gillian are for, so if you fancy jumping on board you'll get a warm welcome. There's not much involved, just being your usual wonderful, positive self and staying in touch.

I hope everything is going well with you.

Gillian x

Wednesday, 8th of September

To Clair

We're having our anniversary a day early to take advantage of the weather and going on a boat trip. I hope you have a good day. xx

To Diana

Thanks, Diana. I hope you're having a brilliant holiday.

My chemo was delayed until next week, so I now start on the 16th. All the more time to enjoy my pixie cut (if that's what it's even called). I did a writing retreat last week with a friend - we've co-written a crazy novel and were editing it. She took a pic of me with my new hair. I've attached it so that you can see your handiwork without me in a mask (I'd just left it to dry on its own). I now have something to look forward to when it grows back in because I actually like it.

Thanks for being such a good friend.

Gillian x

To EKR

I just had to check my letter from the hospital (one of the many) as I have an appointment on the 15th (then I forgot to reply). The appointment isn't until 2.30pm, so the morning would work. Yay! It would be outside at ours, if that's okay because I start chemo the following day and will need to be very careful (although I don't really think I could be any more careful). I'm VERY excited about the hat. It sounds gorgeous. I was offered paperwork for a wig the last time I was at the Beatson and said thanks but no thanks.

We went out on Loch Lomond the day we got married (21 years ago) so Ronnie likes to have a re-do each year (on the nearest body of water, which this year happens to be Loch Lomond again). #TimeFlies #SeptemberInScotland

Thursday, 9th of September

To Johanna

Thank you for our anniversary gift! It was very kind of you to think of us. Thanks also for the chat the other night, Johanna. I really appreciate your words of support. xx

Friday, 10th of September

To Sally

These arrived! How incredibly kind and thoughtful of you. There might have been a wee tear. Thank you! xx

Sunday, 12th of September

To Ruth

Thank you so much for the beautiful flowers! xx

To Victor

Hi Victor,

I hope you had a great trip and a good journey home. It was lovely to see you in Glasgow. I'm sorry for my woeful sense of humour (in Glasgow we would refer to it as my "dreadful chat"). It seems a cancer diagnosis has turned me into the world's worst stand-up comedian.

It was good to talk to you though, both about writing and about my current situation. You're always so encouraging and every encounter, no matter how fleeting, is always in 'high definition'.

Also, I loved my walk home: two miles stomping through the city feeling healthy and strong.

With gratitude,

Gillian

To Sally

Are you responsible for this lovely thing?

To Alan

Hi Alan,

You've no idea how much this means to me. I'm beyond thrilled that 'Daggers' will be included in the anthology. It was a direct response to your brilliant call for submissions. I really hoped it would make it in, but I'd prepared myself for a rejection given all the amazing submissions I knew you'd have. Writing it was exactly the distraction I needed at exactly the moment I needed it. So, thank you.

I start chemo on Thursday. I should have started last week, but it was delayed. So as you can imagine, things are a bit difficult and strange at the moment. I do intend to get through this, though. Out of sheer bloody mindedness, if nothing else. I'll also have surgery, radiotherapy and maybe more chemo. The full trifecta. Having said all of that, I'm doing okay. It was a lot to get my head around, but I'm sleeping again; I've stopped losing weight (I was the incredible shrinking woman for a couple of weeks); and I'm no longer crying while walking the dogs or driving. It's amazing how quickly a thing can be normalised. And today, I got an acceptance from my favourite press. So today is a very good day.

I'd love to catch up sometime for a chat. It would need to be a walk because I do have to be even more careful than normal now, but if that would work for you, I'd love to see you. I'm also hoping for random writing prompts. Yours are always the best!

Thanks again,

Gillian

Wednesday, 15th of September

To EKR

It was great to see you and I love my hat and my pen. It was so incredibly kind of you to take the time and care to make my beautiful hat. X

To Johanna

I've got my pre-chemo bloods, etc. at the Beatson this afternoon. I plan on asking about the injection I mentioned to you, to get a bit more detail about exactly when I need to have it. Thanks again for saying you'd help with it! You've no idea how much it means. xx

To Johanna

Thanks! I think the injection needs to be given within 24 hours of the chemo, and I've to be at the Beatson for 9am tomorrow morning for them to start the treatment. But I'll check the details when I'm there for my bloods today. My plan is to walk this afternoon. It somehow makes me feel better about going if I walk there. xx

Thursday, 16th of September

I start chemo today, so I'll likely be writing and posting about the humanity there is to be found in illness. My community on here are writers, artists, medical humanities folk, MS folk, and people passionate about patient care, so I'm guessing this will be okay. #breastcancer

To EKR

Thank you! I was advised to pack as though I was going on a very long train journey, so I have ALL of the things. Just waiting to be called. x

To Johanna

I have the canula in now and we're waiting for the treatment to arrive. I explained you had kindly said you would do my injection. It's to be done on day 2 or 3 and is subcutaneous. The nurse said she would photocopy the paperwork for you. Thanks again for this! xx

To Johanna

I'm reading a book one handed. It's harder than I would have thought.

To Johanna

I had MS brain there and got my days wrong! It has to be tomorrow evening or Saturday morning. xx

To Karen

I've had saline, my first infusion (90 mins), a 30 minute flush, now I've just started a pre-med infusion (1 hour), then another flush, then my Dexa-bla,bla (another 90 mins, I think). My chemo arrived late so I was sitting with just my cannula in for a couple of hours. It's going okay though. The nurses are nice. Understated but nice. And there's no chat in the seven-chair room. Reading or quiet contemplation seem the order of the day. xx

To Karen

I might be toying with a wig… Claire (sister-in-law) knows someone who does very good ones. I might never wear it, but it might be good to have the option… I've seen the gamut today and there's a woman opposite who I presume has a very good one (she's clearly had a lot of treatment from the whispered chat with the nurses).

To Karen

That's what I'm thinking. I'll text Claire later. They've said no hair by cycle 2 which is in 3 weeks. So I should maybe have decided earlier…

To Karen

Not yet. I took a reaction to the antihistamine, of all things! I'm okay now but they're just going to leave it a little bit. X

To Karen

Ward patients are down. We're a full house. It's all go!

To Karen

I'm on my final infusion. 35 mins to go.

To Clair

Still got 30 mins of my final infusion left. They think I should be ready to go by half six. I had the one they needed to observe first. It's been infusion/saline/infusion/saline all day.

To Clair

No. It was silent. No chat at all.

To Clair

I was the youngest though. The closest in age was a very good-looking woman born in 1964. Next in age was a man born in 1960.

To Clair

They check name, age, and address every time they add a new infusion. I'm sure no one missed anything I said with my loud teacher voice.

To Johanna

I finished at 6.30pm, so could we do closer to 7pm tomorrow? x

To Johanna

That would be great! Thank you so much! Ronnie is just driving me home now. xx

To Johanna

Glad to have escaped and not see another needle until tomorrow night. I had a wee bit of a reaction to piriton, bizarrely, so I needed to be assessed before they proceeded.

To Karen

I'm okay. My tummy feels a wee bit tender, but otherwise, good. x

To S, C, W&J

Thank you for the beautiful flowers. They arrived yesterday, which was lovely timing. I had my first chemo today. I was in the chemo suite from 9am until 6.30pm as I had a number of infusions that had to be interspersed with saline flushes and observations. I did react to one drug, but it was bizarrely the antihistamine that was injected into the port as part of a premed. It was deemed a hypersensitive reaction as opposed to an allergic one, but it did delay the treatment a little. Having said all of that, it was okay. The staff were nice and the day didn't drag in the way you might expect. And I'm feeling okay tonight, so a lot to be grateful for. Including each of you and your healing thoughts and kind wishes. xx

Friday, 17th of September

To Susan

Thanks for reinforcing that I should phone

the helpline. The woman was lovely, said it was a chemo flush that should last 24 hours or so, that I should use an unscented moisturiser (she was having none of my: I've got a not-very-scented moisturiser), and take a Claritin (because I took a reaction to the Piriton injection yesterday). Thanks! X

To Johanna

I feel a wee bit seedy at the moment, so I'm just about to have a slice of toast to see if it'll help. Just after 7 is great. I've to take the injection out of the fridge an hour before, so I'll do that now. Thanks! xx

Sunday, 19th of September

To Susan

Just back from QUEH… I had a horrible night last night, so called the helpline at 8am and they organised for me to be seen at the SATA unit. No infection, just effects of the chemo, which is good (but not pleasant). x

Monday, 20th of September

Elizabeth and Kate

Awful. Sorry. I wish I could say something else. I'm waiting for the Beatson to call to see if they can change the anti-nausea as it's not working. I spent three hours at QEUH yesterday morning because I'd had such a bad night so had to be checked out: bloods, heart trace etc. I hope it starts to improve soon. X

To Father Jim

Just a wee update. I've had a really rough few days with side effects from the chemo. I know you're praying for me and it's much appreciated.

To Father Jim

Thank you. That's really kind of you. It hit me like a truck Friday into Saturday and I ended up in the QEUH for a couple of hours yesterday morning to make sure I didn't have an infection. No more morning Masses for me for a bit, I think.

To Johanna

Thank you. I slept for an hour and don't feel quite so bad now. I even ate an oatcake when I got up because I felt a bit hungry. xx

To Johanna

Even just having been able to talk to you really helped. I think I was at my wits end and am feeling more positive. Ronnie might be a little overexcited as he's now making some chicken noodle soup. I'll try a small bowl. xx

To Johanna

I'm really sorry to bother you. I just took my temp because I was feeling really warm and it's gone up to 37.6. x

To Johanna

I phoned the helpline number, and she said to pack a bag. She'll phone me back to say where to go at the Queen Elizabeth.

To Johanna

Because I have a temperature they've put me in a general area and given me a Covid test. There are people coughing so I told them I felt a bit unsafe. I'm now in a side room and have been told it'll be an hour for the Covid test to come through. x

To Johanna

All I can hear is people coughing outside in the waiting area.

To Clair

I haven't had bloods done yet. But I am Covid negative. Quelle surprise. So at least I'm now in a safer bit of the hospital. X

To Karen

My neutrophils are low, so they need to put me on an IV antibiotic.

Tuesday, 21st of September

To Johanna

They've admitted me. I'm having IV antibiotics. xx

To Karen

Almost finished my three-hour infusion of antibiotics (20 mins to go, I think). It's hard work this trying to be well business!

To Karen

My neutrophil count is 0.1 so I'm in an isolation room.

To Karen

I just wish the infusion could be done. It's making me feel horrible, but I completely understand how important it is. X

To Karen

I'm being nursed by a lovely friend of Suz and Jack though, which was really reassuring.

To Johanna

I slept for about an hour. I'm trying to eat a jelly just now. And my veins are starting to refuse to give up their blood. xx

It seems I'm rubbish at chemo. I was admitted to the QEUH last night and will likely be here for a few days as I'm neutropenic. This isn't the postdoc I would have chosen, but I'm receiving excellent care that is both careful and kind. #breastcancer #medhums

To Johanna

Thank you! Ronnie is going to drop some stuff off just now. I can wave at him through the window, I think. xx

To Molly Jo

I was admitted to hospital last night because I have an infection and my neutrophil count is 0.1. I have my laptop and wondered if we could still have our class but it be more you assessing the best way for me to be with the bed / pillows / breathing, etc.? x

Elizabeth and Kate

I'm neutropenic, which is a bit dangerous, hence the isolation room. I'm doing okay though. I've been sleeping on and off for the first time in days. And I have a view out to the Campsie Hills.

To Johanna

I'm feeling pretty awful again. I've had periods where I felt more normal, but this afternoon hasn't been the best. I'll get there though. Thanks for checking in. xx

To Johanna

Yes. Dreadful diarrhoea (sorry!). It feels like the toilet is a biohazard area.

To Johanna

I know. I've got a lot of abdominal pain, too.

To Johanna

I'm all clammy again. I'm getting a bit worried. xx

To Johanna

They've been putting in calls because I'm in the renal ward but I'm not a renal patient. I think Ronnie's going to drive up because he's worried, but I'm not sure what that will do. xx

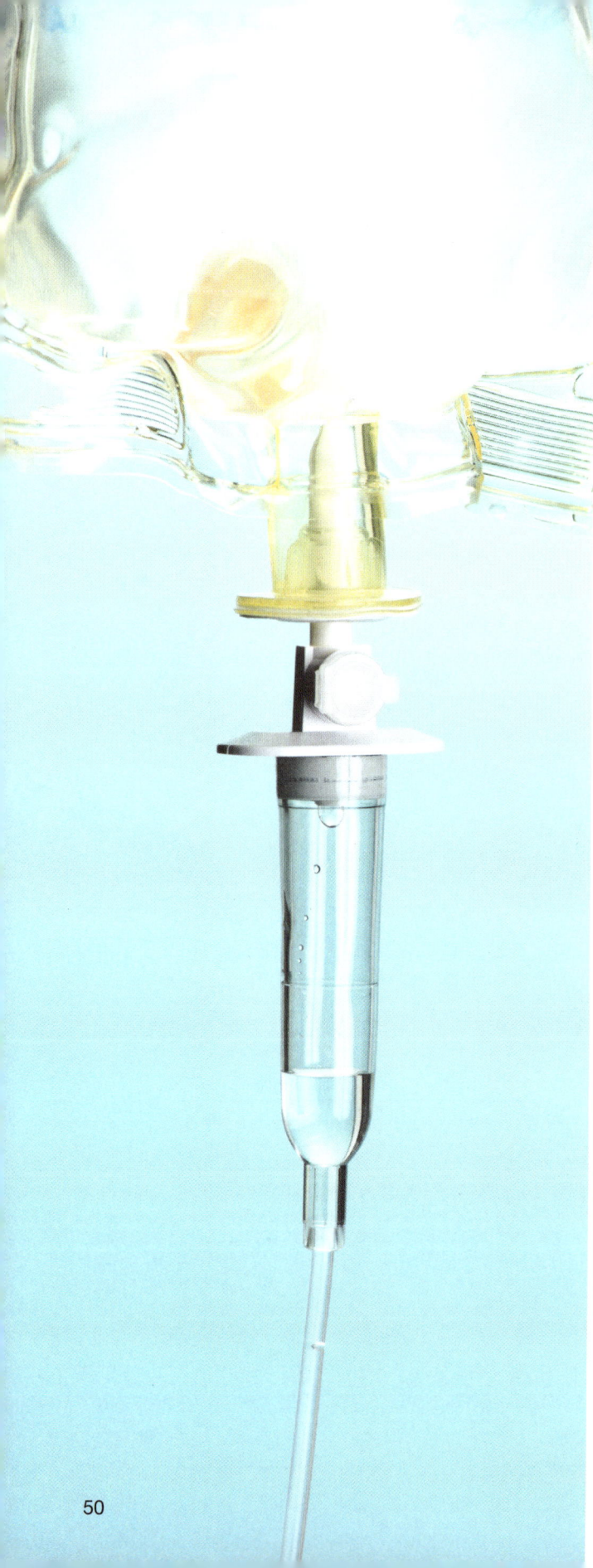

To Johanna

I've just finished more fluids. I had paracetamol for the pain, but it hasn't touched it. I'm due to get more antibiotics overnight.

Wednesday, 22nd of September

To Johanna

I slept most of last night, which was great. I can't thank you enough for the care and support you're showing us. I noticed a real change in Ronnie last night after he popped down. Him being reassured helped me redouble my mental effort to get through this.

To Karen

Haven't had today's results. Apparently, yesterday's ones were concerning. xx

To Johanna

Just a quick update. I'm feeling much better. The nausea has pretty much gone, my appetite has returned, and I have less GI pain. My numbers have also started to creep up (my neutrophil count was at 0.2 today after two days at zero). Thank you again for all your kindness.

To Michelle

Thank you, Michelle. This is the first time I've been on here for a while, which is not to say that you / it haven't been in my thoughts.

It seems chemo is dreadful. Just awful. This is a thing you can know in the abstract without any concept of what it might be to actually know the reality of it. There is also a certain amount of Glasgow bravado that causes you to run into the thing thinking there's nothing else for it so just get it done. Not that you think that it'll be fine. You know it will be dreadful, but you propel yourself forward regardless.

Getting it done, now there's the rub. There's the day itself (and clearly, I can only speak from my experience of the particular breast cancer that I have) and then there are the days that are to follow. It's about these days that I'll now write. Days that are, for now, very much present tense.

I have been a medical boarder, or cuckoo, (my name for a medical patient not able to get a bed in a medical ward) in the renal unit of Glasgow's Queen Elizabeth University for almost three days now, having been admitted after midnight on Monday night. By this point I'd been in the hospital for six hours. The first eighty minutes were spent in the general populace area whilst it was determined whether or not I had Covid (via a lateral flow wing-and-a-prayer test). Having expressed my concern as a chemo patient in a waiting room full of sick people, I was allowed to stay in an examination room. Thanks to a negative test result, I was moved to a chair in a corridor in a Covid secure area and forty or so minutes later, to a receiving bed.

I'm afraid the reality of those afterwards-days has rudely intruded (in the form of biohazard level diarrhoea). More later (words, hopefully).

G x

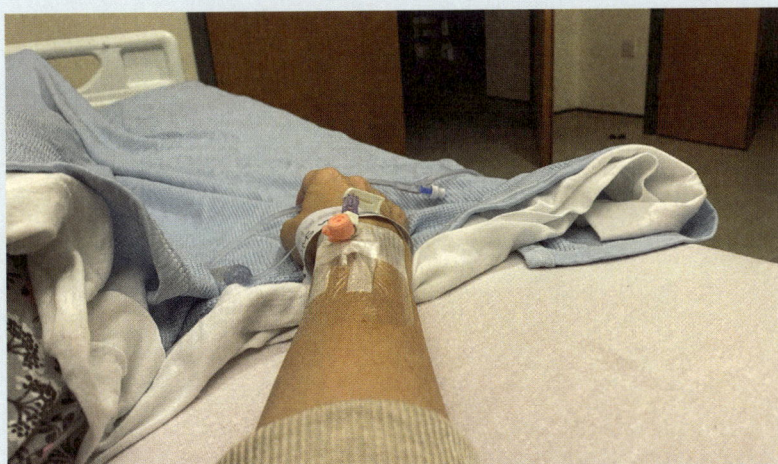

Thursday, 23rd of September

To Victor (05:19 Minnesota time)

I'm really sorry to reach out but I wonder if we could have a call today? I need some advice around advocacy and my care. I'm in hospital as I'm neutropenic and, it seems to me (which makes no sense to anyone else) that my body is reacting to certain things as though I'm hypersensitive (immediate gastric distress, hot flush, red/hot/sore tongue). It's happened with IV fluids (they kept giving them and the symptoms became more severe with each infusion) and this morning it happened when I had a slice of toast and jam. I would never have reacted this way in the past. I'm not sure how to explain it in such a way that I'll be listened to, so would appreciate your advice, if you have any time today.

To Victor

I'm still waiting for a doctor to come and see me. It's at the stage where I'm scared for anything to be put into my body. And thank you so much for answering.

To Victor

I'm a medical boarder in the renal ward, so the staff here are only administering what the medical team prescribe. My care is under the medical team.

To Victor

A healthcare assistant answered my buzzer and said he would mention how I was feeling to the nurse. He also told me that everyone is very busy.

To Victor

I just saw the doctor in charge of my care. Microbiology have confirmed I do have a bacterial infection (campylobacter) but my neutrophils are now 4.7, so she's very happy with me. She thinks I've developed hypersensitivities due to the chemo and asked me just to be careful and take Claritin. She doesn't think I need to worry that it'll become a severe allergic reaction. I feel much better now that she's given me a context to what is going on. I know this won't be an easy journey but understanding what's happening and why is a real help. Thank you again for your support. I really am sorry to have reached out in panic (you should be less nice to avoid crazy, frightened Scottish women from getting in touch). Thank you again.

Elizabeth and Kate

It's too cloudy for my Campsies view today, unfortunately. In good news, my neutrophils had been at zero for two days (meaning I effectively had no immune system) and today they'd jumped to 4.7, which means I'm safe to go home.

Microbiology have confirmed that I have a bacterial infection, but I now have an immune system that should deal with it. I've been getting IV broad spectrum antibiotics for an infection of unknown origin since I was admitted, so hopefully it will clear up soon. x

Elizabeth and Kate

Home this evening. I'm just waiting on my discharge paperwork/medication.

To Karen

I'm waiting for Ronnie to pick me up. Xx

To Victor

I'm home now. Thank you for being there for me. When we spoke a month ago you told me there would be dark times ahead and this morning was the darkest time yet. But in my fear, loneliness, and illness I was able to reach out to you in the act of writing. Writing the aspect of my experience I felt no one was listening to and by doing so I was much better able to articulate what was happening with me to the doctor and as a result I got answers that didn't change or fix anything but that gave me a context to better understand what was happening, which in turn took away some of the fear and loneliness. Thank you. I will try my best not to get to this stage again though because I recognise it's not fair to wail across the ocean with a problem over which you have no control. But I'm very grateful that in my dark time you responded.

Friday, 24th of September

To Susan

I have a temp again so have been told by the helpline to go to the Queen Elizabeth.

To Johanna

I'm in a full waiting room, so let's hope I'm not neutropenic. I do have one of Ronnie's high tech face masks on though.

To Johanna

I'm sitting next to this sign…

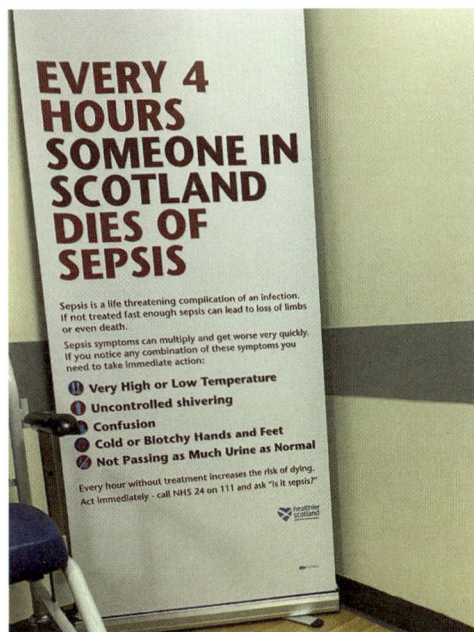

53

To Father Jim

I got out last night, but I'm spiking a temp again so have been sent back to the Queen Elizabeth and am in a waiting room.

To Johanna

The room got very full so I asked the receptionist if I could sit in a more isolated spot, which she kindly did, so I feel safer as I don't have anyone standing over me now.

To Johanna

Still waiting. I think my bloods were done about an hour and 20 minutes ago. I'm a bit lightheaded so I got some water. I hope you're having a good Friday night doing something fun. xx

To Karen

I'm afraid I'm back in.

To Johanna

I just saw a very nice doctor. He explained that my blood count has gone in the opposite direction and is now unusually high, suggesting an infection. He's going to try to get me a bed.

Saturday, 25th of September

To Johanna

Morning! Thank you for checking in. I got a room at 1.30am and it is lovely and quiet. I slept until I was woken to have my obs done, which were fine. BP 104/65, which is much more normal for me. I hope you have a lovely day!

To Susan

I got a bed in a General Medical ward at one thirty. Ronnie just brought me in a boiled egg. They admitted me because my blood count had gone in the opposite direction and was unusually high. It seems my immune system is being its usual rogue self.

To Karen

I'm in until tomorrow. My neutrophils are over 40, so they'll check again in the morning.

To Karen

I have fish fingers, chips and beans ordered for dinner. x

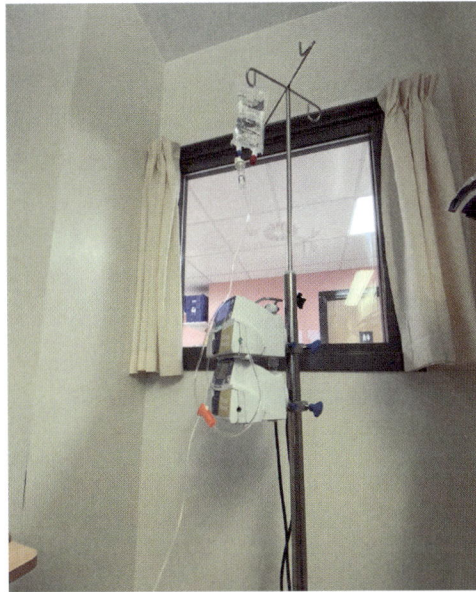

Apparently I'm also rubbish at being discharged. I was back in the QEUH within 24 hours. (boo!) Hopefully I'll be back home tomorrow. I knew this would be a hard road, but it seems that's no preparation for the reality. What I wouldn't give for some good old Glasgow swagger.

I may be back in the QEUH, but what a view I have from my window. #MotherGlasgow

To Father Jim

I was admitted last night, but at least I have a great view from my window. Thanks for all your prayers. I really appreciate the support.

Elizabeth and Kate

I'm actually feeling much better in myself, but I think the reality of the diagnosis hit me today, maybe for the first time, so I've been a blubbering wreck. I'm not sure there's much to be done other than just experience the emotions as they arrive.

Sunday, 26th of September

To Susan

As they would also say in Glasgow, I'm hingin like a washin.

To Susan

Still in the QEUH. They're going to do my bloods again this morning and let me out if they're happy with them. I still feel dreadful, but the nausea and abdominal pain have pretty much gone. If you have any magic potions, speak up.

To Hilary

Thanks. I'll be okay. It's just post chemo stuff. Hopefully it'll go more smoothly next time. xx

To Karen

Do you want a challenge…? Ronnie's been unable to locate Robinson's Lemon Barley Water. He could only find lemon on its own. xx

To Clair

I have a notion for a slice of carrot cake…

To Yvonne

Thank you. And thanks to Doug! I do need some company but you're right that I can't really see people, so maybe we could figure out some gentle FaceTiming (gentle because everything is feeling a bit harsh and rough just now). I was incredibly lonely in the hospital last night and just didn't know what to do. I know I have great friends and family, but I was here on my own and I've never felt so alone. I'm thinking I'll need to figure out how to ask for help because I've now realised, I'm just not going to be able to do this on my own. xxx

To Father Jim

My wee heart was very sore. I'm feeling a bit better today as Ronnie has been here since ten. I'm hopeful they'll let me out today. There's still a bit of a question over my bloods, but hopefully they'll be good enough to get out.

✉ Monday, 27th of September

To Alison

Hi Alison,

I realise it's the September weekend, so I'm not sure if anyone is working, but if there is, I'd appreciate if someone could give me a call.

I've had a difficult time since my first lot of chemo and would really appreciate the opportunity to speak to someone. I was admitted to QEUH last Monday as I was neutropenic and had an infection. I was discharged on Thursday, readmitted on Friday and discharged again yesterday. I've been feeling quite anxious and alone and would really appreciate the opportunity to talk to somebody.

Many thanks,

Gillian

To Karen

Things still aren't great, but I'm doing the best I can. x

To Karen

I contacted the breast cancer nurses this morning, but the message said no one would be picking up any messages until Wednesday. X

To Karen

It's a bank holiday.

Tuesday, 28th of September

To Susan

Ronnie just got me to come out the front to get some vitamin D. I'm feeling a bit better but still have diarrhoea, so I'm not sure how to get nutrition to stay in my body. I had a challenging morning trying to organise to get bloods taken tomorrow as per my discharge letter. Three calls to my GP (each with a 20-minute wait in their telephone system), one of which was dropped by them when I was put on hold. And an equally lengthy call to the community phlebotomy service. They clearly want to keep my brain active. x

Wednesday, 29th of September

To Susan

I'm starting to feel much better… I'm in the suntrap garden.

To Susan

I spoke to my oncology nurse. She said that there are many ways to skin a cat and that I shouldn't worry about the next treatment because they'll figure out how to make it easier for me. Maybe weekly chemo as opposed to every 3rd week. She said they would do whatever they could for me. And my GP surgery phoned to say they would fit me in for my bloods.

To Jenny

It was lovely to see you on Facetime. Something like this happening makes it clear what's important and who's important. xxx

Thursday, 30th of September

To Sally

Thanks, Sally. I started to turn a corner a couple of days ago so am feeling a lot more like myself again, thank goodness. I'm trying to build myself back up before my next chemo session, which is a week today. Thanks for checking in and letting me know you're thinking about me.

To Susan

In today's news… seems like my hair is coming out. But I am still feeling much better than I was. x

To Susan

I have an MRI tomorrow afternoon. How do they MRI your breasts? I remember a friend going for one in the US and I think she said they had her lie on her stomach…?

To Susan

Thanks. I like to mentally prepare, and MRIs aren't my favourite thing, so I'm trying to get into a good head space. Can the lymph node be imaged at the same time?

To Susan

Thanks. Any MRI strategies? I'm changing my mindset (notice I'm eliminating the word try) to thinking about it as a friendly space…

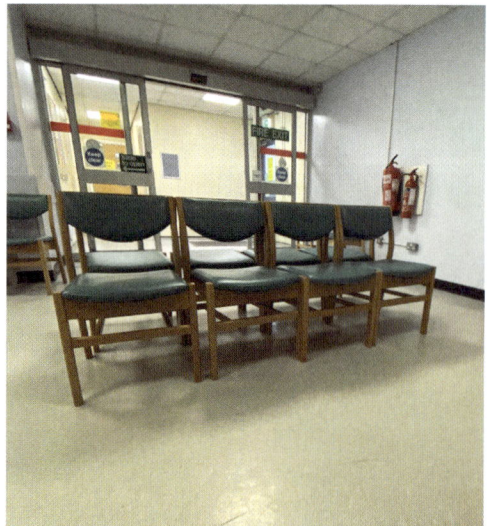

October 2021

Friday, 1st of October

To Father Jim

Thank you. I'd appreciate that. I've got an MRI at 3.15pm today, so I'm trying to get my head in a good place for it.

To Karen

Scan done. Ridiculously happy. Xx

Saturday, 2nd of October

Elizabeth and Kate

So… my hair started coming out in clumps yesterday and by today it was painful to the touch (I'd heard that's the point at which you need to shave it to minimise the discomfort). Ronnie phoned Diana (our hairdresser for the last 15 years) and she said to come to the salon after 6pm (the Rainbow Room in Uddingston). She was absolutely brilliant. And now I am bald-ish. X

Elizabeth and Kate

My Irish mother over FaceTime, having been warned she was about to see me without hair said, 'Gillian, I don't know you.' She recovered quickly and beautifully. After a moment she said, 'Ach it only takes a minute to get used to. And you have to remember, we knew you as a baby and you were bald then.'

To Cousins

My hair started coming out two weeks to the day after chemo, in small clumps at first and then in handfuls (what thick hair we have!). Ronnie phoned the hairdresser we've both gone to for 15 years. She told him to bring me at 6pm when the salon closed. She was great; she did it slowly; had great chat. And I much prefer it to balding with hair coming out in my hands.

Sunday, 3rd of October

To Clair

Wake up, sleepy head! It's a beautiful morning!

To Susan

Hairless

To Susan

Now all the face emojis look like me.

To Susan

I woke up this morning and thought: a week ago today Susan came over and did meditation with me and I was a wee lost soul. Thank you. I turned a corner that day. xx

To Susan

I've started visualising a time when I'm the one helping; when I'm there for someone else.

Tuesday, 5th of October

To Molly Jo

I don't have hair anymore. I thought I should let you prepare yourself before you see me over facetime. x

To Sandra

Thanks, Sandra. I really want to be able to write my way through this experience in the way I have with MS, but it's behaving like a more difficult beast. If I can though, I will. The fortnight after my first chemo session was rough and included two hospital stays. I was so unwell I was just trying to get through time in five-minute blocks, so no writing. I turned a corner last week though and have felt so much better since. My next chemo is Thursday, blood work dependent, so I'll need to see what it brings.

Thank you for giving me your thoughts on those pieces. I've been a bit lost as to what to do with this village (that's too small to be a village) that I seem to want to write about. It's very different from my usual work, which is a mix of narrative non-fiction about illness and fiction exploring the lived experience of illness. For my doctorate I wrote a novel, Brodie, narrated by a copy of The Prime of Miss Jean Brodie that's literary fiction on the face of it, but for me was just a way to explore what it feels like to have MS - the copy of the book is really a more gossipy, opinionated version of me... to my surprise I got an agent, less to my surprise, Brodie has now had a number of polite (sometimes very nice) no thank yous.

I really hope I'll be well enough to come along next week.

With best regards,

Gillian

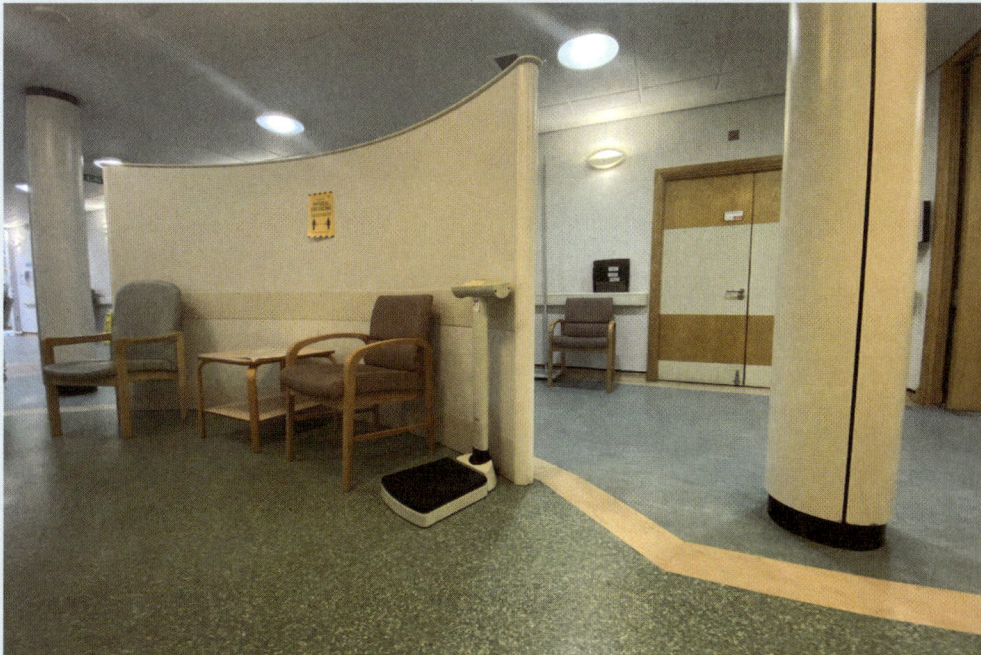

Wednesday, 6th of October

To Susan

I'm sitting in the Beatson waiting for my pre-chemo appointment. But it's a beautiful day outside and I'm planning on walking home. I was weighed when I arrived… 7 stone 4 pounds. I hope you're having a lovely day so far. x

Beautiful day in Glasgow. Lovely walk home from the Beatson after my pre-chemo appointment. Very glad to be fit to do so after my brush with neutropenic sepsis a couple of weeks ago. #BreastCancerAwarenessMonth

To Johanna

I was just about to text to update you. They're going to keep me on a three-weekly cycle but decrease the chemo by 20%.

They hope that this time it won't be too toxic for me. She also said that I had had neutropenic sepsis, and she thought the campylobacter was a bit of a red herring (a pretty awful red herring!), so fingers crossed it won't be quite as bad this time. Also, I was going to ask if you would be able to do my filgrastim injection again, if you're around. xx

Thursday, 7th of October

Chemo Day 2. I've been making slow progress with this great book. Nothing to do with it; everything to do with me. Thanks @NewishPuritan, the short chunks I'm reading it in are brilliant. I can also recommend chunks of ginger in hot water for nausea. #amreading #breastcancer

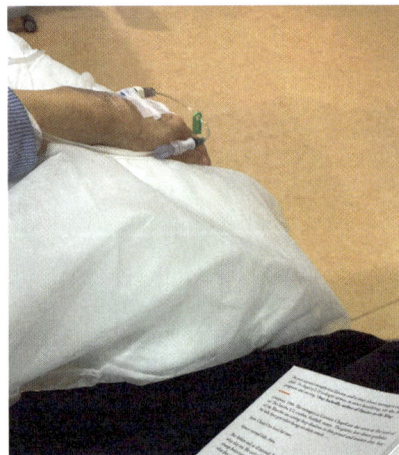

To Karen

There was drama this morning (I'd been removed from the list). It's going fine now. Feeling a bit ropey, but only a bit. xx

To Ronnie

Thanks. I'll message again when I know more. I should be done with the chemo infusion about 2.15 and then they do a 15 minute flush. I don't know if they need to watch me for a set time afterwards. They did the first time, but I don't think they will this time. I'll ask when they come to remove the chemo bag. x

To Ronnie

15/20 minutes from now I can leave the chair, so if you were in the car park you dropped me off in at about 3.15…? X

Came home from chemo to find this little Etsy beauty had arrived. It's lovely and soft and it's good to add a scarf to my fab hats. And with the blue cardigan, it makes for the colours of a St. Ninian's uniform à la the 1980s. #LifeInAScarf #StepBackToKirky

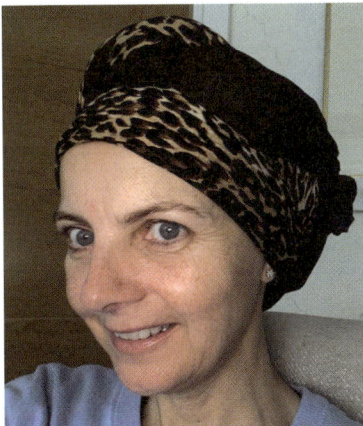

To Cousins

Chemo Day 2 done and dusted. Let's hope for an easier onward path (they reduced the dose of the main drug by 20% in the hope that will help). Also, this scarf I ordered weeks ago arrived for me while I was out. With the cardigan it's the old St Ninian's colours!

To Johanna

Sorry for not writing sooner. It was quite the day. If you're able to give me the injection when you get home tomorrow, that would be great. I finished treatment at 3.30pm today. xx

 Friday, 8th of October

To Karen

I'm okay. I've felt ropey since not long after I got home yesterday but I'm taking it that means my body is clever and was alert to what was going on this time. I'm hoping the 20% reduction will help.

To Johanna

That's great. Thank you. I'm just hoping the filgrastim injection kicks in more quickly this time (rather than three days after my neutrophils hit zero). xx

Elizabeth and Kate

Luckily for me, round two didn't come round fast at all and I had a good week of feeling almost well and feeling like myself. Today started as the kind of disaster I may well write about.

I'd been accidentally removed from the list. I wondered what was going on when the receptionist's smile disappeared, and she told me to take a seat. The only free one was way down the corridor closest to the day unit, which meant I got to witness a different woman accosting the unit sister and loudly complaining about some woman who had just pitched up… it wasn't until 15 minutes later when someone came out of the day unit and told me there was no chair for me, that I realised I was that woman.

She said she was going to take me up to a ward and they'd send someone up later to start off my treatment and because it was a ward I had to be treated like I might have Covid so it would be an isolated room. The poor staff nurse I was handed over to - I was crying because I was petrified of being given the wrong treatment (I'd been told I'd get a reduced dose - 20% less - to try to make it more manageable) and that no one would be able to see if I took a reaction (I took one last time to one of the premeds but luckily I was in the busy day unit so could alert someone immediately).

She told me not to worry that she would speak to the ward sister. I also phoned the breast cancer outpatient area to ask them to let my main nurse know what had happened. The sister was just brilliant. She listened to me, empathised, apologised for what had happened, said they would make sure I was safe and that she would get their pharmacist to check the premed had been removed and that the main chemo drug had been reduced, which she did.

The pharmacist also came to speak to me to reassure me and then brought me Zovirax when I asked if it was a problem that I had a cold sore on my lip. Then my main nurse phoned and talked me down (she also apologised that I'd been described as 'some woman who had just pitched up') and then 15 minutes later the day unit sister came to bring me down for a seat, so my treatment started at 11 instead of 9, but everything after that went well (unpleasant but well). And the lovely ward sister after listening to my tale of woe said, you know for someone with no hair you've got amazing eyelashes, like a cow.

To Alison

Hi Alison,

Thanks so much for speaking to me and coming to see me yesterday. It really helped reassure me. I know how busy you are, so I really appreciate you taking the time.

I started to feel pretty ropey not long after I got home. Mainly nausea but also general gut discomfort. I took one of the Cyclizine and not long afterwards felt even worse: dizziness, light-headedness, fast pulse, so I haven't taken anymore. It wasn't as bad as my reaction to the Ondansetron, but it still worried me. I had wondered if it was one of the things making me feel bad in the hospital, but I was getting so many things, I couldn't tell.

I do also have Metoclopramide, so took one of those at bedtime. It didn't seem to make much difference, which was my experience last time, but I don't have any negative reaction to it. I'm feeling pretty nauseous again today so am just sipping hot water with chunks of ginger, which seems to help a bit, but I wondered if there's anything else you could suggest?

Also, I got a letter today with an appointment to see Dr Kerr at 9.30am on 28/10. I'm meant to report to the MacMillan day unit for my next treatment at 9am that day, so wanted to ask about what I should do.

Thanks again for your help yesterday!

Gillian

To Susan

I'm sipping hot water with chunks of ginger… It seems safer than the anti-nausea drugs that make my pulse race and my head dizzy.

Saturday, 9th of October

To Johanna

I'm taking everything very slowly and easily today. I've done a meditation and am sipping hot water with ginger (I've also had a kiwi and a boiled egg, for good measure). I hope you have a great day.

To Johanna

I'm going to phone the helpline number because I'm feeling shivery and that's one of the things it says to phone about. My throat has also got a bit tight and sore. I don't want to phone, but I think I probably should. xx

To Johanna

The number is still busy and saying to call back in ten minutes.

To Susan

I finally got through and they told me to go to the SATA unit at the QEUH. I'm in a side room and they've done a heart trace, a Covid test, put a cannula in and taken bloods. And the staff have been the nicest to date. I'm going bald-headed, which I think helps.

To Johanna

I'm still clammy and shivery… this was the pattern last time before my temp started spiking. I'm just hopeful I don't have another failed discharge, which is how it started the Sunday morning after my first chemo.

To Ronnie

I'm going to be admitted, but I don't know when they'll find a bed.

Sunday, 10th of October

To Johanna

I was admitted at midnight into the ward attached to the SATA unit. Someone popped their head round my door about an hour ago to ask how I was feeling, and I told her sweaty and pretty horrible. She just nodded and left, and no one has been since. I admit I'm feeling pretty anxious again (and hot and sweaty and sick).

To Johanna

Still in ARU5 with no sign of moving but they have said Ronnie can bring me in some hot water with ginger and some food. xxx

To Johanna

I'm still in the ARU. They're still trying to get me a medical bed. xx

Monday, 11th of October

To Susan

I was transferred to Ward 11C last night. The staff are very good (friendly and caring). They've taken cultures and will wait for the results before letting me go, which sounds like at least a day. It feels like I'm now under the same medical team as last time and that they are fully aware of what's going on with me. They're going to try to get someone from acute oncology to see me, but no guarantees. I'm up, showered, and sitting at the window looking out at Glasgow with a t-shirt fashioned into a headscarf on my head. I hope you have a lovely day. x

To Alison

Thanks, Alison. I'm in Ward 11C now. They've cultured blood and urine and will keep an eye on me while they wait for the results.

I'm still feeling pretty rubbish but I'm

no longer shivery/clammy, so that's a big improvement.

Many thanks,

Gillian

✉️

To Sandra

Hi Sandra,

I'm sorry to miss the class tonight. I'm in the Queen Elizabeth after my chemo. It seems my body is struggling to cope with the treatment, but I'm hopeful I avoid sepsis this time. They are keeping a close eye on my bloods and me, so that's reassuring.

I hope it's a good class tonight and I look forward to feeling better and coming along to the next one.

With best wishes,

Gillian

📞

Elizabeth and Kate

I was clammy and shivery on Saturday afternoon, which are symptoms you have to phone the helpline about. They sent me to the hospital. When I was admitted my temp was 35.2. It fell to 35 then 34.8, so they had to use something called a bear hugger to heat me up. That was much less fun that it sounds. They're just keeping an eye on bloods and cultures now and hoping I avoid sepsis this time. Scary and miserable and a bit dull all rolled into one. xxx

📞

Elizabeth and Kate

They've let Ronnie come in a couple of times. He's very good. I don't think I would cope as well if it were reversed.

📞

Elizabeth and Kate

Thank you, both of you. You really are a support network for me. I feel you holding me up and it makes a difference. X

📱

To Johanna

They're still waiting on the cultures. My neutrophils are still high, so fighting anything that's there, I'm guessing. I managed to eat (in small portions) some chickpea dahl for dinner and I'm sitting at the window just now enjoying the cityscape. xxx

📞

To Kirsten

My goodness that is such a powerful poem. You are incredibly talented. And I love the screwdriver and battery chat! It's what a little bald lady on the 11th floor of the Queen Elizabeth needs. xxx

Tuesday, 12th of October

To Karen

Haven't seen a doctor yet today. Feeling a bit grotty, but that's okay. I hope you have a lovely time with Rhys. xx

To Karen

A challenge if you choose to accept it… Susan phoned me today and was a fount of wisdom. One tidbit was that when she worked with Professor Kenneth Calman (or Kenny as she calls him), he gave patients pan drops for the bad chemo taste (he'd spent weeks having different patients try different mints apparently and pan drops were the winner). Is there any chance you could try to find some…? xx

Wednesday, 13th of October

To Kirsten

Thank you for the voice notes. It makes me feel less alone to have your voice in this hospital room. Sending much love to you and Queen Scout. xxx

To Karen

I'm feeling better (not well, but no longer like I have something in addition to the post-chemo stuff), so I'm hoping my bloods tell the same story. It's a bit random in terms of when someone might come

to see me because I'm a cuckoo again (on a surgical ward). I think 2pm is the earliest I've ever seen someone. My bloods were done about half eight, so they'll be available by now, I'd think. X

To Ronnie

The nurse checked my bloods and the numbers are all within range today, so fingers crossed. Apparently, there are doctors on the ward, too, so maybe I'll hear soon. xx

Lovely view from the 11th floor of the QEUH out over the city. Fingers crossed my bloods are looking just as good and I can get out today. #MotherGlasgow

To Ronnie

I can go home whenever you can get here. xxxxxxx

To Karen

Any pan drops…? The horrible taste in my mouth is horrible.

To Karen

Yay! I hope Professor Calman's research was sound.

To Susan

I'm home and my sister brought me pan drops, which work! God bless Sir Kenneth Calman. And you for passing on his highly researched finding! Thank you.

To Johanna

I'm feeling so much better than I was. And I'm so grateful for your texts and support when I was in the hospital. My bloods had been on an improving trend and looked good today, so the lovely doctor was happy for me to go home. She said she also noticed a big difference in how I was looking (my colour was back). xxx

Thursday, 14th of October

To Cousins

I got home about 4pm yesterday and slept well last night. My plan is to focus on eating a small meal every two hours or so. It seems to help with the nausea and should help with the weight loss. Project Get the Pounds Back On!

To Susan

I listen…

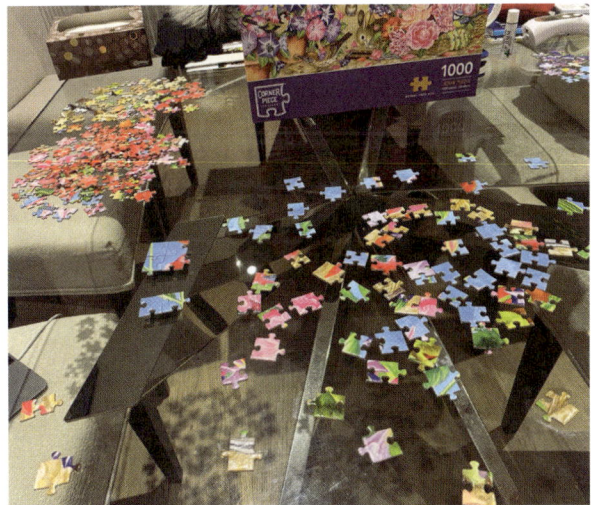

Saturday, 16th of October

To Susan

My morning was good. I was even in my old uniform of denim dress, black tights and boots. And I wore the rat wig. My energy started to dip about two and has been free falling (and the feeling of general unwellness is lurking). This has been the pattern over the last few days. And then I normally rally the couple of hours before bed. So more good hours than bad (I am back in pyjamas and a beanie hat). How are you? How's your weekend so far?

Tuesday, 19th of October

To Cousins

Poor Ronnie! The dogs have completely given up on me. He's now their number one human (slave).

And Daisy is chief food negotiator.

Wednesday, 20th of October

To Susan

Rat-wig with a scarf…

To Johanna

Aargh! I've not been feeling great this afternoon and now my temperature is all over the place. I took it half an hour ago and it was 34.8! Ronnie took his to check the thermometer is accurate and he was 36.9. I put on a hat and a scarf, and it jumped back up. I've been trying to get through to the helpline for the last half hour.

To Susan

I'm back in the Initial Assessment Unit at the QEUH. I started to feel unwell late morning: hot/cold/abdominal pain. I took my temp about ten to four and it was 34.8. I put on a hat and a scarf and phoned the emergency helpline.

To Susan

My temp did go up to 37.4 before I left the house. It's that same old hot/cold thing again. Hopefully my bloods are good, and they'll send me home.

To Johanna

Still waiting for bloods to be taken. It's a busy place. xxx

To Ronnie

Bloods just taken. Put in a seat in a little side bit by a nurse I saw the last time I was here.

To Johanna

I'm still running hot and cold. Hat on. Hat off. Hat on. Hat off.

To Johanna

It'll be two hours for the bloods, anyway. I'm an old hand at this now. xxx

To Ronnie

I'm tired, miserable and nauseous.

To Ronnie

Other people are allowed people with them… if you wanted to come and keep me company…

Thursday, 21st of October

To Karen

I was admitted about 1.30am and had blood cultures done just after 2.30am. I was in the main area in a bed but not a room (with the light on until after four) and then got wheeled to a side room with a curtain, which is where I am now. Maybe 15 minutes sleep… They admitted me because my white cell count is high, suggesting infection.

To Johanna

I was supposed to have an appointment with my surgeon at 9.30am this morning. I told the doctor who admitted me, and he said they'd leave a message for him.

To Johanna

Andrew Walker just phoned me. He was very nice and said the important thing is for the oncology team to look at what's best for me going forwards. He said there are options, and they might even bring surgery forwards. It all sounded quite scary, but I understand it's just the situation I'm in right now. Thanks for checking in and for being there. xxx

To Susan

Ronnie made me a cauliflower curry, which was lovely. My tummy is a wee bit sore now but will be fine. I got a call from my main nurse who said they were going to have to come up with a modified plan for me… she mentioned weekly chemo again and the possibility of going to surgery. I'll know more next Wednesday (although there was a mix up, so I currently don't have a time for that appointment).

Friday, 22nd of October

To Isobel

Hi Isobel,

Thank you for my lovely plants and card. It's so good of you to think of me.

I look forward to thanking you in person when this is over.

Love,

Gillian x

My second cycle of chemo has also been (unsurprisingly) tough, but I'm on day 15 and I'm grateful for every card I've been

sent and the lovely flowers, perfect gifts, and messages that appear, as if by magic. In this lonely season, I know I'm not alone. Thank you. #breastcancer

Monday, 25th of October

To Gitte

Thanks, Gitte. It has been difficult. I'm on a tough chemo regime that's not been going well. I've been hospitalised four times since I started on 16th Sept. One of those times was with chemo-induced sepsis, so very scary. I've had two treatments so far (it's a three-weekly cycle) and I'm due my third on Thursday, but I'm meeting with the oncologist on Wednesday who may decide to change the plan. This could be to weekly chemo (as that would be less toxic), to go straight to surgery at this point, or to continue with the current regime, which I've been told is less likely. It's a bit scary, but he's very good and I trust his decision.

I look forward to a time after all of this and would love to show you Glasgow when it's over and just a memory.

Gillian x

Tuesday, 26th of October

To Alison

Hi Alison,

I'm writing to ask if my husband can come to my appointment tomorrow. If so, he could wait in the cafe downstairs until I'm called.

Many thanks,

Gillian

Twitter post with link to my website - www.sunshinescot.com

I wrote a short thing. I have fewer words these days. (some people may be relieved about that)

It's been a while. A while of not writing.

A while of having nothing to say.

Except certain phrases:

Don't get cancer.

It'll be fine.

It is what it is.

I say them often. On a loop.

Not to the same people.

I seem to reserve *Don't get cancer* for friends. People my age, or within fifteen years of my age, give or take. And when I say it, I mean it. Like I can prevent cancer from happening with words; as though I can ordain it to be so; demand that this not happen.

An imperative; an incantation; a command.

I don't want anyone else to live this experience and yet I now know it's a concrete possibility. There's nothing I can do to stop it. Except issue this directive and cross my fingers that words have a power I don't possess.

Family members are most likely to get *It'll be fine*.

And it will be fine.

I feel it in my water and in the kindness and good wishes that encircle me.

I feel it in the treatment I receive. I feel it in the care I'm given. [I've learned that treatment and care are not one in the same. This is a thought for another time. A time when I have more words.]

It is what it is seems to be for everyone. It's indiscriminate and uttered most frequently.

I'd like to have more words. But I don't. Not yet.

I've been told this is a season. A season that will pass.

When it does there will be words.

I promise.

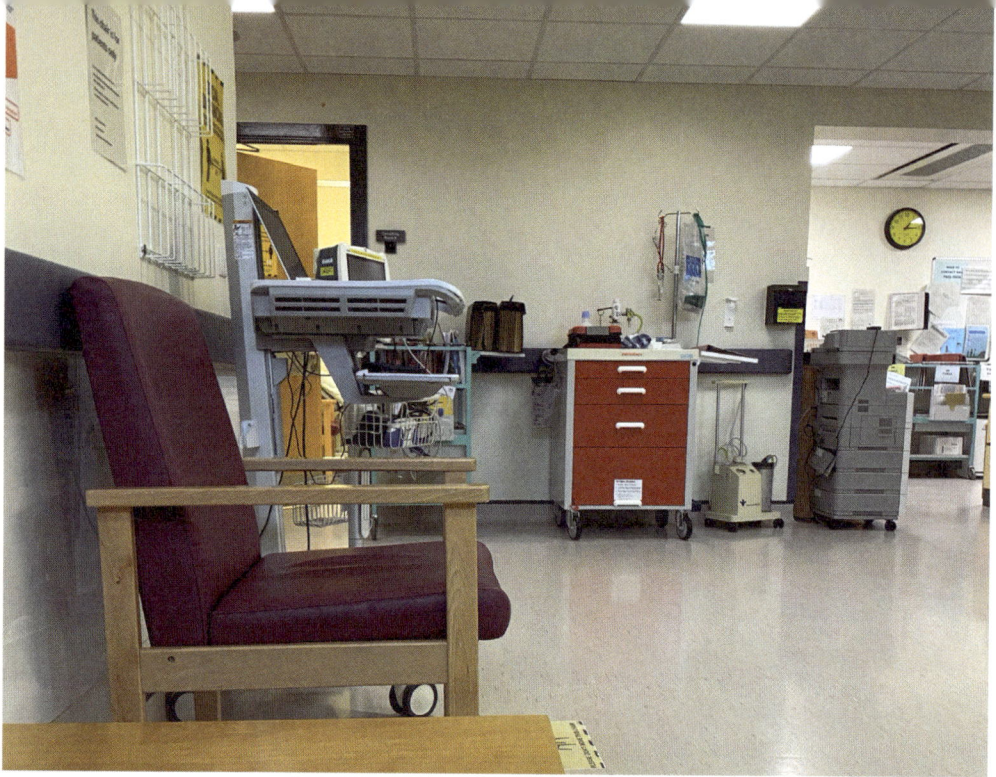

Wednesday, 27th of October

Elizabeth and Kate

I'm doing okay. I have an appointment with the oncologist today (1.20pm) at which I'll find out what he's decided to do… keep going as is (unlikely now but a possibility), switch to weekly chemo, switch chemo, or go straight to surgery… nothing sounds terribly good (my preference would be weekly chemo, but what do I know). I trust his decision and will get behind it mentally (after a wee cry, possibly).

Elizabeth and Kate

It couldn't have gone better. We're going to try weekly chemo, but it will be stopped if my body still can't cope. (PLEASE let my body cope). The drug is related to what I've been getting but not identical and has a much lower risk of sepsis. And he wants to start next week instead of tomorrow as I'm still not fully recovered from the second treatment (so I have a recovery week and

he says it will have no negative impact, only the potential of a positive one because he wants to give me the best chance of coping with the weekly chemo).

AND he can't be sure but thinks the lump may have shrunk a little and might be softer. I know this sounds ridiculous, but it feels like I've won the lottery. xx

Sunday, 31st of October

To Karen

Better but not 100% yet. We walked about 2 miles. Longest since I started. X

November 2021

✉️ **Tuesday, 2nd of November**

To Laura

I'm so sorry I've not written or facetimed. I think about you every morning with all good intentions and then, at night when the day is over and I'm exhausted, I realise I didn't write or call and I'm very sorry!

My pyjamas and dressing gown arrived a few weeks ago and they are just lovely (so soft!). Thank you for always thinking about me and giving me such lovely gifts.

This experience is tougher than I could have imagined.

I have weekly chemo for the next six weeks (if my body can tolerate it). I will then have a couple of weeks to recover (maybe slightly longer because of Christmas) and then it'll be surgery. After surgery, I'll have radiotherapy. I've been told that once I'm through the surgery, I'll start to be able to get my life back. I'm very much looking forward to that. And I'm very much looking forward to seeing you again when I'm at the other side of this.

With all my love,

Gillian xx

📱 **Wednesday, 3rd of November**

To Karen

I hope you're feeling a bit better today. I was going to drop a little something over for Pete (plus your container, waterproofs, and the liquorice Ronnie got for you). When will someone be in…? xx

🐦 **Thursday, 4th of November**

A lovely pre-chemo walk in the autumn sunshine with the dogs and their giant shadows. I start six weeks of weekly chemo this afternoon. Fingers and toes crossed my body copes better with this new regime. #breastcancer

📱

To Ronnie

Still in the waiting room, waiting. xx

To Ronnie

I've had IV steroids and the ouchy thigh injection and now have a half hour saline bag running before the paclitaxel. xx

Thanks to a brilliant recommendation from a good friend (and former teaching colleague), I'm spending my third session of chemo listening to The Prime of Miss Jean Brodie on BBC Sounds. #ForTheLoveOfMuriel #SparkTherapy

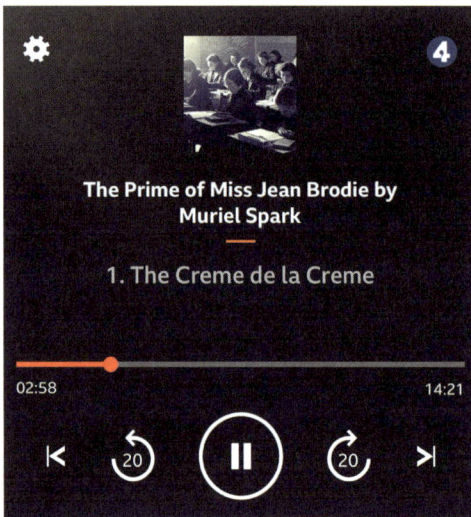

To Ronnie

I had a reaction to the paclitaxel so was given a rescue steroid and they're now giving me more saline after which they'll try it again more slowly. I could be here for a while.

To Ronnie

They just restarted it. xx

To Ronnie

I should be done in 20 minutes. xx

To Karen

I hope Pete had a lovely day and enjoyed his cake. xx

Friday, 5th of November

To Karen

Steroids… can't sleep with them, can't live without them.

To Clair

Hoping you and Nic have a lovely warm blast of a time. xx

To Clair

The rule is - don't think about your sick pal when you're away. Your only job is to relax and enjoy yourself. And that's an order! xx

On day 30 cards started appearing on the kitchen table each morning. Today's marked day 50 of treatment, which seems unbelievable (at points I've just been focused on getting through the next 5 minutes). Thanks for all the love and support that's getting me through.

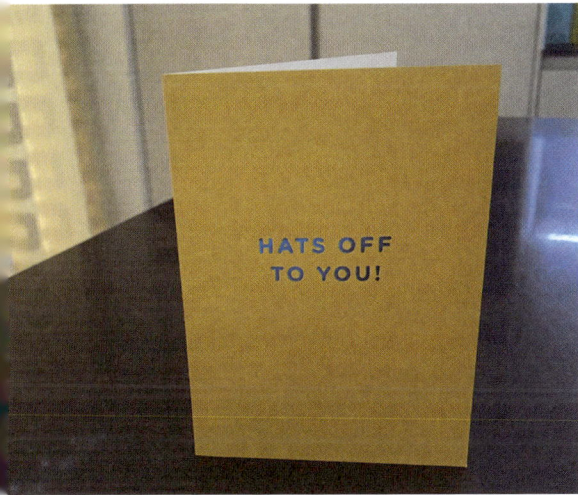

To Johanna

I hope you had a lovely break! How are the dogs doing with the fireworks? Fergus is terrified. Hamish and Daisy are nonplussed. I hope yours are okay. xxx

Saturday, 6th of November

To Misti

Thank you. Resilience. A wonderful tale, expertly told. Your timing is perfect.

I met with the oncologist for a pre-chemo appointment last Wednesday. After

discussing the options fully, it was clear his preference was to switch to six weeks of weekly chemo. He also gave me an extra week off as he felt I wasn't well enough recovered from cycle two to have the best chance of tolerating the new regime, so I had my first weekly chemo this Thursday.

Of course, there was drama. I'd had the saline infusion, the premeds, the ten-minute antibody injection in my thigh, and then they started running the bag of paclitaxel (my new chemo drug; the old one was docetaxel). I was merrily listening to an abridged version of The Prime of Miss Jean Brodie (it's on BBC Sounds and is very good) when, just minutes in, it felt like an elephant had sat down on my chest. I told the closest nurse who said, 'You're looking very red.' She stopped the paclitaxel and started giving me recovery medication through the iv, which, unnoticed by me, had been sitting just off to the side. They did repeated obs (blood pressure etc.), a heart trace, gave me a saline infusion and then, as everything had settled, waited a further hour and restarted the paclitaxel more slowly (it went in over two hours as opposed to one).

I was completely fine the second time around, which was a relief because my oncologist has told me that if this doesn't work, he'll need to stop my treatment (for now) and refer me for surgery.

Almost two days on and I'm feeling okay, chemo okay as opposed to normal okay, but not dreadful (although I'm almost scared to type this in case I jinx it...)

Thanks again for the gift of story.

Gillian x

To Susan

I'm feeling a bit rubbish but not QEUH rubbish. I was just ogling a pink wig, but at £350 it's not ever going to find its way here! How's your weekend going?

To Susan

Well… I'm still in quite a bit of abdominal discomfort, which makes eating more functional than for pleasure. I have something small every two hours. My favourite is curry. Ronnie's doing a great job of them (good variety of veg and things like turmeric, ginger and cumin versus anything too spicy).

My concentration isn't stretching to reading books at the moment, so I'm listening to them instead. Loving this cosy crime gem. Thanks, @OlgaWojtas! #gettingthroughchemo

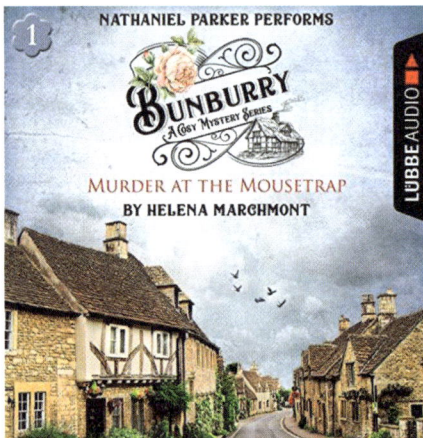

I'm trying to walk my way through chemo (when it's not pouring with rain). Tonight we circled the Kelvin, taking in Alexander 'Greek' Thomson's sixty steps. Brilliant. (Okay so strictly it wasn't night, but it was DARK at 5.30.) #exerciseoncology #Glasgow

To Alison

Hi Alison,

I got a letter about an appointment with you at the Beatson at 11am tomorrow. My brain is a bit scrambled, but I thought maybe we'd spoken about it being over the telephone (that could just have been last week). I'm glad to come in though as I don't think I'm managing to keep weight on (I am trying), so it would be good to be weighed before this week's chemo. Also, I know I said I didn't want a wig prescription, but I've changed my mind, so if it's still possible, I'd appreciate getting one from you.

Many thanks,

Gillian

To Johanna

I'm doing okay, thanks! Saturday was my worst day. Every other day has been much more manageable. I had my pre-chemo bloods this morning; I've got my pre-chemo clinic appointment tomorrow and then back at the Beatson for weekly chemo 2 on

Thursday. I actually much prefer this level of oversight and the sense on getting things done/ticking things off. I'm also not feeling dreadful, which makes a huge difference. I took Fergus for a walk on his own this afternoon. He loves pretending he's an only dog. I hope your week is going well. xxx

![WhatsApp] **Wednesday, 10th of November**

To Cousins

Thank you. I really appreciate everyone's thoughts and love. xxx

![WhatsApp]

To Ronnie

Still waiting… x

To Ronnie

Seven stone two pounds…

To Ronnie

The 10.40 appointment just went in…

To Ronnie

Actually… she was in and out… As far as I can tell, I'm next.

To Ronnie

Could you come and get me, please? x

To Ronnie

I'm next in line to get bloods. Will be done before you get here. x

![WhatsApp]

To Karen

My bloods weren't good enough, so they sent me to get another full count. If I don't hear anything it means they were better and I've to go for the chemo at 1pm tomorrow. If they phone, it means it's postponed for a week. I had a big cry about it. Poor Ronnie. I feel a bit better after the big cry, though. xx

![WhatsApp] **Thursday, 11th of November**

To Susan

I'm in the chair, so my white cell count must be good (or good enough). And I have a nurse I really like.

![WhatsApp]

To Clair

There was no call, so I showed up at the Day Case Unit (the euphemism for chemo area). xx

To Clair

Only 40 minutes left. Lots of premeds, an hour to let them percolate and then the chemo going in in 1hr 45mins. xx

![WhatsApp]

To Ronnie

The saline is going in now. xx

To Ronnie

There was air in the line so another few minutes. x

Tuesday will be 2 months since I started chemo. Tuesday is also the day I go for a wig fitting thanks to @Beatson_Charity (my hair came out in handfuls 2 weeks in). Today I created a 2020/21 hairstyle album to remind myself of myself pre-chemo cut/pre-bald. #breastcancer

To Susan

It was a record. Only four hours. I didn't get the antibody treatment / needle in the thigh as it's only every third week, so hopefully that'll make a difference to how I feel this time.

Friday, 12th of November

Sleep is elusive. During yesterday's chemo I had 2 different IV steroids as premeds (the 2nd was due to my reaction last week to the new chemo drug). I've tried my usually trusty Headspace meditations + sleepcasts to no avail, so I'm off to Bunburry. #cosycrime #booktherapy

To Karen

The two premed bags of steroid did for me. Two hours sleep (one for each bag?!). I'll set an alarm for an afternoon nap to get me through the day. I hope you have a good Friday. xx

To Karen

It wasn't terrible. I listened to sleepcasts, music, and a cosy crime novel. I like to mix it up. xx

Tuesday, 16th of November

Thank you @Beatson_Charity! I had a lovely wig fitting with Rhona today. Such careful and kind care. We decided on a cheeky bob, which has been ordered in creamy toffee... An uplifting experience from the moment I arrived at the welcome desk. #breastcancer #carefulandkindcare

Wednesday, 17th of November

To Jenny

Rhona advised a modern wee bob called the Codi. She also advised a lighter colour and has ordered creamy toffee and then a shade lighter and one darker for me to try… she'll call when they arrive.

To Jenny

Thank you. I have struggled with loneliness, but it seems when I feel it, I'm least able to reach out. I just had my pre-chemo call and yesterday's bloods are good enough to go ahead with tomorrow's chemo. And that'll be another one done. xx

To Clair

Crazy steroid purchase number 68… Your Christmas jumper might have arrived… Age 12? Why, yes! xx

To Clair

And I want to hear about the new Christmas jumper day you're initiating at work… the trainees will love it. Promise. x

To Clair

Oh. And I got a phone call to say my bloods are good enough for chemo tomorrow. (tiny) yay

Thursday, 18th of November

To Susan

Yes. I had porridge and seeds for breakfast number one, walked Fergus around Wilton Street and then had breakfast number two of spelt flakes, almond milk, and a chopped banana. My day unit slot is at 1pm, so I'll leave in an hour with a packed lunch of an almond spread sandwich. It's all about two hourly eating…

To Cousins

Weekly treatment three of six. I'm three hours in, one hour to go. The weekly treatment certainly gives more of a sense of being able to count down, which helps. xx

Friday, 19th of November

Chemo day and the cocktail of two different pre-med steroids it involves turns chemo night into a sleep-free event. Luckily when my appetite for listening to books wanes, there's this beauty by @IAMKP. #musictherapy #gettingthroughchemo

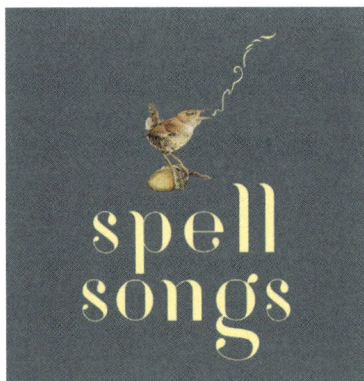

spell songs

To Misti

It's a hard slog but so much better than the teetering on the edge of hospitalisation that characterised the 3-weekly treatment. And I actually appreciate all the extra activity that comes along with it: pre-chemo bloods on a Tuesday, pre-chemo meeting on a Wednesday, chemo on a Thursday. This level of oversight feels a lot safer. And it lends itself to counting down… I had weekly chemo number three of six yesterday, so in three weeks (tick, tick, tick) this bit will be done. (My first chemo was on the 16th of September, which seems years ago now.)

G x

To Cousins

Thank you, Marie. I'm sipping hot water with ginger as I write (my way to manage the nausea). xx

Elizabeth and Kate

The chemo was the usual level of fair to middling trauma, which actually I've normalised now, so the answer is fine. The cocktail of steroids did mean I only managed just over an hour of sleep last night, but they also still have me a little buzzed, so there's that. Only the nausea has kicked in so far and it's not terrible as long as I keep drinking hot water with small chunks of ginger. Apologies for the level of detail. How are you? Have you got nice plans for the weekend?

Beautiful morning walk to my appointment at the Beatson. #walkingtherapy #Glasgow

To Elizabeth and Kate

In good news, three weeks today I'll be done with the 'death is an actual listed possible side effect' taxol-type chemo. I'm counting down the days (and marvelling that I've managed to put more than 60 of them between me and that first chemo day). Phew.

I wrote a piece of fiction today. A tiny moment of a story. From start to finish. It's the first time I've managed it since starting chemo. The first time I've been able to lose myself in fiction. It felt good. #writingtherapy #gettingthroughchemo

To Elizabeth

Dear Elizabeth,

I saw something on twitter yesterday about a piece of flash fiction and I followed the thought. It was wonderful to write fiction again. So distracting.

I'm sending it by way of conversation. :-)

G x

Evergreen

Maura had needed to walk and cold though it was, this was her place. She spoke as their boots tramped a path littered with debris from the high winds. Between swathes of hat and scarf she could tell he didn't understand. What was visible of him offered only pity.

She tried again to explain. Her hand arched up and over, reaching across the horizon to the pines that edged the length of the loch. The trees had been here before her, she said, and they would still be here, after. Tall. Evergreen. She told him that sometimes those trees were all she could think about; she had no other thought.

Maura could see it made little sense to him.

He was lucky.

She no longer had the luxury of not knowing. She understood what it was to have an expiry date; what that meant in the very bones of you. And she knew what the knowledge of it does to your head.

The doctors hadn't come right out and said it, of course. Instead, they had talked in terms of treatment and how it wasn't what it used to be. It's not like it was in the 1950s, the doctor said, not meeting Maura's eyes.

The 1950s. That was when her granny died of it. Her dad's mum.

There's a freedom in not knowing, she thought, and she could almost remember how it felt. Not knowing. Not knowing what it was like to see those trees by the loch and be unable to help yourself; your only thought: they were here before me, and they'll be here long after.

Maura saw the trees again. In her head this time. Tall. Evergreen. Destined to stretch up into the sky for millennia. Or until they're cut down for no good reason, she thought. Cut down by someone who doesn't know; someone who doesn't understand the sense of ease that comes from the fact those pines were here before you. Before your parents. Before your grandparents, even. Watching the loch on the day they were born.

She saw a girl she knew only from photographs, her dad's mum, playing as a child beneath the green of their branches; playing beneath the green of their branches in a moment before Maura existed. As her granny ran and danced, Maura thought, it's okay not to exist when it isn't your time. Her own moments, more noticeable in number now, were as and when they should be.

His voice broke in.

'It's best not to dwell, Maura,' he said.

'No. I suppose not.'

'And anyway, things are advancing all the time. You'll outlast us all.'

It's not that she hadn't heard it before, but somehow coming from him it was worse.

She pushed her scarf down and turned to face him.

Maura flashed that smile – her old one, from before – and said, 'I might just do that.'

THE END

✉️

To Elizabeth

Thank you! That's given me really interesting thoughts to think. I hadn't considered working it into something more, but I might. It was almost just a conversation starter with the universe. Using fiction to tease out something about the impact of knowing what you've always known but never really understood.

My day has been a bit nausea and fatigue filled. It's almost as if yesterday's effort (which was no effort at all at the time) of writing/thinking has taken a toll on today. But the march continues regardless: chemo bloods today; pre-chemo Beatson appointment tomorrow; chemo on Thursday. This week. Next week. The following. Then a breath. Hopefully (there was a whisper about more chemo hard on the heels, fingers crossed that doesn't happen).

Your beautiful hat made a trip to the laundrette today. The ladies there are lovely. They are very fond of Ronnie and Fergus, so it felt a little like I was intruding.

Thank you again. I miss this sort of conversation.

G x

📞 **Wednesday, 24th of November**

To Ronnie

Seven stone three pounds today (that's up from last week). x

To Ronnie

It's all that good food you make me. xxx

📞

To Cousins

Waiting to go in for my pre-chemo appointment. They weigh me every time and it's always been on a downward trajectory, but today I was up, so that's good! Fingers crossed my blood results are good, too. xxx

📞

To Ronnie

My bloods aren't good enough so I'm waiting to have them redone. I've to get them done here on a Wednesday from now on. xxx

📞

To Clair

That is the BEST news! I'm so happy for you. And proud of you. xxxx

To Clair

I'm at the Beatson waiting for my bloods to be redone. That news was exactly what I needed. I have a big smile that wasn't there before. xx

📞

To Kate

I'm actually feeling okay (I just want my bloods up!). I was entertaining Alison (the breast cancer nurse) with hair loss and haemorrhoid chat earlier. I'm thinking a career in stand-up beckons.

Thursday, 25th of November

To Cousins

Waiting in the chemo corridor. My appointment was at 10am. I didn't hear anything about my bloods, but she said they would redo them this morning if they're still too low. xxx

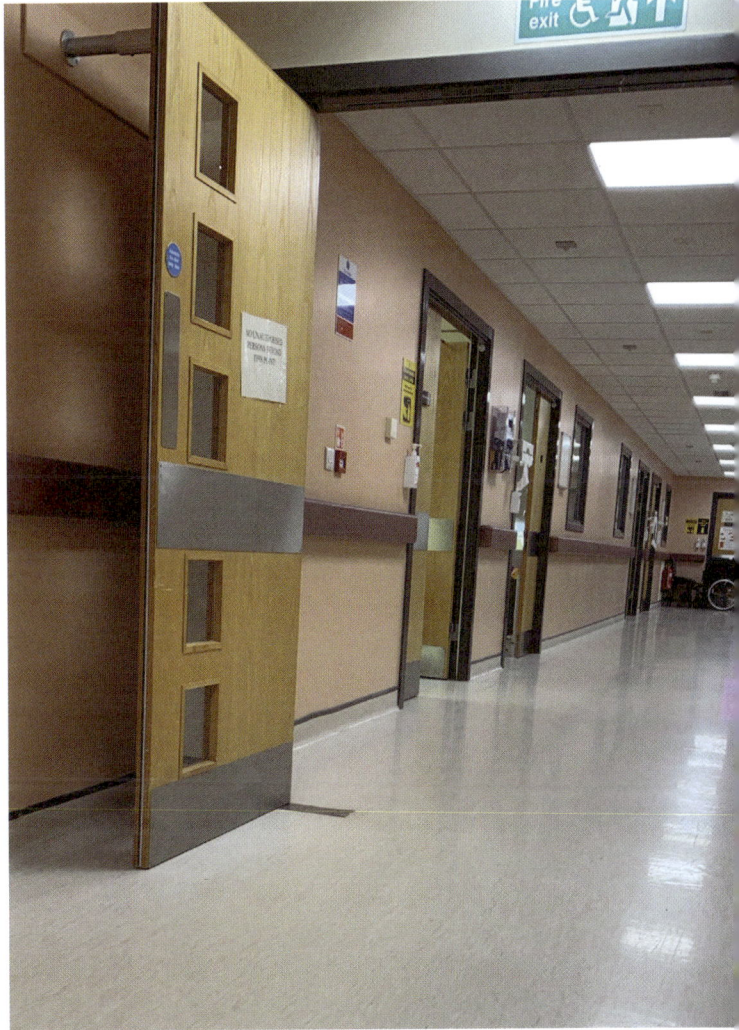

To Ronnie

I'm on the post- pre-med flush, which is an hour. I'm still waiting for the injection into the thigh, which they always do pre-chemo. xx

To Ronnie

My battery is getting low, for some reason… so hopefully it'll last until I'm done. xx

To Ronnie

I'm just waiting for them to remove my cannula

To Cousins

I got taken after about an hour. I'm just home now. I get a ten-minute subcutaneous injection into my thigh every third week, so today was the day. It stings like billy-oh to start with, but it's a great drug (combo of pertuzumab and herceptin), so I'm more than happy to put up with it. xxx

Elizabeth and Kate

Happy Thanksgiving, Elizabeth!

To Clair

It was fine. (except for the needle in the thigh bit) In better news, I had a message to say my wig is in.

To Clair

Have I told you how proud of you I am…?! I am VERY proud of you. (and that's me without any alcohol for months… Sober as a Sheriff…)

Friday, 26th of November

Chemo night. The two different IV steroids have me wide awake. I just watched Effie Gray and I'm now going to listen to some Headspace sleep music in the hope of an hour or two (of rest if not sleep). The lovely thing is that I'm another one down. #gettingthroughchemo

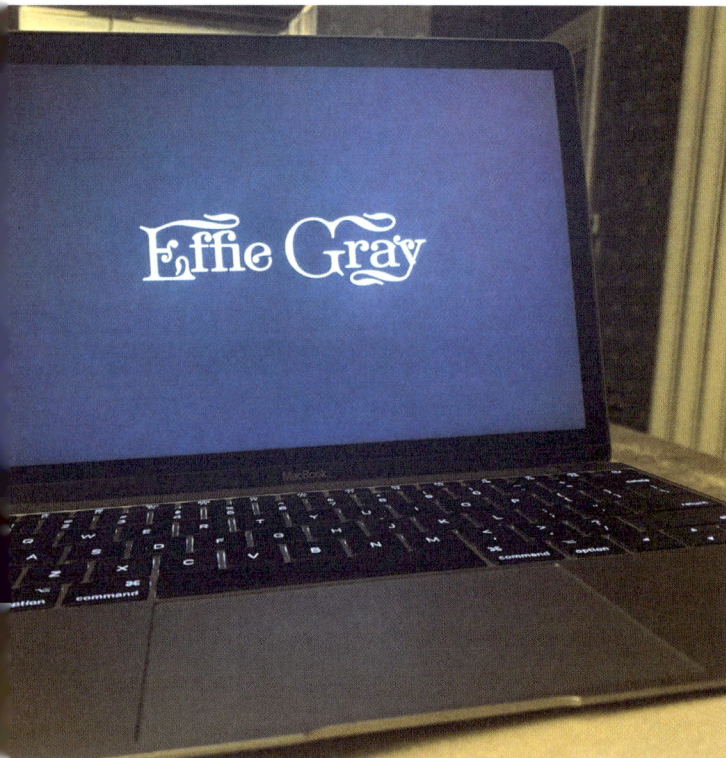

To Clair

Happy Friday… I got you a wee extra CONGRATULATIONS gift (I blame the steroids). Are you around tonight for a walk by or at the weekend for a walk… xx

Elizabeth and Kate

I'm still as high as a kite. Was just in the shower having done all manner of cleaning and tidying… I'd love a Zoom when you're up for it this morning. I'm collecting my wig at 1.30pm and have a telephone GP appointment at 3pm.

Saturday, 27th of November

Thanks to @ekreeder who braved a Zoom with me yesterday while I was still hyped up on steroids and let me talk about trees and the crazy ideas I'd had in the wee small hours for creative work related to this experience. So grateful for my @UofGWriting family! #gettingthroughchemo

To Karen

Would you believe I've almost finished all the pan drops…! If you're wherever you got them, could you get some more please? I've got enough left for few days. xxx

Monday, 29th of November

Thanks to the steroids, I now have a list of 12 projects I'd love to undertake as a result of this illness experience. I've joked (I've been employing a lot of black humour) that this is the post doc I never wanted, but maybe some useful work can come out of it. #creativetherapy

✉️

To Sandra

Hi Sandra,

I'm looking forward to the class. This might sound silly, but I feel I have to warn you that I'll have hair this time, thanks to a blondish bob of a wig. I'm not sure why I feel compelled to issue a warning, but it seems it's what I do. :-)

See you soon,

Gillian

📞

Tuesday, 30th of November

Elizabeth and Kate

Sounds good! I can provide a hot lunch to keep us warm and full… these days there's always a sweet potato curry on the go… (thanks to Ronnie)

December 2021

Wednesday, 1st of December

To Karen

They've switched me to Wednesday bloods because of my Tuesday fails so I'll get them done when I go for my pre-chemo appointment this afternoon (2.20pm). This week was a bit more of a slog. I am thinking I might walk to my appointment though… xxx

It was stubbornness more than sense that made me walk to my pre-chemo appointment at the Beatson this afternoon. It was a beautiful walk (if chilly), so I'm glad I'm so thrawn. #gettingthroughchemo

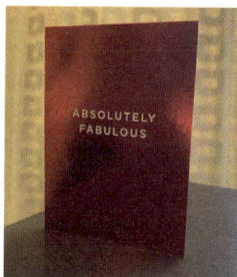

To Karen

Sorry for not replying. Alison will let me know if there's a problem with my bloods. I had a really good appointment with her. Our chats are becoming the highlight of my week. And I walked there, but not back. And I'd put on another two lbs! xx

Thursday, 2nd of December

To Karen

Thank you. Just hoping my bloods will be okay. The nosebleeds are a bit worse, so I'm hoping that's not a sign of anything. xxx

Today will be my 2nd last chemo (for now) (of this type of chemo). According to the card waiting for me on the kitchen table this morning, it's also day 77 and hair or no hair, wig or no wig, I'm #AbFab (I think Ronnie might have started to lose the plot). #gettingthroughchemo

To Ronnie

Alison came to see me. She had chased up my genetics result. It's negative. I have none of the mutations they look for. Thank goodness!!!!!!

To Ronnie

So good. I cried a little. How good is she to do that and then come and find me to let me know. xx

To Cousins

My Wednesday bloods were okay so I'm in the big chair with the cannula in my hand. And my clinical nurse specialist came to see me to tell me the genetic testing had come back negative. So that was great news in terms of the amount of surgery I'll require. They took the blood for the genetic testing back in August, so it was great to finally hear and get good news. xxx

To Cousins

Thank you! It means I can avoid a preventative double mastectomy and ovary removal, so it's a huge relief.

Friday, 3rd of December

To Clair

Thanks to steroid craziness, I've ordered some things for Sebastian the Bird and Susan the Bird and I'm hoping you'll let them live in a wee corner of your garden…

xxxxx

To Clair

And you're in for a bumper Christmas of random stuff.

Saturday, 4th of December

To Clair

The blackbird swag hasn't arrived yet…

Sunday, 5th of December

To Karen

Thanks. The banana bread is delicious!

Tuesday, 7th of December

To Johanna

I had the appointment with the surgeon. He said he can't feel the breast lump anymore and that the lymph node is less obvious, too, so the chemo seems to have done its job (thank goodness!). There was no more mention of additional chemo pre-surgery and he said they would make sure the MRI was an urgent request. He also said I'd need a pre-surgery appointment at radiology in Gartnavel to have something inserted into the breast to direct the surgery (I can't remember what he called it). I'm very relieved and grateful. I don't quite know how to process the news yet other than I know that it's good. Thanks again for your friendship and support. Our walk was exactly what I needed on Sunday.

Wednesday, 8th of December

It was too miserable to walk to the Beatson, so I had to drive to my last pre-chemo appt/pre-chemo bloods of the year. Annoying as that was (I'm a stubborn creature of habit), it says a lot for the Glasgow weather that I've been able to do it up until now. #gettingthroughchemo

Thursday, 9th of December

To Karen

Thank you. I wasn't feeling great yesterday, so hopefully today will be better (even with the chemo). xx

To Clair

Thanks for all the brilliant support. I couldn't have done this without you. Just couldn't. xxxxx

To Ronni

Still waiting…

To Ronni

Almost finished the premeds. Then it'll be an hour flush. Then the chemo…

To Cousins

Chemo eight of eight. One hour to go. xxx

To Susan

Yes. An hour and a half to get a chair, but strangely the time passes easily. An hour to go now. Oh. And another blown vein.

An hour to go and chemo 8 of 8 will be over. And the lovely, incredible nurses have made the room as festive as infection control allows. #carefulandkindcare #gettingthroughchemo

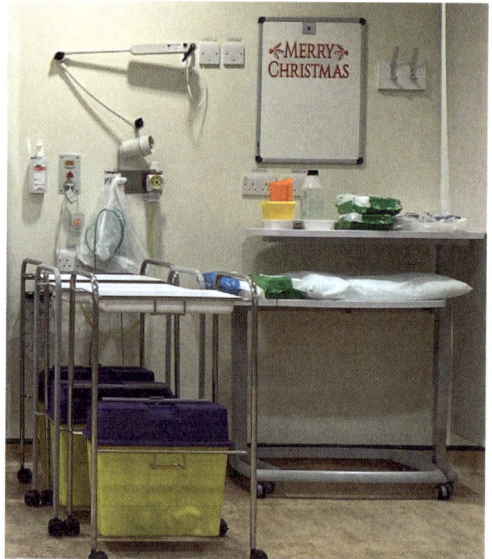

Friday, 10th of December

A stunning 5 hours sleep on chemo night. My mind has now been up for a bit though: bright, alert, and full of chat. #steroids #allofthethoughts #gettingthroughchemo

I had a great meeting with my lovely agent today. It was so good to do something normal. I'm not doing much writing at the moment, but I am still thinking, planning, and making a lot of notes. #stillme

Saturday, 11th of December

Two days post-chemo session 8 of 8, so forgive the face, but isn't my wig from @Beatson_Charity just lovely. Thanks to all who work, volunteer, and support this brilliant charity.

Monday, 13th of December

According to the card that was waiting for me this morning, it's day 88 (since starting treatment). For anyone familiar with my foibles, you'll know it should be a good day. The only thing better than an 8…? Two 8s. #gettingthroughtreatment #luckynumber8 #loveanevennumber

Wednesday, 15th of December

To Alison

Hi Alison,

Just to let you know that Dr Kerr gave me a prescription for the suppositories. I've put it into the pharmacy.

Also, I left a couple of boxes of chocolates at the desk for area two. Hopefully you'll get some.

I hope you have a lovely Christmas. Thanks for giving me such great care! It's made all the difference in the world to me.

Gillian

To Karen

I feel pretty rubbish, but that's okay. I went for a sleep this afternoon and woke up confused in a… *was that all a dream* sort of way. Oops. Apparently not. I checked to see if I had hair. xx

To Karen

I think there might be a bit of a wallop in the tail of the weekly chemo. Dr Kerr told me today that I'd done extremely well to get through it.

To Clair

Hey! Do you have any time later to pull your pal out of a big old hole of sadness… You know scrappy wee me though, I'll probably have scrabbled out all on my own in two shakes of a lamb's tail. xx

To S,C,W&J

Just a wee update for my American support team. I had chemo treatment number 8 of 8 last Thursday and have met with both the surgeon and the oncologist to discuss next steps. If my MRI scan next Wednesday shows there has been good progress, it will give the green light for surgery. I hope you're all well and are enjoying the festive season. Thank you for all your love and support.

To Sally

I've really appreciated your support. You've been so thoughtful and have often done something at just the right moment. This is a hard slog and friendship and support are vital.

Thursday, 16th of December

To Libbe

Thank you so much for the beautiful flowers and card. It's wonderful to see those adorable faces!

You've been on my mind in the last couple of days. I kept intending to write with an update, which I'll give you now. I had chemo session number eight of eight last Thursday. The next step is an MRI next Wednesday. If it shows that the chemo has done its job, it will give the green light for surgery in early January.

My chemo was changed to weekly after two 3-weekly treatments because I'd been dangerously unwell after each one. I've done so much better on the weekly chemo (no more infections or sepsis!). I know that everyone's prayers have been so important in keeping me safe. I'm trying to recuperate now and get my body ready for the surgery.

Thank you again for the flowers and kind words. They certainly brightened my day!

Much love,

Gillian x

Friday, 17th of December

To Molly Jo

I'm really sorry but I'm not feeling well today so won't be able to do our class. I'm hoping this doesn't lead to another hospitalisation.

To Johanna

I'm afraid I'm having an overnight at the Beatson. I felt dreadful this morning with abdominal discomfort and other unpleasantness. Thankfully when I phoned the emergency line at lunchtime, they let me go to the Beatson for assessment. My bloods are actually looking okay (neutrophil count is 3.5) but they want to keep me overnight just to make sure. I hope you're having a lovely time with family. xx

Saturday, 18th of December

To Johanna

Your messages were lovely. I was awake on and off, so they were a nice companion. I was so excited to finish chemo last week so was doubly devastated to start feeling horrible on day 8. I am feeling a lot better than I did yesterday morning though and my bloods are okay, so I should be out this morning. I'm glad you're having a wonderful time with family. You deserve it! xx

To Ronnie

I have a message from the vet centre asking you to call Aileen.

To Clair

Better than yesterday but still a bit yucky. I should get out at 4pm today. xx

Wednesday, 22nd of December

I'm having a pre-surgical MRI in just over an hour to help assess if the chemo has done its job. The MRI scanner was one of my research objects. We have a bit of personal history, too. #medicalobject #medicalsubject #talkingobjects

To Karen

It was horrible, but it's done, thank goodness. x

Thursday, 23rd of December

Elizabeth and Kate

Thank you. I had the MRI yesterday. It was surprisingly tough. I thought I was mentally prepared, but I lost the head game early. I still managed to stay in for the full 45 minutes though. I'm guessing I'll hear the results next week. I hope you're both having a lovely festive period. xx

Friday, 24th of December

To Clair

Happy Christmas Eve! I hope it's a jolly holiday today… And in case you're interested… my top three Sheriff wig names are… Mildred, Mabel, Maud…

To Clair

Three more choices… Hattie, Joan, Barbara… (the Carry On shortlist)

Saturday, 25th of December

To Cousins

A very happy Christmas! Thank you for all your love and support this year. xx

January 2022

Saturday, 1st of January 2022

To Karen

Happy New Year! xx

Sunday, 2nd of January

To Laura

Sorry! I only saw this now. I wasn't feeling very well today (or yesterday). It seems chemo is the gift that just keeps giving. Maybe we could FaceTime tomorrow? xx

Wednesday, 5th of January

To Georgi

You've rumbled me. I haven't been great and couldn't face inflicting it on you. It seems chemo has ensured that my guts are actually garters (if being garters means they're completely f**k*d). I have felt a bit better yesterday and today though, so YAY. Just in time to meet with the surgeon tomorrow at 10.30am (I got the call today to say I have an appointment tomorrow) to find out the results of the MRI scan I had two weeks ago, which will also mean them giving me all the gory details of 'the next steps'.

G x

Thursday, 6th of January

To Father Jim

I got a call yesterday asking me to come for an appointment at 10.30am today to talk to the surgeon. He'll let me know the results of the MRI scan I had two weeks ago and will explain the next steps. I'll let you know what he says. I am a little bit nervous this morning.

To Karen

The scan appeared to show that the lymph nodes have responded well and that there's been a partial response in the breast. This means they don't have to remove all the lymph nodes, probably he'll just take three. I would have preferred to have heard something more positive about the breast, but it's better than no response. He also said that the important measure is the pathology. Depending on what it shows they may have to take bigger margins and more lymph nodes, or not. The date for surgery is the 24th. There's a problem in that I need to have magnetic seeds inserted and the clinic that does it is fully booked before that date, but they're going to try to have me fitted in. x

To Susan

That kick up the arse made me smile. Thank you! He had the scan on his screen while he talked to me, so I could see the tumour sitting there with a stubborn look on its face. (I like Janey Godley's tumour being called Bunty, but I don't want to name a thing I just want gone).

To Clair

Was just wondering when you fancied a walk… xx

Elizabeth and Kate

I feel a bit lost if I'm honest, but I'll get there. The words 'partial response' seems to have knocked me off balance. I think I just need a couple of days to get back on an even keel. I wanted him to tell me it was gone, which was unrealistic but maybe just human nature. Thanks for being there. It means a lot.

Sunday, 9th of January

To Susan

Thank you! As always, very helpful! I'm currently a little bit mad at a website for post-surgical bras. It declares that breast cancer survivors were involved in the design process, which is great. But why not just say people who have had surgery for breast cancer?! Language is important (which is evidenced by the tailspin I almost went into after the reminder that there are survivors and there are those who don't).

To Susan

Have I mentioned how glad I am that your head is packed full of useful stuff?! I contacted a friend (son-in-law-to-be of good friends) and he's going to come here at 12.30pm next Saturday. He's lovely, Irish, and dual qualified as a nurse and a physio.

Monday, 10th of January

To Georgi

Sorry that it's taken me such a long time to reply. My head was mince. I'm getting to the other side of the initial impact of all the news now, but it's not been easy. Lots of little dragons and beasts to be sealed tightly in dragon and beast-proof glass jars.

I now have the following things scheduled… a pre-op assessment (Friday at 11.30am), a magnetic seed insertion procedure (next Monday at 9.30am), and a pre-surgery Covid test (next Friday at an as yet undisclosed time). In addition to a confirmation that surgery (if all those things go as they should) will definitely be on the 24th.

I'm having to figure out how to live and breathe in the in-between times.

G x

✉ Tuesday, 11th of January

To Zoe

Thank you, Zoe! That was very kind of you.

Thanks also for the bra tip. It feels like I should figure some of this stuff out beforehand. I ordered one from an Irish company, so we'll see what happens with that. The local bramonger sounds much better, though.

Thanks again!

Gillian x

🐦 Friday, 14th of January

Mindfully breathing as I wait for my pre-op assessment.

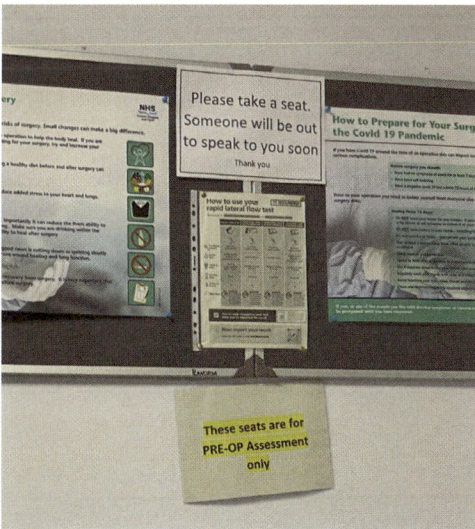

📞 (WhatsApp)

To Ronnie

Just finished. Walking home. x

🐦 Sunday, 16th of January

To distract me from tomorrow's hospital appointment (magnetic seed insertion), I'm focusing on these lovely January flowers. #snowdrops

📞 (WhatsApp) Monday, 17th of January

To Susan

Waiting to be called for magnetic seed insertion. My name wasn't on the list so apparently my breast nurse is going to come down…

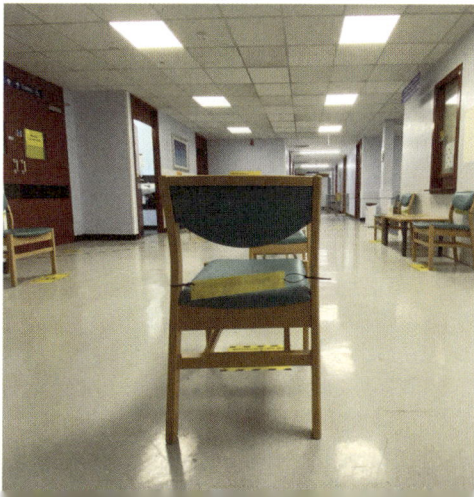

To Ronnie

The procedure has been done. I'm waiting to have a mammogram done to check they have been positioned correctly. x

To Ronnie

That's okay. I need to go back to the clinic once I'm done here. They don't have me on the list there either. x

To Ronnie

Could you come and get me?

I'm grateful to be on the other side of magnetic seed insertion. The radiologist was brilliant. She infused the clinical space with humanity and care. #carefulandkindcare

To Karen

There was a bit of a mix up to start, but I got squeezed into the clinic and the radiologist was lovely. I didn't get the one they thought they'd organised. Instead, it was the one who did my biopsies. I'm very happy it's done. Just rest, recuperation and fresh air from now until next Monday. xx

To Karen

She asked for a long green needle and I told her I'd renamed it broccoli quiche. When she was done, she asked me to write down the name of the journal because she wanted to read the piece I'd written. She

seemed genuinely interested in being able to experience the procedure from the other perspective. xx

Wednesday, 19th of January

To Susan

My sister just sent me this. Since she started bulk buying Pan Drops, Asda have doubled the shelf space for them…

To Susan

Maybe it's also because I keep telling folks in the Beatson about them. You should demand a share in the profits.

To Hilary

Thanks! I really appreciate that. They're going to keep me in overnight because I became very unwell after a previous surgery. It was 20 years ago though and I'm told anaesthetic is very different now, so I'm hoping it'll end up just being overcaution. x

I had my pre-surgical PCR at Gartnavel this morning. This is my second Friday in a row at pre-op assessment. The staff are lovely. They do all their tests/paperwork with grace, care, and a reassuring manner. #carefulandkindcare

To Clair

Thanks. The pre-op staff are very nice. I'm just trying to manage the nerves now. Please give my love to the lovely Lynches. xx

To Georgi

Thank you, best pen pal. I really appreciate you writing (and the words that you wrote). My brain is a bowl of the mushiest peas, which renders me incapable of constructing anything approaching the response I might like to write. Suffice it to say the days have been going too quickly, hurtling me towards something I fear. Something who's name I'm becoming less able to speak. Wah. And. Gah.

But I will be fine. I will. (this is my mantra)

And I'm grateful that you'll be there on the other side.

Sending love and best wishes for a time when there's less health/medical stuff. And more writing that's lovely.

G xx

Surgery is on Monday so even though it's a bit drizzly I'm spending time outside focusing on January flowers. #JanuaryRose

To Katie

That's a lovely picture. Thank you.

I've been thinking about you also and I've composed a number of emails, in my head. I am very sorry about your dad and wanted to send love to you, but the chemo got the better of me and the email was never written. Sorry.

It is lovely to hear from you. I don't have a good history with surgery, so I'm mainly trying to manage my anxiety levels. The app Headspace was recommended to me right at the beginning and it really has been a great help to me. I also find getting outside to be very important.

Wishing you all the very best,

Gillian x

To Susan

Thank you for my lovely gift. SO thoughtful and SO helpful.

To Clair

Sorry! I was packing my hospital bag. Just about to have dinner then go to 5.30pm Mass online. Can I phone you afterwards? xx

To Cousins

Thanks, everyone! I really appreciate all the support and care. xxx

To Johanna

Thank you. You are so lovely. I really appreciate you checking in. xxx

Monday, 24th of January

To Karen

In the surgical assessment area. The anaesthetist has been to see me. He was very nice and very reassuring. The surgeon got me to sign a consent form and despite the mask etc., I could tell it was Mr Walker. I'm just waiting to be sent to nuclear medicine. xx

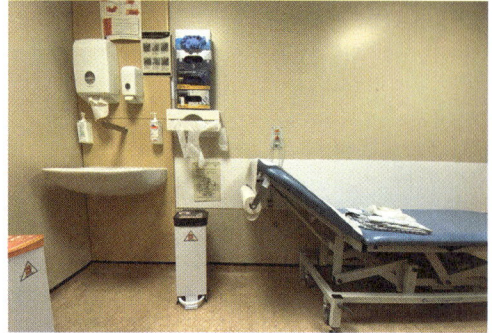

To Karen

Thank you. Nuclear Medicine injection done. xxx

To Father Jim

Thank you. In the ward about half an hour post-surgery. A bit sore and nauseous but very glad to be on the other side.

To Father Jim

Ha! Of surgery! I really want to be on THIS side.

To Hilary

Thanks! In the ward now. Sitting on a chair sipping chopped ginger in hot water (I brought the ginger in). I really appreciate you checking in, Hils.

To Johanna

In the ward. I asked to sit in a chair because I was feeling nauseous. I'm sipping chopped ginger in hot water. Very grateful to be on this side of surgery. xxx

To Susan

To Susan

Sitting on a chair in the ward. I didn't last long in bed.

Sitting up in the ward post-surgery, sporting my compression socks. Grateful to be on this side of it.

Tuesday, 25th of January

To Ronnie

I should be ready to go in about half an hour. x

To Ronnie

Change of plan. I need bloods done so the discharge will be delayed.

Wednesday, 26th of January

To Susan

About to go out for a wee dog walk. I'm guessing that's okay. I'm going to take Daisy and let my mum take Hamish.

I'm gathering artefacts for a writing project that's simmering in the background, waiting for a time beyond. It'll be an archive of all that accompanied diagnosis and treatment, including images charting the experience. This arrow was drawn pre-surgery. #medhums #talkingobjects

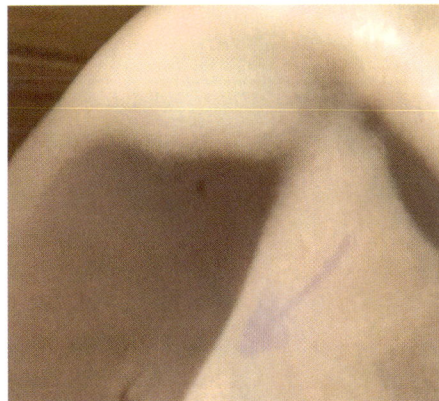

Elizabeth and Kate

Just thought I'd check in. I'm now a bit sore and feel a bit hungover, but otherwise good. I've been doing my physio regardless and have had two walks today, one on my own in surprisingly pleasant drizzle. Here's a photo of the arrow they drew on me to make sure they got the right (right) breast. It feels a little scary that it's necessary… xx

Thursday, 27th of January

To Johanna

I'm okay. A bit sore and finding it hard to find a comfortable way to arrange my body for sleep (which sounds very silly), but I know it'll just be a matter of time. xx

To Susan

I think I did something stupid. I lifted a couple of heavy things with my left hand thinking that would be okay as it's the non-surgical side, but I've got more pain on the right side now and am wondering if I shouldn't be lifting heavy things with either hand.

In other news… I could open a florist…

To Susan

It was, in fact, the transporting of six flower/water filled vases from sink to table…

To Susan

I've been doing my exercises like a gold star is depending on them. I'm just about to go out for another walk. I promise no more heavy lifting even with the left hand!

This was left in an envelope on the kitchen table, which is surprising because I've been sore and grumpy since I got home. I can't even imagine how hard it is for the other person. In other news, the card also told me it's day 133 since treatment started. #breastcancer

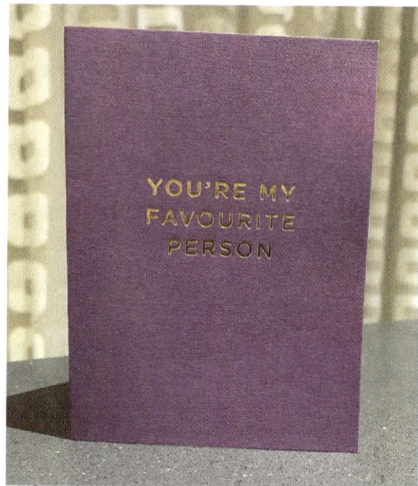

Friday, 28th of January

To Molly Jo

Here are the exercises I was given at the hospital.

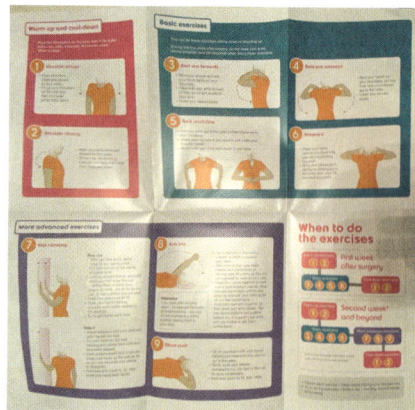

Saturday, 29th of January

To Clair

We're heading out for a dog walk in five. xx

📞

To Jen

It felt a bit traumatic, just because it's surgery in the midst of everything, but it went without incident. I see the surgeon on Thursday to have the wounds checked and to find out the results of the pathology. I'm trying hard to manage the stress about that by focusing on the physio and on taking each day as it comes. How are you? I hope you had a lovely birthday. x

📞 **Sunday, 30th of January**

To Hilary

Thanks for checking in! It's still a bit sore but much better than it was and I'm able to do all the exercises without any problems. I see the surgeon at 11am on Thursday. I'm trying hard not to think about it too much beforehand. xx

📞 **Monday, 31st of January**

To EKR

I'm doing okay, thanks. Annoyingly sore, but I'm pretty good at ignoring pain. I'm also doing all my physio like a teacher's pet. How are you? I hope your week has started well. X

February 2022

Tuesday, 1st of February

To Father Jim

Thanks for keeping me in your prayers. There's a bit of a battle in my head at the moment because I'm back to see the surgeon on Thursday morning so that he can check the wounds and let me know the pathology of what he removed, which will determine treatment going forwards. I'm really hoping I'm able to move onto radiotherapy, but I may have to have more surgery and/or more chemo first depending on the results.

Wednesday, 2nd of February

To Michelle

Hi Michelle,

I hope your week is going well and that I'll see you later today at Maggie's meeting.

I was going to go and write something in our google doc, but after so long my laptop doesn't seem to have any memory of where I can find it (and I'm still as technically incompetent as ever). To add to the problem, I no longer have access to my university email, so can't look back through our previous correspondence.

I'm not sure exactly what I would have written, and I seem unable to write with the same freedom in an email that I would have done there, so it will just need to remain a mystery. Suffice it to say, I'm doing okay just now (I'm nine days post-surgery), but I may be less good after the appointment with my surgeon tomorrow at 11am, at which we'll discuss the pathology of what he removed and my treatment moving forwards.

Sending all good wishes,

Gillian

Thursday, 3rd of February

To Susan

The news could have been better. I need more surgery because he didn't get clean margins (pre-cancerous cells) and there was still cancer in the lymph node (although not in the other two that were removed) so they're recommending a targeted antibody/chemo protocol. I have an appointment with my oncologist next Wednesday, so he'll explain more. My next surgery is on the 17th. I had a big cry but no screaming or stamping of feet.

To Susan

Thank you. The crying is still coming in big waves, but I'll get there.

To Susan

You win the best response of the day. Thank you. Nose wiped. Feet stamped.

Friday, 4th of February

I had my first shower in 11 days (I'd been having shallow baths, so I wasn't that smelly). It meant I could wash my hair, what there is of it, for the first time in all those days (maybe I am that smelly). Hair that's almost at the 60s Mia Farrow stage of regrowth.

Sunday, 6th of February

To Clair

Are you back home? Do you fancy a walk…? xx

Monday, 7th of February

To Michelle

Well, it really has been a while. A while of writing very little and of narrowed everything. My life has shrunk down to coping with cancer: the thought of it; the reality of it. There are, however, days when, for hours at a time, I am able to win the head game and just be. These mostly happen outside, which can be a challenge in winter. Even a mild Scottish winter. Mild is a relative term here. The Scottish winter is indeed mild when compared to those in Neenah, Wisconsin, but decidedly awful if I think back to the winters of St Petersburg, Florida.

Today is cold and damp. But the temperature is above freezing and there have been a couple of dry spells in the midst of otherwise unrelenting drizzle, so I managed a decent dog walk.

I'm in an in-between place.

In-between surgery one and two (the surgeon didn't get clean margins, although what was in the margin were pre-cancerous cells; cancer cells being completely gone from the breast). Surgery two is scheduled for next Thursday.

In-between hearing from the surgeon that my oncologist recommends a particular antibody/chemo protocol due to the cancer cells that had stubbornly stayed in one lymph node (the same lymph node that had been biopsied at the outset; he removed two others that had no cancer cells) and sitting down with the oncologist to learn the detail of his plan. That will happen this Wednesday.

At the moment the discomfort being caused by cancer is mainly psychological. A lot of the physical symptoms of the chemo have subsided, although, some do remain. And the post-surgical pain is manageable (I'm an old hand at pain management and do my physio exercises like there might be a gold star on offer). The discomfort therefore lives in my head and in my gut (where fear seems to reside): the problem being thoughts and the feelings they conjure, unbidden.

I use the Headspace app, which helps. But I still catch myself in an unhelpful spiral. Usually, the nausea in my gut alerts me to the fact that my thoughts have slipped off-piste and have begun to hurtle down a black run.

I have to say, no one has asked what help I might need in this regard. I am a car from which parts need to be removed (in surgical terms) and one to be tinkered with in order to keep it running a bit longer (in oncology terms).

In the meantime, the car is lost, driving aimlessly in hostile terrain.

It seems that careful and kind care would at least ask the question, which is just one of the reasons why its cultivation is so important.

Sending love and solidarity from Scotland.

G x

To Karen

Wordle? I haven't heard of it. I'll have a go. My brain isn't quite what it was though.

To Karen

I'm completely stuck!

To Karen

And now I've lost where it is on my phone!!!!

Tuesday, 8th of February

I had a lovely Zoom with @georgi_gill today during which we discussed my transitional hair. We decided it's currently channeling Renton and have our fingers crossed it will embrace a Jean Seberg phase very soon. #palsareimportant

To Hilary

Thank you for my beautiful flowers. It was really kind of you to send them. xx

Wednesday, 9th of February

Elizabeth and Kate

I had a good appointment with the oncologist. He's great. He spent an hour and fifteen minutes with me. He talked through the pathology and whilst it wasn't perfect, there still being a remnant of live cancer cells in one lymph node, he said it was really pretty good (no live cancer cells in the breast, just some pre-cancerous ones and no cancer cells in the other two lymph nodes). He used the word cure for the first time. Before they only used the word treatable, but today he said that in 8/9 cases out of 10 of breast cancer that looked like mine is looking now, the person would be cured, assuming they had all the treatment now planned (breast surgery to achieve clean margins, radiotherapy, and nine months of this new drug: T-DM1). If my pathology results had still shown live cancer cells in the breast and a spread to other lymph nodes, my chance of a cure was 3 out of 10, so whilst I'm daunted by what's ahead, I'm grateful for where I am now. He said he hadn't been sure I would be able to make it through all the chemo I had before Christmas. Thank goodness I did! xx

To Karen

Are you around for a FaceTime? xx

Thursday, 10th of February

To Father Jim

I saw the oncologist yesterday afternoon and he talked me through the pathology in detail. He said that while it wasn't perfect it was pretty good. The next treatment is a bit daunting - it's 14 3-weekly cycles and 3 weeks of daily radiotherapy - but he said what I've been through already was much harsher. I have the surgery next week to try to get clean margins and then, if they do, the new treatment should start by the end of March.

Friday, 11th of February

To Johanna

Thank you. I struggled so much at the start and will be forever grateful for the friendship and support you gave me. For the moment, I'm just setting my sights on getting through surgery on Thursday and hoping it'll be my last one. I hope you have a lovely weekend! xx

Saturday, 12th of February

To Karen

My first three at Wordle.

Sunday, 13th of February

To Jen

Thanks, Jen. I appreciate all the care and support we get from you. I'll be having treatment until mid-December, but it gives me a much better prognosis, so I'll get on and do it. x

Monday, 14th of February

I have my Covid test tomorrow and will then isolate until surgery on Thursday so my sister and I used my last day out for a wee bit to look for the family grave of our great great uncle, sculptor William Shirreffs. We scoured Glasgow's Western Necropolis until we did.

Tuesday, 15th of February

Elizabeth and Kate

I know I'm the only one obsessed with this, but two days before surgery two I have hair (extremely short but full coverage), eyebrows AND eyelashes. I'm taking this as a win.

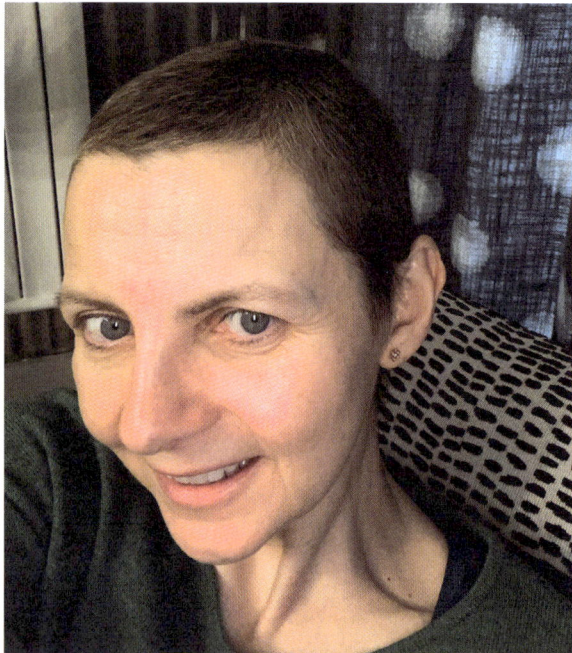

Elizabeth and Kate

It seems the problem with the hair etc is that you look sick without it. Like a cancer patient in a film. So, I am totally obsessed with every last eyelash. I know I don't look the picture of health yet, but I'll get there. A good thing about the next treatment is that I shouldn't (although they can't give a 100% guarantee) lose it again. A bad thing is that it causes weight loss, something the oncologist doesn't want me to do anymore of.

Elizabeth and Kate

It's good to talk. I realise now I was feeling a little bit low before sending that message. Reaching out into the void and a hand appeared. Thank you.

Elizabeth and Kate

I tried to write earlier but it was sticky and stale. I need the wind to change, like Mary Poppins. I'm glad you're writing. Something for future me to read. Future me has a to do list that keeps growing. In a good way.

Thursday, 17th of February

To Susan

I've to report to the Gartnavel surgical admissions unit at noon, so had my light breakfast at 6.30am (two slices of seeded bread with almond butter). Hopefully it was light enough! The suggestion was tea and toast. I'm guessing I can still drink clear fluids because it says I've to have a glass of water at/before 11am.

To Ronnie

Anna was here to see me. She said if you want to call afterwards to check on me it would be the ward you would call due to the time of day. xx

To Ronnie

Ward 4A. They don't have anyone before me, so I'll be taken soon. xx

To Ronnie

I'm just in the ward. Feeling pretty rubbish, but here. xx

To Cousins

Back in the ward. Feeling a bit sick and sore but sipping my magical ginger in hot water so I should be good soon. x

---

Friday, 18th of February

To Ronnie

Are the dogs loving the snow? x

To Ronnie

I'm ready whenever you're here…

Happy to be back home. They were discharging folks early doors in case the weather got any worse. And in other good news, I had a distant view to the @UofGlasgow tower (through the window netting).

To Johanna

I was back in the house before 10. Very happy to be home but feeling that restless, slightly sad way the anaesthetic makes you and a bit sore as, due to my weight and sensitivity to other drugs, I can only have a maximum of 4 paracetamol a day, so I've only had 1 so far today. Ouch. I hope you're having a good Friday. xx

To Susan

Thank you. I'm feeling a bit crummy - sicky, lightheaded - but otherwise okay.

To Clair

R and I are going out for a wee walk without dogs. I'll wave (with my good arm) on the way by. xx

To Clair

Been and back. Your white planter needs a wee clean…

Surgery two brought two arrows. The one on my arm was drawn while I was still awake; the second one was a wee surprise. #talkingobjects #breastcancer

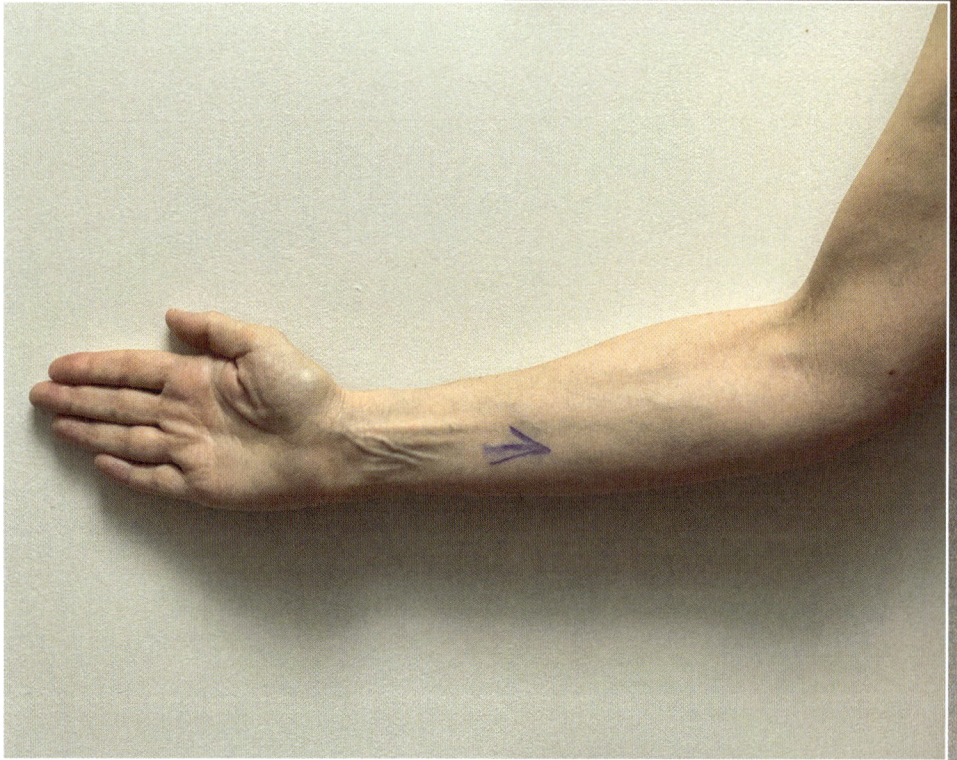

114

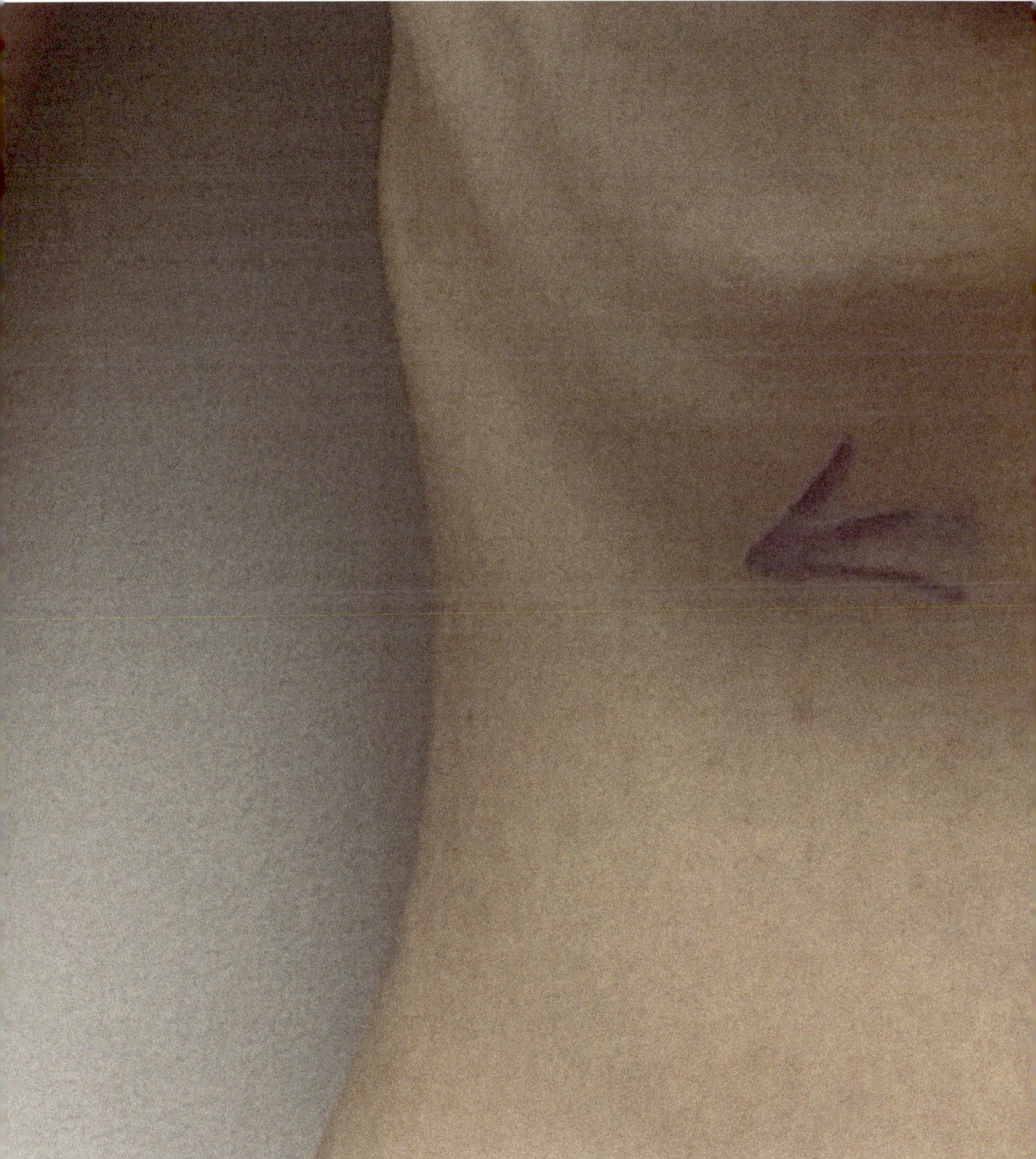

Elizabeth and Kate

More arrows! The registrar must have drawn the one on my torso once I was anaesthetised… x

To Laura

I'm still a bit sore and a bit nauseous, but I got home yesterday. I'm sure I'll be feeling much better in a couple of days. How's your mom? xx

To S,C,W&J

I had my second surgery on Thursday and got home yesterday. The staff made sure they did the discharges early in the day as they were worried about the snow… Here's the view from the window of what they were so concerned about… Ha! You can tell I'm not in Wisconsin anymore!

To S,C,W&J

To be fair, the forecast was also for 90 mile an hour winds, which we might describe here as 'a wee bit blowy'.

Monday, 21st of February

To Clair

Do you want some sweet potato, butternut squash and carrot soup (with cumin)? xx

To Karen

I'm doing okay. I didn't feel at all well yesterday but am where I should be now. It was almost like a delayed response in my gut to whatever drugs they'd given me. Annoying but not permanent. x

To Father Jim

I hope you're having a great, relaxing, sunny time. I got your message when I was back in the ward after surgery, and it was a lovely message to get. Thank you. I got out on Friday and have been resting and recovering since. I see the surgeon on Thursday to find out if he got clean margins this time. He told me he was hopeful but that there were no guarantees.

Tuesday, 22nd of February

Elizabeth and Kate

Happy 22.2.22! There will be a smile affixed to my face all palindrome-day long.

Elizabeth and Kate

Fantastic! I'll raise a mug of fennel tea to you both at 22:22 (and 22 seconds).

I was having not the best morning (6 days post surgery 2 and 1 day until I'm told if the surgeon got clean margins or if I need more surgery) and then the post arrived. I have been shown such love and kindness through this whole process and it means so very much. Thank you.

✉️

To Misti

It's SO good to hear from you. I've begun a follow-up email in my head numerous times, but it never reached my fingers.

I'm six days post surgery two. It's definitely better done in skit form, so I'll leave any description of the experience to a future Zoom. I find out tomorrow if he got clean margins. His words on the day were that he was hopeful but there were no guarantees.

My fingers and toes are crossed that he did (I shared a 4-bed ward after surgery two with a lady who had just had her third surgery on that very quest), which would mean I have three weeks to recuperate (mainly from not-gone-yet chemo side effects) before I start the new treatment.

Gillian x

Thursday, 24th of February

This is Hamish's pleeease-throw-me-another-snowball face. An antidote to pre-hospital-appointment nerves. #HappyFlattie

To Cousins

Just back from my appointment. He got clean margins, so I don't need any more surgery. xx

To Father Jim

Just back home after an appointment with the surgeon. He got clean margins this time, so I don't need any more surgery. I'm so grateful.

To Clair

He got clean margins! Thanks for being there every step and every tear of the way, best pal. xxx

To Molly Jo

He got clean margins! It means no more surgery. And we can focus on getting my body ready for the antibody treatment and radiotherapy. I have three weeks to rest and recuperate before it starts.

Elizabeth and Kate

I meant to tell you, Kate. I was wearing my lucky scarf today. And not to be too nuts but… today is day 161 since treatment started (adding up to 8 and a teeny tiny palindrome) and it's the 24/2 (adding up to 8 and a sort of teeny tiny palindrome). A good day for good news.

Friday, 25th of February

To Hilary

Thank you for all the support you've given me through this. The care and the flowers and the messages to let me know you were there. I needed it all and appreciate it so much. I know I still have a long way to go, but it feels like the hardest part of the journey is behind me now. xx

Saturday, 26th of February

To Clair

Yay!!! I'm up for a walk when you are… 10 mins…?

Sunday, 27th of February

To Clair

Have you Wordled…?

To Clair

How you got from tramp to chant can only be described as black magic!

Enjoying the late-February sun with the dogs. #NatureIsNurture #DogTherapy

Monday, 28th of February

To Clair

Happy Monday! Have you Wordled yet…? Xx

To Clair

And despite having different first words we both went for chore then choke…!

March 2022

To Diana

Hi Diana,

I hope you're well! Since I last saw you, I've finished chemo and had two operations. I saw the surgeon last week and he told me he had got clean margins with the second surgery, so I don't need have to have a third one. Yay!

In other exciting news... I have hair. It's incredibly short but is getting thick (especially at the top). I've just booked an appointment with you in three weeks. Partly because I'd love to see you, but also because it would probably look better (especially at the back) with a little tidy up (there are wispy bits) and it would be good to get your advice on what I should do as it grows back in.

Gillian x

P.S. I also have eyelashes again and one and a half eyebrows!

🐦 Thursday, 3rd of March

The first sign of #breastcancer for me was unintentional weight loss; then I noticed the lump. The weight loss continued as my body coped poorly with chemo, so before my next treatment starts, I'm focused on maintaining and gaining, hence today's breakfast. #firsteverfoodpic

🐦 Friday, 4th of March

I'm using twitter to capture my illness experience as it's easy on energy levels. When I do start to write again, I'm thinking I'll tackle a braided essay on hair. Maybe that's why my phone just randomly decided to share a photo of when I had too much of it thanks to lockdown

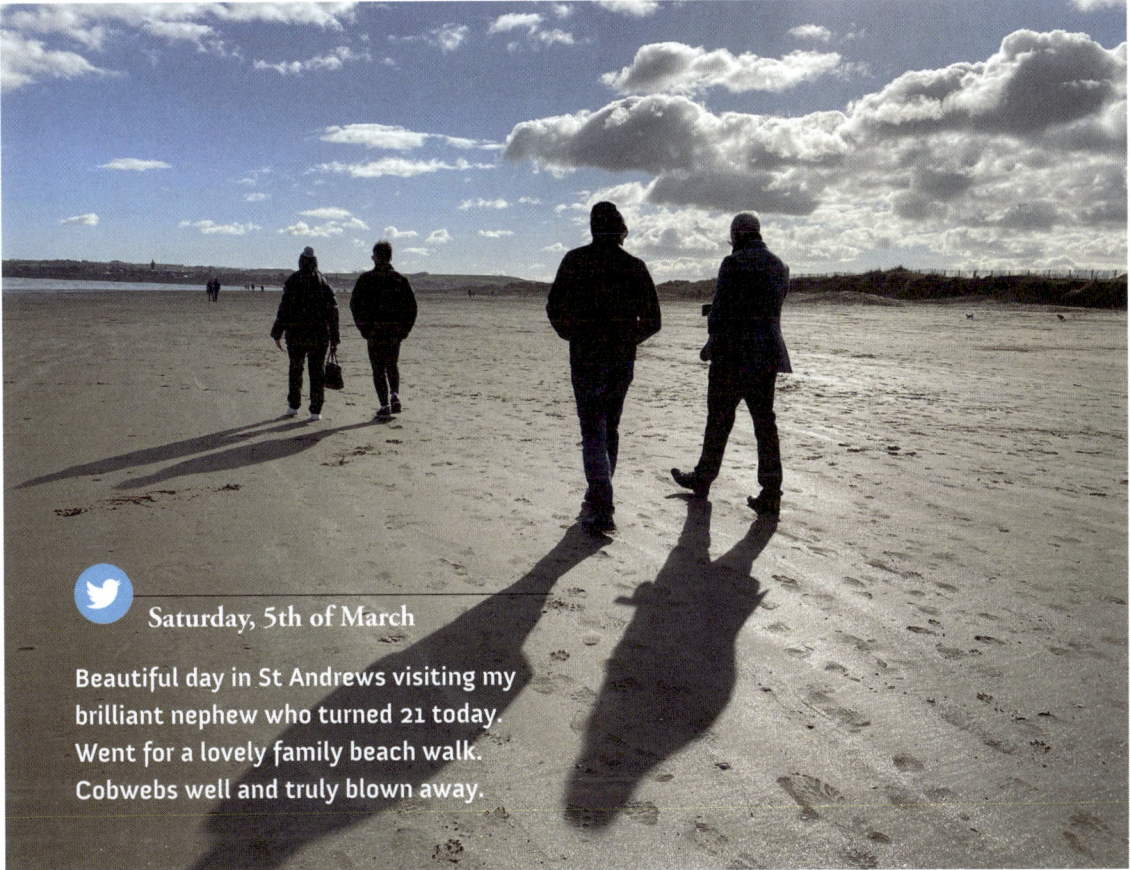

🐦 **Saturday, 5th of March**

Beautiful day in St Andrews visiting my brilliant nephew who turned 21 today. Went for a lovely family beach walk. Cobwebs well and truly blown away.

🐦 **Sunday, 6th of March**

Tea and a chat in my pal's Glasgow garden was a sanctuary post-diagnosis. Today was our first chance to have garden-time this year and it was just as therapeutic as I remembered. #friendship

🟢 **Monday, 7th of March**

To Karen

I noticed a lump on Hamish. The vet can see him on Thursday, but Ronnie is in meetings, so I'll need to take him. I should be okay to drive. It might just be a little uncomfortable with the seatbelt. x

Thanks to the Glasgow sun, I was able to have my weekly @Beatson_Charity befriender call outside today. Daisy was keen to get in on the action.

✉ **Tuesday, 8th of March**

To literary agent

Hi Sarah,

I hope you're well.

Sorry for the delay in responding. I know it was in no way your intention, but I was a bit devastated by your email. I received it the day of my first surgery and I didn't have the mental reserves to face the reality that Brodie might never be published. I know I seem practical/pragmatic/realistic and I am, for the most part, but I was sad that we're almost at the point of pressing pause, much as I understand why that might be. I suppose I'm just not as resilient as I normally would be. The last six months have been more difficult than I could ever have imagined.

Having said that, I realise I can't just ignore what needs to be done, so I wonder if you have time to have a Zoom call later this week or next week to discuss the pitch?

I've had a couple of weeks to recuperate after my second surgery, but I have an electrocardiogram and my fourth Covid jag today and a couple of hospital appointments tomorrow (oncology and radiology), so thought I should email before I get swept back up.

All the best,

Gillian x

Waiting for my echocardiogram. I had one pre-chemo in September, too. The staff are, as always, lovely.

A lovely, therapeutic walk back from my Beatson appointment this morning. Chilly but beautiful with spring flowers along the way. #WalkingTherapy #Glasgow

Wednesday, 9th of March

I have two hospital appts today, so I've been doing some prep (noting down questions etc). Thanks to @vmontori I understand the importance of meaningful conversations. I've also been thinking about the person within the patient / the person within the clinician. #carefulandkindcare

Thursday, 10th of March

I had good appointments yesterday. Nothing was rushed, all my questions were answered and the conversations were careful and kind. There was even some polite laughter at my horrible jokes. The dates have changed slightly, so I have three weeks to rest and recuperate.

Friday, 11th of March

To Clair

I skin-of-my-teethed Wordle today. That's what I get for doing it early. xx

To Karen

Sorry! I meant to reply yesterday. The vet biopsied two lumps yesterday. She found one under his front leg also (which I presume, from personal experience, to be a lymph node). She's going to phone me today. X

To Karen

He's a star. He always jumps in and out for me (never for Ronnie who ends up having to lift him in and out). X

Monday, 14th of March

I'm taking advantage of having had my 4th Covid jag last week and not starting my next treatment until the 31st to get out and about so despite the Glasgow rain I walked to the Waterstones on Byres Road and bought these two beauties. It was great to be in a bookshop again.

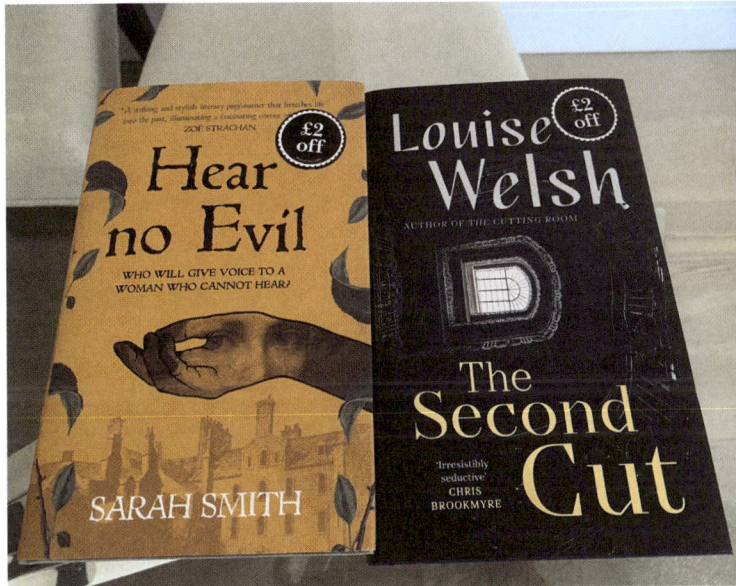

Tuesday, 15th of March

To Clair

Did you Wordle? Have you Wordled? Did you? Have you?

To Clair

Now? Now? Now?

To Clair

I thought TEASE was a little SAUCY…

Wednesday, 16th of March

I started treatment six months ago. A neighbour (who won't know this) handed in flowers today. It feels representative of the kindness I've been shown throughout. I'm grateful for all the messages, cards, books, baking, hats, scarves and flowers. #kindness #community #day181

🐦

Thursday, 17th of March

Today's post included a schedule for my radiotherapy, which I now know will start four days after I begin my new immunotherapy/chemo treatment. There may have been some deep breaths. Tomorrow's appointment is for a CT scan and tattoos...

🐦

I'm very excited that this appeared in my Audible library today (I'd pre-ordered it). The perfect distraction for my upcoming hospital appointments. A murderous mission from cauldron to castle... Can't wait! @OlgaWojtas @SarabandBooks

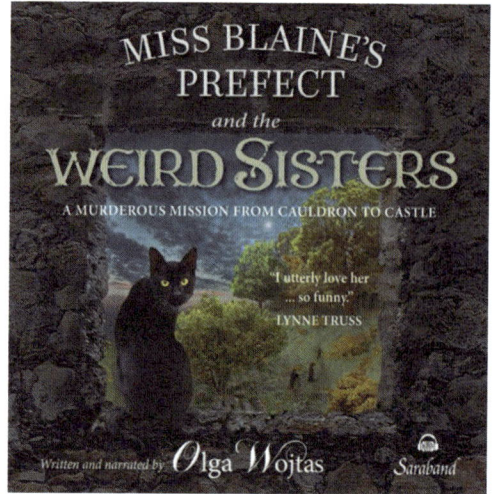

MISS BLAINE'S PREFECT and the WEIRD SISTERS
A MURDEROUS MISSION FROM CAULDRON TO CASTLE
"I utterly love her ... so funny." LYNNE TRUSS
Written and narrated by Olga Wojtas — Saraband

🐦

Friday, 18th of March

Waiting to be called for my radiotherapy planning appointment: CT scan and three freckle-sized tattoos. Breathing deeply.

NHS Greater Glasgow and Clyde — Beatson West of Scotland Cancer Centre - Radiotherapy Appointment Schedule

Patient : Shirreffs, Gillian   Patient Id
Oncologist :

Date	Time	Appointment Type	Location	Hospital
18/03/2022	09:20 AM	Planning Scan	Simulator 1	Glasgow Beatson
04/04/2022	10:12 AM	First Treatment	Treatment Room B	Glasgow Beatson
05/04/2022	10:12 AM	Daily Treatment	Treatment Room B	Glasgow Beatson
06/04/2022	10:12 AM	Daily Treatment	Treatment Room B	Glasgow Beatson
07/04/2022	10:12 AM	Daily Treatment	Treatment Room B	Glasgow Beatson
08/04/2022	10:12 AM	Daily Treatment	Treatment Room B	Glasgow Beatson
11/04/2022	10:12 AM	Daily Treatment	Treatment Room B	Glasgow Beatson
12/04/2022	10:12 AM	Daily Treatment	Treatment Room B	Glasgow Beatson
14/04/2022	10:12 AM	Daily Treatment	Treatment Room B	Glasgow Beatson
15/04/2022	10:12 AM	Daily Treatment	Treatment Room B	Glasgow Beatson
18/04/2022	10:18 AM	Daily Treatment	Treatment Room B	Glasgow Beatson
19/04/2022	09:18 AM	Daily Treatment	Treatment Room B	Glasgow Beatson
20/04/2022	10:18 AM	Daily Treatment	Treatment Room B	Glasgow Beatson
21/04/2022	10:18 AM	Daily Treatment	Treatment Room B	Glasgow Beatson
22/04/2022	10:18 AM	Daily Treatment	Treatment Room B	Glasgow Beatson
25/04/2022	10:18 AM	Final Treatment	Treatment Room B	Glasgow Beatson

To Clair

Tattoos: 3. Wordle guesses: 5.

Saturday, 19th of March

To Clair

Let me know if you want any "early" morning swanning before you head off. I sat out the front with a cup of tea and it was ROASTING. My chemo skin definitely needs factor 50 and a sun hat. xx

To Clair

11.30am sounds great. Could you come by me for a quick walk with the dogs to empty their tanks…? I have three dogs and two hands… and an Auntie Clair nearby who they love very much.

Sunday, 20th of March

To Linsey

Hi Linsey,

It was nice to meet you on Friday. The photos look good. I don't love myself with short hair, but I'm absolutely fine with you using one of them. And I do love Hamish in a picture (maybe one where you can see his lovely pink tongue as he's hard to photograph with all that black).

I hope you're having a lovely, sunny weekend.

Very best,

Gillian

Tuesday, 22nd of March

To Ruth

Thank you for the card! It was so good to see your handwriting and read such nice words. Please thank EK also. I got her card today, too. How lovely! They both cheered my spirit. I can't wait to see you both (and Josh!) again. xx

Wednesday, 23rd of March

To Molly Jo

Great! Thank you! I was walking a lot today and have done 'the thing' to my right hip, so I'm about to do knee sways, bridges, and some rolling out.

Thursday, 24th of March

MS nerve pain reminded me yesterday that I do also have multiple sclerosis. Today it's making itself heard loudly and clearly, which puts paid to most of today's plans. My focus will instead be on breathing, sitting for a little bit in the Glasgow sun, and gentle stretches.

Friday, 25th of March

To Laura

I'm doing okay. The Scottish spring has been beautiful (highs of 60 and sunshine with a chill in the wind). There are lots of daffodils out now. I start my next treatment on Thursday of next week and radiotherapy on the Monday of the following, so I'm trying my best not to engage with the anticipatory anxiety that keeps sidling up alongside me. xxx

Saturday, 26th of March

To Karen

We've put the table and chairs out for the birthday/Mother's Day lunch. X

Tuesday, 29th of March

At my GP surgery waiting to be called for my pre-chemo bloods.

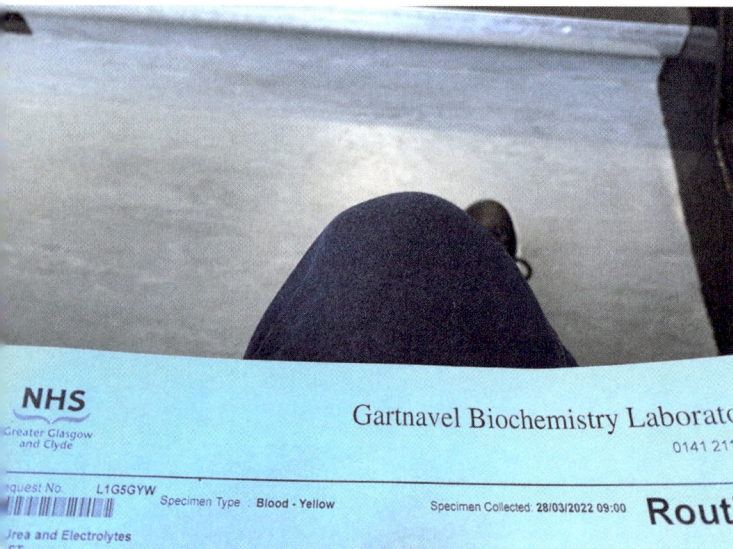

To Clair

Wordle took the total PISS out of me today! xx

Thursday, 31st of March

To Ronnie

That's it just up now and it runs for an hour and a half. It took three attempts to get the cannula in.

To Karen

It took three attempts to get the cannula in and we've had a couple of leakage incidents (a slightly faulty valve). The infusion has been up and running since about half four, so it should be done about six. xx

To Ronnie

It's beeping and saying end of infusion…

To Ronnie

Just a ten-minute saline flush to go and I'll be done. x

To Ronnie

Heading out now.

To Susan

I hope you've been enjoying all the sunshine. I love your tulips. I had my first treatment of the new drug today. It took three goes to get the cannula in…

To Susan

I'm feeling okay, but a little bit delicate. I took an anti-nausea about ten minutes ago.

I start my new treatment tomorrow so I'm enjoying the chilly March sun whilst focusing on noticing. #natureisnurture

April 2022

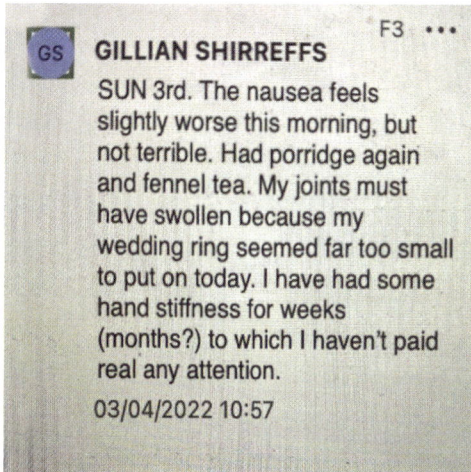

GS **GILLIAN SHIRREFFS** F3 ...

SUN 3rd. The nausea feels slightly worse this morning, but not terrible. Had porridge again and fennel tea. My joints must have swollen because my wedding ring seemed far too small to put on today. I have had some hand stiffness for weeks (months?) to which I haven't paid real any attention.

03/04/2022 10:57

Sunday, 3rd of April

To Susan

It's been okay, thanks. I have a spreadsheet now to keep a note of what happens (because a fish has a better memory). There's space for comments, which might give you a laugh. It's like the diary I kept when I was 12! Here's today's entry… (there'll soon be one with: Played monopoly. Karen cheated. Had fish fingers, beans and chips for tea).

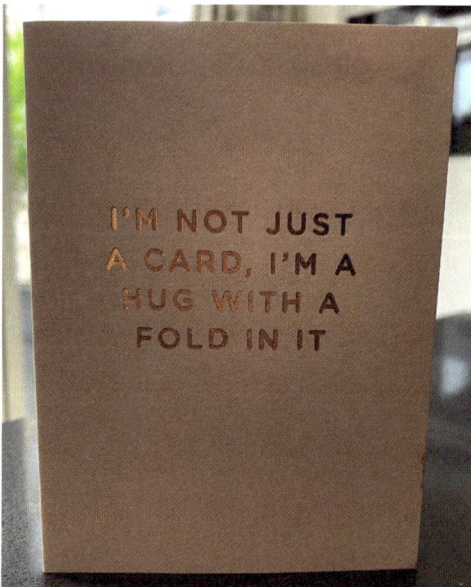

I'M NOT JUST A CARD, I'M A HUG WITH A FOLD IN IT

Monday, 4th of April

According to the card that was waiting for me in the kitchen today, it's day 200 of treatment. It's also the day I start 15 treatments of radiotherapy (at the very precise time of 10:12). And for those of you who know about my 'numbers thing', it's 4/4, so that has to be good.

To Karen

If you want to do anything later, let me know. I'm about to walk the dogs with mum. The radiotherapy took about 30 mins today and should be less on future days. X

To Karen

I have my Beatson befriender call 1.30pm–2pm and was wondering about popping over after, if that would work for you…? X

To Karen

I'm now feeling quite nauseous, so I'm going to stay here. I'll maybe have a lie down and see if that helps. X

To literary agent

Thanks, Sarah. I'm feeling pretty nauseous, but this has cheered me up.

Gillian x

To Clair

FATAL and MADLY are our two best Wordle words of the day.

Tuesday, 5th of April

Waiting to be called for radiotherapy session number two. Once again, at the very precise time of 10:12.

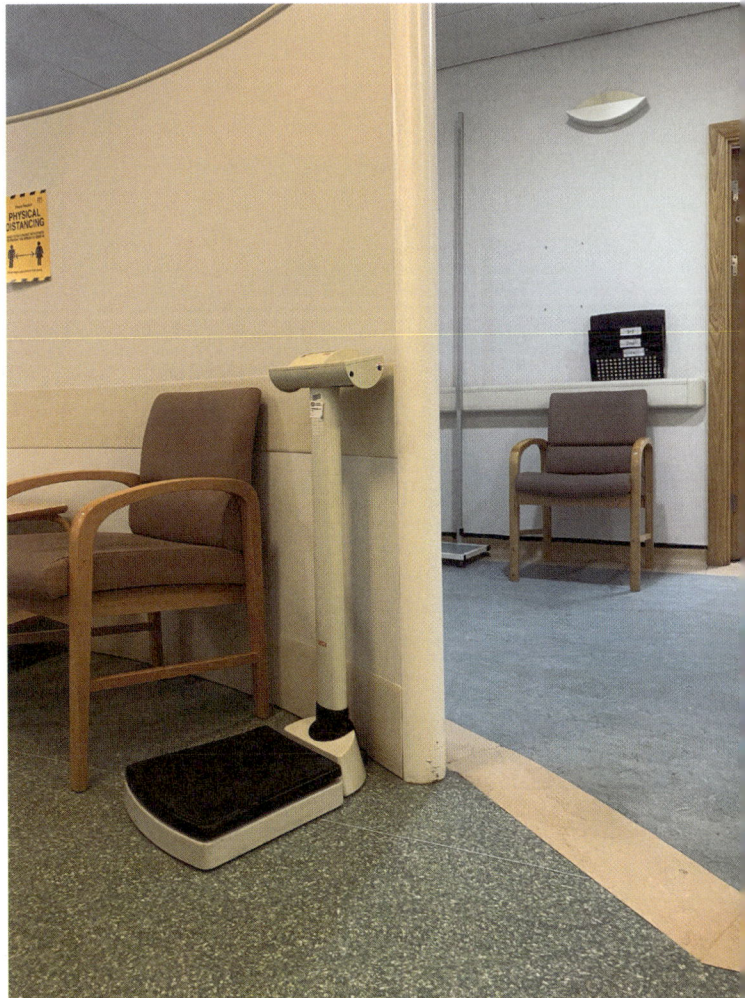

Wednesday, 6th of April

Sitting outside treatment room B at the Beatson waiting to be called for radiotherapy number three (at 10:12).

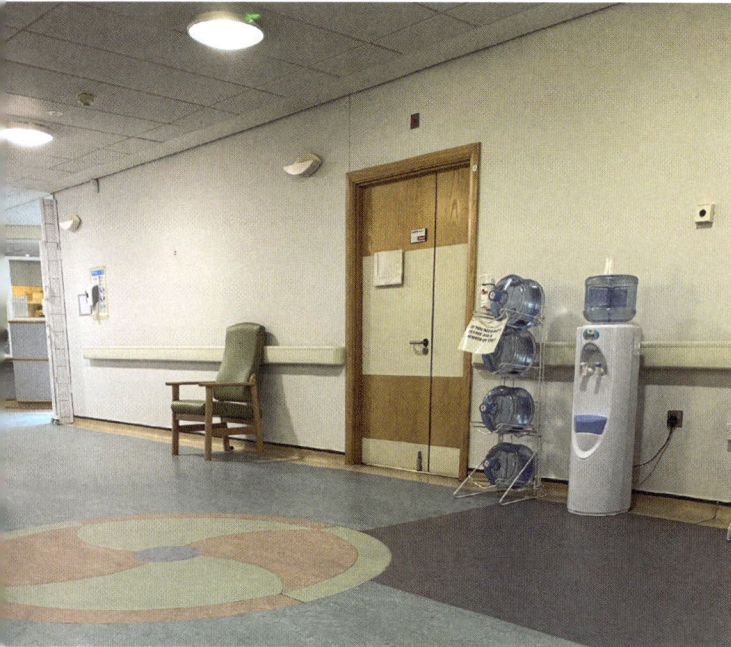

Thursday, 7th of April

Admiring the beautifully tended garden outside the Beatson on my way in for radiotherapy treatment four (at 10:12). #FocusingOnNoticing #NatureIsNurture

Friday, 8th of April

Today is radiotherapy 5 of 15. I've brought Anne Boyer's brilliant, beautiful, visceral The Undying. When I read it during my doctorate, I had no idea I'd be living elements of it a few years later. I'm annotating in a different colour: in conversation with myself. #medhums

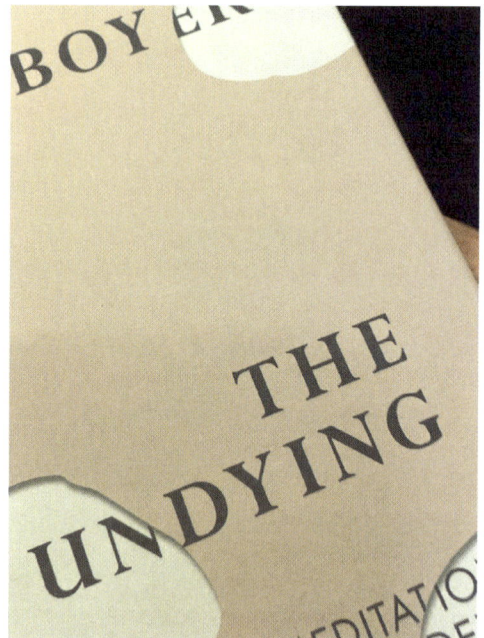

Saturday, 9th April

To Sam

I'm okay. The antibody/chemo hasn't been as symptom-free as hoped, but I'm getting there now (ten days on). I also had the first 5 of 15 radiotherapy treatments this week. x

Sunday, 10th of April

MS fatigue + radiotherapy fatigue + chemo side effects = FATIGUE. My weekend therefore wasn't the best, but Ronnie got me some pansies to fill an empty flower basket sent by a dear friend after my second surgery, which made me happy. #NatureIsNurture

Monday, 11th of April

After radiotherapy this morning I went to a Look Good Feel Better session at the Maggie's Centre. It was a lot of fun with lovely participants and great volunteer tutors. My sister's friend happened to be there, so there's a pic of my ugly mug.

Elizabeth and Kate

I was at the Maggie's for Look Good Feel Better today. My sister's pal happened to be there too, so there's photographic evidence. I thought as you've had to see all the bald/sick pics, I should share. x

Tuesday, 12th of April

Waiting to be called for radiotherapy 7 of 15 (still at the very precise time of 10:12).

Wednesday, 13th of April

To Father Jim

The Beatson asked me to come in, so I'm waiting to be seen and get some bloods done.

Today is a day off radiotherapy (the machine is being serviced) but I've ended up in the Beatson anyway with an unexplained rash. Waiting to be checked over / get bloods done.

To Ronnie

Bloods were done about two hours ago. It doesn't look like chicken pox or shingles. The Advanced Nurse Practitioner has spoken to the registrar who will come to see me and possibly prescribe a steroid cream. It just seems to be a bit of a mystery.

This is a wonderful service. I've been having a weekly call from a brilliant Beatson Befriender since November. I'd definitely recommend trying it out. (And Hamish looks quite handsome in the photo.) #ItsGoodToTalk

Thursday, 14th of April

To Ronnie

Radiotherapy done. I'm now up in Area 2.

To Ronnie

Waiting at pharmacy for oral steroids and a different antihistamine.

To Ronnie

I saw Alison. She was all over it… like a rash (ba boom)

To Gitte

Hi Gitte,

It's lovely to hear from you. Spring arrived here in March, which was a lovely month. April has been a bit colder and wetter, but we've had lots of colour for weeks, which is really cheery on a dog walk.

I'm not sure how much of my recent 'stuff' you know (my memory is shocking at the moment, so I'm not sure when we last 'spoke'). I had surgery in January and February. The second one was because there had been pre-cancerous cells in the margins (I had two tumours in my breast, one of which was still pre-cancerous and it's much more difficult to get clean margins in that case). Thankfully they got clean margins in the second surgery, so I was sent on to the next stage of the journey (radiotherapy and a new antibody/chemo treatment).

I'm in the midst of radiotherapy now (I'll have treatment 9 of 15 today) and I've started the new drug treatment (on March 31st). I have 13 more 3-weekly cycles of it left. It's quite tough just now, but nowhere near as bad as the original chemotherapy.

I'm looking forward to a time when I'll be feeling better and I hope that part of that will be getting to see you in Scotland, Denmark, or both.

I hope the spring arrives for you very soon!

Gillian

Today is seven months since I started treatment. Despite the 'niggles' with the new treatment and the radiotherapy, it feels good to be here (day 212) so we went for a lovely, bracing walk. #LochLong #WalkingTherapy

To Laura

I'm doing fine. The double whammy of new chemo and radiotherapy had taken a bit of a toll but overall, I'm okay. How are you? How's your mom? xxx

To Karen

I'm doing okay. Still a bit itchy but otherwise unremarkable. It seemed to be of interest (in a *we have no clue but it's interesting* sort of way). X

To Karen

Otherwise, I'm actually feeling quite chipper.

Saturday, 16th of April

To Karen

I'm feeling much better. Chipper has moved to normal service has resumed (with some itch thrown in). xx

Monday, 18th of April

I finally plucked up the courage to ask if I could take a picture of the machine. In very exciting news (if you're me), they then asked if I'd want a pic taken during treatment tomorrow. Of course, I would! #medhums #talkingobjects

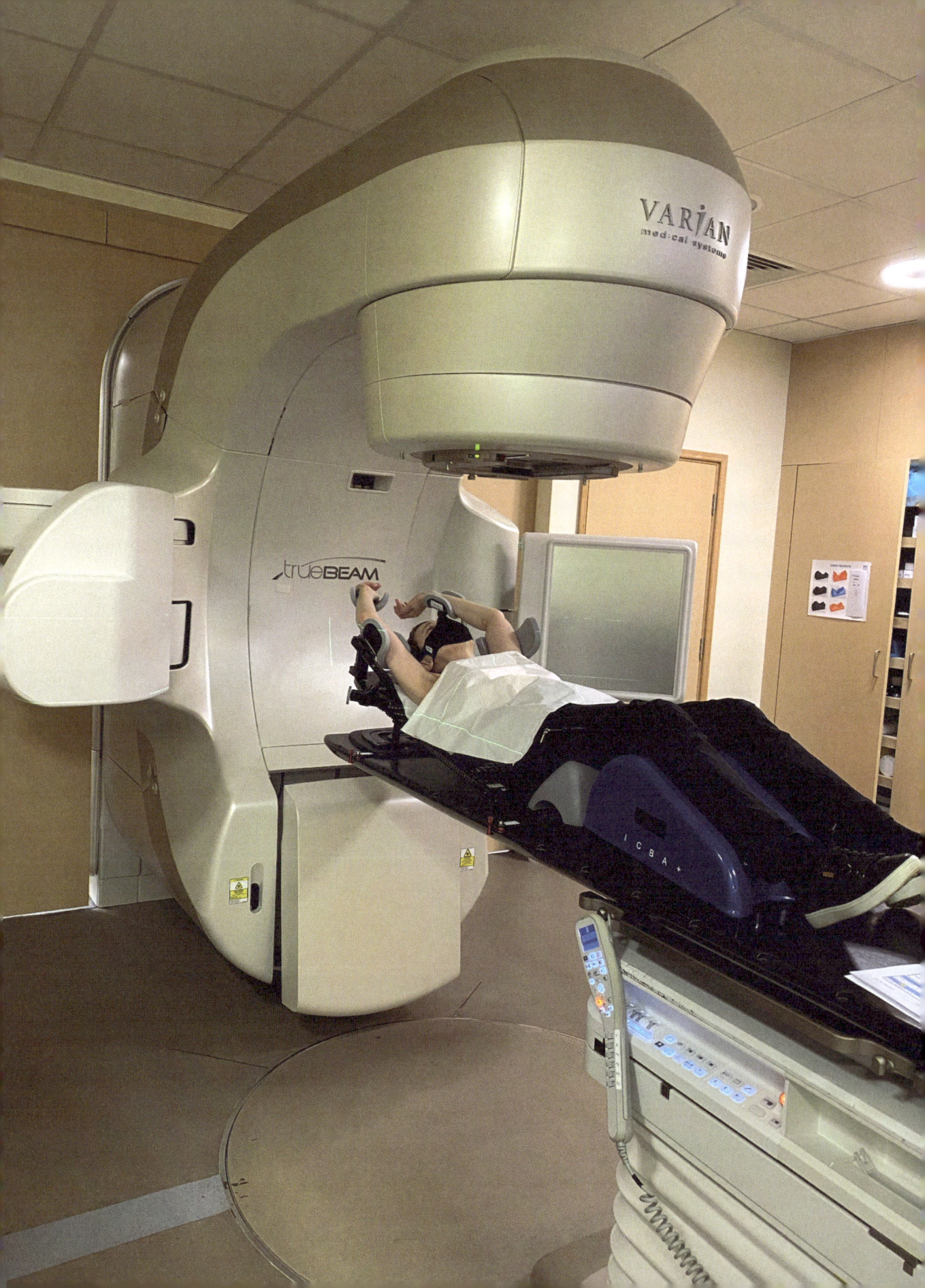

Tuesday, 19th of April

My doctorate explored the relationship between medical object and medical subject and the way in which subject can become object and object can become subject. It seems life has become research. #medhums #talkingobjects

To Molly Jo

I meant to tell you… they let me take a picture of the machine and today they took one of me just before treatment. I thought you might find it interesting to see (and the position I have to stay completely still in for the entire time).

To Karen

Starting to become uncomfortable around the radiotherapy area. I was advised to stop wearing a bra today, so maybe next I'll get a job presenting a gardening programme. X

Wednesday, 20th of April

Waiting to be called for radiotherapy treatment 12 of 15 at today's very precise time of 10:18. Outside in the grounds of the Beatson, spring is just showing off. #NatureIsNurture #GlasgowInSpring

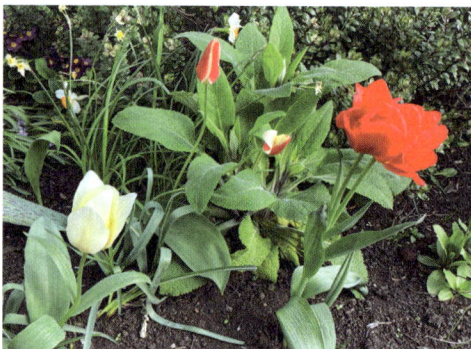

Thursday, 21st of April

| Reflect | **Stats** | Buddies |

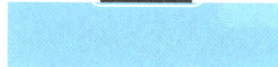

⏱ TOTAL TIME MEDITATED
158 hours

🎧 SESSIONS COMPLETED
580 sessions

⏱ AVERAGE DURATION
16 minutes

The head game is real today. I have radiotherapy treatment 13 (of 15) in the morning and TDM1 treatment 2 (of 14) in the afternoon. Thank goodness for the Headspace app. I downloaded it within a day or so of starting chemo.

Waiting to be called for radiotherapy treatment 13 of 15. I was told at reception that the room has been changed so I'm waiting outside room E instead of room B. It's very silly to be disconcerted by such a small thing, but I am. Or maybe it's the number 13…

Waiting to be called for TDM1 treatment 2 (of 14). #andbreathe

The nurse got the cannula in first time (which is the first time that's happened in forever) and I'm so incredibly grateful (the mantra worked @georgi_gill). Today I'm going to attempt a wee bit of writing inspired by Alan @thiwurd's excellent homework task.

To Karen

It was an accidental dial when they were moving me downstairs. My treatment will run just beyond six, so I need to move down to the main chemo area, IV stand and all. x

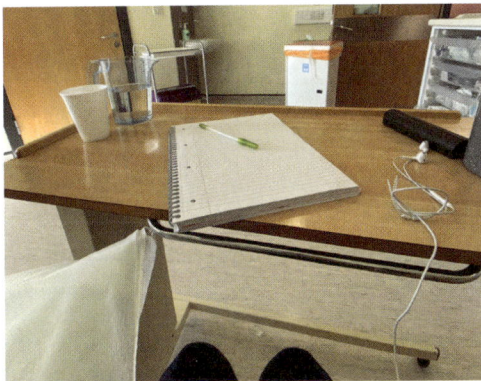

To Ronnie

My infusion pump is beeping. Just waiting for someone to come and take the cannula out. X

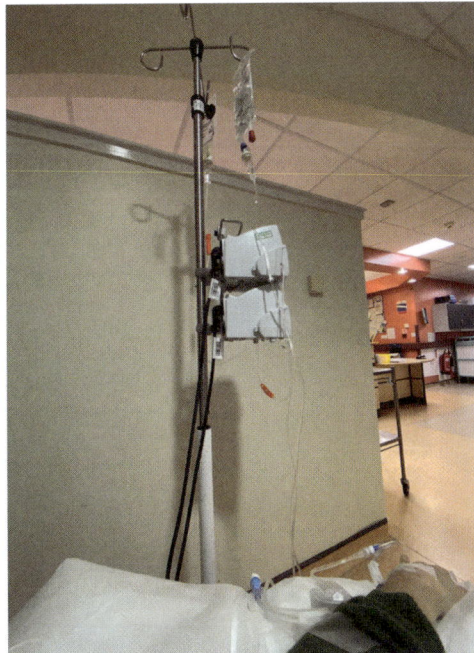

139

Friday, 22nd of April

Waiting to be called for radiotherapy treatment 14 (of 15) at the very precise time of 10:18. Outside in the grounds of the Beatson, spring is showing off again. #NatureIsNurture

Day 218

From sunshinescot.com
Friday, 22 April 2022

It's 218 days since I first walked along the corridor to the Macmillan Day Case Unit at The Beatson West of Scotland Cancer Centre. 214 days since I was admitted to the Queen Elizabeth University Hospital with neutropenic sepsis. A day since I last walked along the corridor to the Macmillan Day Case Unit.

In the meantime, I've had another four unplanned hospital admissions and two planned ones in three different hospitals. The unplanned four were for chemo-related infections and the two planned ones were for surgery.

It's a lot.

And that's okay.

But it's a lot.

I cry more than I did. It comes on unexpectedly and has a primordial quality. It mainly happens when I'm alone, but sometimes there's a witness.

In my mind's eye I see the face of a friend. I facetimed her from hospital 200 days, or so, ago. I didn't speak. I just cried.

The moment is etched in my memory and whilst I wish it hadn't happened, for her sake, it's a reminder that I'm not alone in this. That those who love me are willing to be there even in my most difficult moments; to witness emotion I struggle to identify – anxiety, despair, fear, grief, hopelessness?

Today I cried for reasons I can't pinpoint. Yesterday I had the double whammy of radiotherapy (13 of 15) and an infusion of TDM1 (2 of 14), so it might simply have been exhaustion. For the first time in 218 days though, I wanted to write about it.

Writing has long, for me, been a way to better understand illness. In my case, multiple sclerosis. To help make sense when there seems to be none.

The desire to return feels good.

Like I'm becoming me again.

![Twitter icon]

Saturday, 23rd of April

Beautiful late afternoon looking for heart-shaped rocks on the loch shore. #LochLong #NatureIsNurture #WalkingTherapy

![Twitter icon]

Monday, 25th of April

Waiting to be called for radiotherapy treatment 15 of 15 at the very precise time of 10:18.

![Twitter icon]

I've been ticking the appointments off one at a time each day when I get home. This page is now ready to be stored with my other artefacts of illness. #TalkingObjects #MedHums

NHS Greater Glasgow and Clyde

Beatson West of Scotland Cancer Centre - Radiotherapy Appointment Schedule

Patient: Shirreffs, Gillian Patient Id:

Oncologist:

Date	Time	Appointment Type	Location	Hospital
18/03/2022	09:20 AM	Planning Scan	Simulator 1	Glasgow Beatson
04/04/2022	10:12 AM	First Treatment	Treatment Room B	Glasgow Beatson
05/04/2022	10:12 AM	Daily Treatment	Treatment Room B	Glasgow Beatson
06/04/2022	10:12 AM	Daily Treatment	Treatment Room B	Glasgow Beatson
07/04/2022	10:12 AM	Daily Treatment	Treatment Room B	Glasgow Beatson
08/04/2022	10:12 AM	Daily Treatment	Treatment Room B	Glasgow Beatson
11/04/2022	10:12 AM	Daily Treatment	Treatment Room B	Glasgow Beatson
12/04/2022	10:12 AM	Daily Treatment	Treatment Room B	Glasgow Beatson
14/04/2022	10:12 AM	Daily Treatment	Treatment Room B	Glasgow Beatson
15/04/2022	10:12 AM	Daily Treatment	Treatment Room B	Glasgow Beatson
18/04/2022	10:18 AM	Daily Treatment	Treatment Room B	Glasgow Beatson
19/04/2022	09:18 AM	Daily Treatment	Treatment Room B	Glasgow Beatson
20/04/2022	10:18 AM	Daily Treatment	Treatment Room B	Glasgow Beatson
21/04/2022	10:18 AM	Daily Treatment	Treatment Room B	Glasgow Beatson
22/04/2022	10:18 AM	Daily Treatment	Treatment Room B	Glasgow Beatson
25/04/2022	10:18 AM	Final Treatment	Treatment Room B	Glasgow Beatson

![Twitter icon]

Tuesday, 26th of April

I'm a bit numbers obsessed (with a fondness for even ones and palindromes thrown in). Today is 222 days since I started treatment for cancer. I remember longing for spring and easier days ahead. #Day222 #SpringInGlasgow

Wednesday, 27th of April

Elizabeth and Kate

I had quite the dream last night. We met up at my favourite Neenah restaurant. There was a lot of cheese (I don't eat cheese!). Elizabeth - you had a glass of whisky. Kate - you had a glass of Belgian wheat beer (very precise!) and I had a fennel tea. Regardless, we had a lot of fun shouting over ridiculously loud music.

Elizabeth and Kate

I'm afraid I don't know the provenance of your whisky, Elizabeth (but Town Council definitely stocked some decent Scottish ones). I DO however know that Kate's beer was a Belgian wheat beer as she extolled her love of it during the dream.

Thursday, 28th of April

To Alan

I do love a homework task. Thanks, Alan. I'm not sleeping as well as I could, so I'm loving it even more than usual.

Unfortunately, I can't go along on the 12th. It's a chemo day and much as I'd love to be at a wurd event again, I know I'll not feel well enough.

Hopefully next time!

Gillian

TWO-HUNDRED WORD STORY FOR HOMEWORK

I regret clipping the heel of one of the smaller boys. Of course, I do.

At the time it felt like my only option.

He yelped, and in the ensuing commotion of teenagers pushing and shoving, I weaved my way through the throng and stepped onto the bus.

I climbed the staircase to the top deck.

It wasn't a disaster: there was only one other person, near the back, hunched forwards, his eyes down, texting, or asleep. I dropped my rucksack and scarf onto the front seat. From my vantage point, I could see the boy and his pals. Laughing and shoving. He was fine.

As the bus turned onto the Great Western Road, I rummaged in my pocket for the key. I should have handed it back, but no one had ever asked so there was no harm, really, and I'd be in and out before anyone else arrived.

The front door needed a wee shove, just like I remembered. My rucksack was heavy on my back, and I could feel the edge of the spray can, digging in. I walked through the office. Everything looked the same. His desk was a study in neatness.

For now.

THE END

✉

To Jacqui

I enjoyed doing my wee homework piece. Over the next nine weeks I'm planning on creating and then living vicariously through some truly dreadful characters. :-)

Looking forward to reading yours!

G x

🐦 **Friday, 29th of April**

When I was 'discharged' from radiotherapy on Monday, in addition to being given a helpful leaflet and good wishes, I was told that the peak of symptoms should be in 7-10 days. As a distraction, I'm focusing on noticing. #NatureIsNurture #SpringInScotland

May 2022

Sunday, 1st of May

To Clair

If you're free and up for a walk later, give me a shout. xx

Monday, 2nd of May

To Susan

I must have used my witch powers because I was thinking about you earlier. I have the most ludicrous hair and was going to offer you a laugh by showing it to you (think the worst short haircut of 1982). I think I need some serious scarf action. Or a paper bag. Otherwise, I'm doing okay. I finished radiotherapy a week ago today and look much less like I've been dipped in a deep fat fryer now. They've given me some different meds that made cycle two of the TDM1 much more tolerable, so that's good. If you have time to split your sides laughing at my hair at any point over the next couple of days let me know. I'll walk slowly by your garden sporting my 'do'…

Tuesday, 3rd of May

To Alyssa

Hi Alyssa,

I have a quick question about your Connect Fest call for proposals. Does the research have to already have a home/

be linked to an institution? My current project (Artefacts of Illness) is grounded in my current illness experience and builds upon my doctoral research, which explored the relationship between object and illness. It's only at the early stages and I'm just doing it on my own. I had hoped to explore postdoc options, but I found the lump in my breast just as I was beginning to do so.

It sounds like a great event, so I wanted to check if I'd be eligible to submit a proposal.

With best regards,

Gillian

To Alyssa

Thanks, Alyssa! It sounds really great. I'll get to work on a proposal. Regardless of outcome, it'll be a good way for me to work through my thoughts.

Thanks again,

Gillian

Wednesday, 4th of May

To Clair

I hope today is a good day. Your wee Campsie pal is happy… putting on weight (seven stone five pounds) and just did Wordle in 3 for the 2nd day in a row.

To Elizabeth and Kate

I hope you're both well! I'm now nine days post-radiotherapy (yay!) and I'm doing better this TDM1 cycle (cycle 2 of 14) due to them giving me different meds to help with the side effects (mainly a new anti-nausea).

I saw a call for proposals for a work in progress event at the CCA in June and am sorely tempted to submit something for my Artefacts of Illness project. It would also be really nice to feel part of a creative community again as I'm feeling a little bit bereft at the moment.

I just thought I'd mention it, in case either of you have any thoughts about whether or not it makes sense (I definitely trust your brains/judgement over mine at the moment)... here's the info...

G x

Saturday, 7th of May

The postman brought this brilliant card today and it warmed my heart. Thanks @Yvonnewallace32 for producing the wonderful, kind, funny boys of Fruglas Studios! #thepineappleofpositivity

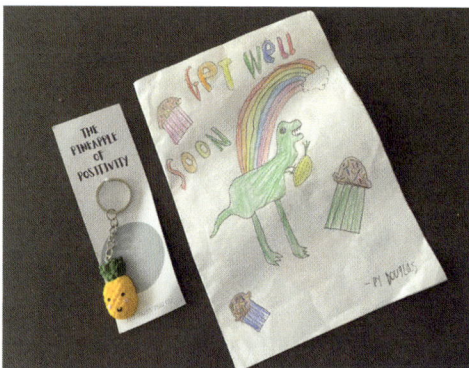

Monday, 9th of May

It's chemo week, which means tomorrow I go for my pre-chemo bloods, Wednesday is my pre-chemo appointment and Thursday is my third infusion of TDM1. My plan is to take all the deep breaths I need and go out for walks when I can (rain, rain, go to Spain).

Tuesday, 10th of May

I'm wondering if I've upset the universe. I'm just in from pre-chemo bloods and the kettle isn't working. I'd saved my once a day coffee for after, as a reward (I hate needles). Not to be thwarted, I'm going old style. #coffeefixfixed

Wednesday, 11th of May

Waiting to be called for my pre-chemo appointment. From what I overhear my notes aren't where they should be. I'm wondering again about the universe and if I have done something to annoy it... #sorryuniverse

To Ronnie

I hate chemo week.

Thursday, 12th of May

Even though I'm not on hardcore chemo anymore, I'm still not a big fan of chemo day. But I do love a perfectly timed piece of post. #friendship #care

To Katie

I loved getting this email, Katie. Thank you. I need all of the sunshine today, so am revisiting it and those beautiful tulips. I love the thought of the sun being their mainstay and the mainstay of that oh-so-very-pleased-with-itself grass.

I've been thinking about, and writing about, trees, of late. I've attached a short piece of fiction that was about me trying to work through the early days of this illness experience. I've attached it by way of sharing and conversation.

I hope you're well. Maybe we could have a virtual coffee, or a walk in the sun, in the not too distant future.

G x

To Susan

My blood pressure was high last time and I explained it was due to the anticipatory anxiety of it taking three goes to get the cannula in. My chemo times are all 3pm, to give plenty of time for the nerves to build…

To Ronnie

I couldn't get a space so after fifteen minutes of driving around the car park I knocked on the window of a man who was reading and explained I had chemo at 3pm. He took pity on me and gave me his space. x

Waiting to be called for TDM1 treatment 3 of 14. #chemoday #deepbreaths

To Johanna

It was lovely to see you last night and your lovely dogs. Texa is getting so big! Good news from the Beatson today… the nurse got my cannula in on the first attempt. xx

To Johanna

I'm feeling okay. I've had an anti-nausea tablet (prochlorperazine) and am just taking things easy. I'm feeling quite proud of myself that I drove to and from chemo as Ronnie's away. xx

Friday, 13th of May

To Johanna

Thanks. I'm feeling okay (touching all of the wood!). I'm about to have breakfast and then the anti-nausea tablet that takes over an hour to dissolve under my lip, so hoping that keeps away the nausea that's threatening. I hope you have a brilliant Friday! xx

Saturday, 14th of May

Today's favourite find… a three-headed daffodil. #FocusingOnNoticing #SpringInScotland

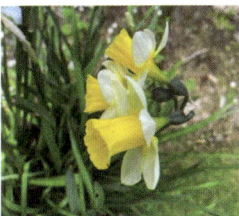

Sunday, 15th of May

The first few days after treatment can be a wee bit of a slog. Being outside in nature definitely helps (as do my new anti nausea meds). #NatureIsNurture #FocusingOnNoticing #DistractionTherapy

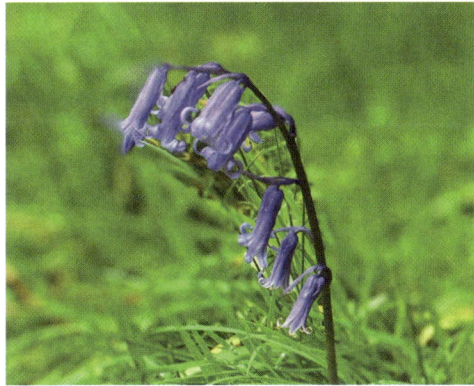

Thursday, 19th of May

To Sam

It was no problem! I had Fergus with me as I was taking him to stay with my mum and dad for a couple of nights (Ronnie's away, it's chemo week so one less dog is helpful, and they love him). He certainly enjoyed being in the waiting room seeing other dogs.

Friday, 20th of May

To Jenny

I'd love to get together. We could meet up with Yvie at Rouken Glen like we used to… All we need is some dry weather. I can't wait to finish this treatment and get back to more normality. x

Had a lovely time drinking coffee in my sister's garden this afternoon. I'm really enjoying how well I feel during the middle week of the three-weekly TDM1 cycle. #gratitude #coffeetherapy

Sunday, 22nd of May

I was out visiting my mum and dad today. All eyes (and ears) were on their ever-popular bird box. #birdwatching #hungrychicks

Monday, 23rd of May

To Alyssa

Thank you so much, Alyssa! I'm thrilled to be part of Connect Fest and am very much looking forward to it.

With best regards,

Gillian

To Clair

I don't think Fergus has enough toys…

Tuesday, 24th of May

It's 250 days since I started treatment. These beauties arrived today. #Day250 #breastcancer

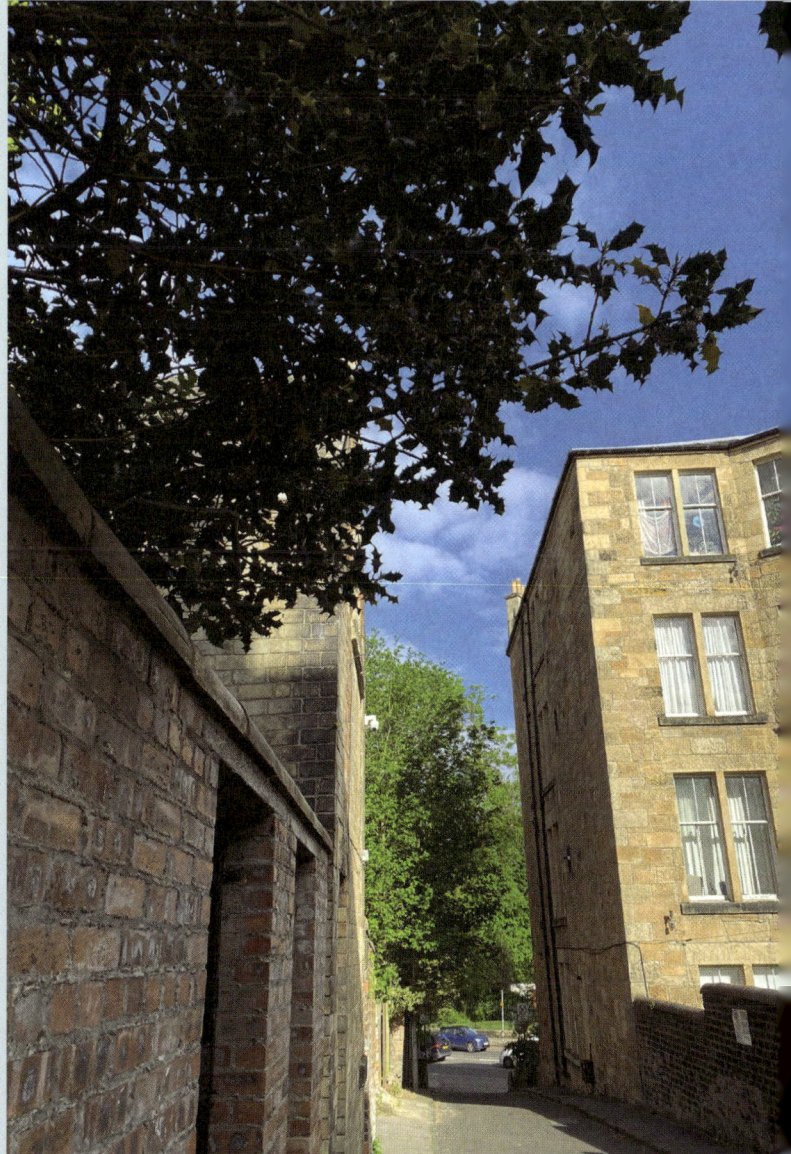

It's day 250, so I've written a thing. #breastcancer

SUNSHINESCOT.COM

Just after eight this morning, I went for a dog walk. It was unzipped jacket with a light scarf sort of weather. Beautiful blue sky. I was keenly aware of the pavement beneath my feet, the dogs' leads in my hands, and a deep sense of gratitude.

I've been aware of a milestone approaching. Day 250.

250 days since I began treatment for breast cancer, which, in my case, was chemotherapy. 250 days since I walked along a corridor at The Beatson West of Scotland Cancer Centre to the Macmillan Day Case Unit. 250 days since my first infusion of Docetaxel.

What I couldn't have known on that Thursday was that three days later, just after eight in the morning, I would phone the Beatson emergency helpline to say I was spiking a temp. Or that I would be told to go immediately to the Queen Elizabeth University Hospital, be sent home a few hours later, then phone the emergency line the next day to say I was still spiking a temp and felt dreadful.

I couldn't have known I would spend six hours that Monday in a busy, noisy Emergency Department waiting to be seen by a doctor, and when I was, and my blood results came back in the wee small hours, that I would be told I had sepsis.

250 days ago, I had no idea those things would happen. I also didn't know that I would have four further unplanned hospital admissions. Or anything about the 'bear hugger' I would be put in at some point during my third emergency admission because my temperature had dropped so low due to a chemo-induced infection.

I think it's fair to say that back then I was pretty rubbish at chemotherapy. Had it been an exam, I'd have been lucky to scrape a C.

I'm better at it now.

Granted, the treatment I've been on since March (TDM1) is very different from the chemo I had pre-surgery, but, even so, I'd like to think I might be edging towards an A.

My body's ability to cope with TDM1 is just one of the things I was grateful for on my dog walk this morning. I also felt gratitude for every bit of kindness and care I've received over the last eight months. From doctors, nurses, pharmacists, medical secretaries, receptionists, folks at the brilliant Beatson charity, from my family, from neighbours, from friends old and new.

In the last 250 days I've had eight cycles of pre-surgical chemo, two surgeries, fifteen sessions of radiotherapy and am now in cycle three (of fourteen) of TDM1 treatment.

I lost my hair, my eyebrows, my eyelashes, my sense of safety, my sense of dignity (did I mention the campylobacter infection that accompanied the sepsis...?), but not my terrible sense of humour.

I couldn't have managed it without each and every person who wrote me an email, sent me a text, posted me a letter, hand-drew me a card, knitted me a hat, gave me a scarf, bought me thick woolly socks, sent me flowers, went for a walk with me, made me banana bread, supplied me with Pan Drops, sent pyjamas across the Atlantic, carefully chose a book for me, dropped off a care package at the door, said a prayer for me, or took a moment to wish me well.

Getting to day 250 takes a village.

I'm very grateful for mine.

Friday, 27th of May

I've developed an interest in the idea of 'the invisible archive'... things patients don't have access to that relate to them/to their treatment - records, charts, conversations, etc. I'd love a clinical perspective, if anyone is up for a chat... #medhums #talkingobjects

Saturday, 28th of May

To Karen

We're over in Uddingston picking up a booster collar for Daisy (long story involving her having a 5 cm crystal removed from her bladder on Friday and peeing her way through two surgical suits and me being up with her since 5am). Monday would be good. I'm going for a dog walk with Clair at 2.30pm. Maybe I could come to you afterwards…? xx

Sunday, 29th of May

To Karen

I haven't felt brilliant for days, but thought it was something and nothing. I woke up today feeling horrible. I phoned the helpline and was sent to the QEUH. Before we left, I was sick twice. I'm now here in a side room (the staff are lovely), waiting for bloods/Covid test to come back. X

To Ronnie

Bloods aren't back yet, but a very nice doctor has been in to see me and wants me to stay for 24/48 hours. I'll let you know more when I do.

To Ronnie

Could you remember Daisy has to have her antibiotic at lunch and supper. It's the one in the fridge. x

To Clair

Feeling dreadful. Just sat sitting waiting for a doctor to come and speak to me. I've had a bag of fluids. xx

To Ronnie

I can go home because my bloods were completely normal. He thinks I have a tummy bug but I also an immune system to fight it. Yay! Could you come and get me?

To Clair

I was given the option to stay overnight and be monitored or go home and promise to keep up my fluid intake, so I'm going home. Yay. xx

Monday, 30th of May

To Johanna

I'm doing okay. I feel a wee bit like I've been hit by a truck, but I haven't been sick since yesterday morning and don't feel like

I will be again. My plan is to take it easy, drink loads of boiled water (that's cooled down) and try to start eating again with some bland food. I'm a very well-behaved patient. Thanks for checking in! I hope you're well. xx

✉️

To Alan

It was great to see you on Friday, Alan. I really enjoyed the walk. I hope I didn't manage to pass on the sickness bug that must have been brewing away under the surface and landed me in hospital for a few hours yesterday.

The homework was a great distraction over the last few days, so thanks again for a brilliant task.

Gillian

💬
Tuesday, 31st of May

To Susan

Daisy is doing well. She's being checked back over by the vet on Thursday so we're hoping for a clean bill of health. She seems very happy in herself. I hope everything is going well with you. It's back to treatment week again, so pre-chemo bloods today, two different appointments (hours apart) at the Beatson tomorrow and chemo at 3pm on Thursday. (treatment week: my least favourite of the weeks)

💬

To Susan

Actually, I've missed a trick. I should also have mentioned the SPECTACULAR vomiting on Sunday morning. I could have won a prize.

📞

To Clair

Just tried to Facetime you. My hair is looking even more comedy than normal, so I thought I should share…

June 2022

Wednesday, 1st of June

To Clair

Enjoy your night with the birthday twins. xx

To Ronnie

Dr Kerr seems to think the episode that landed me in the QEUH was more due to toxicity from the TDM1. I was offered a dose reduction… I've asked if I can try one more cycle on this dose and then review… I'm still hoping it was a sickness bug.

To Ronnie

We've agreed to give it one more try. I hope I'm not being silly.

To Ronnie

There's scope for two dose reductions and apparently they often need them over the course of the treatment.

A lovely walk home from the Beatson. #WalkingTherapy #FocusingOnNoticing

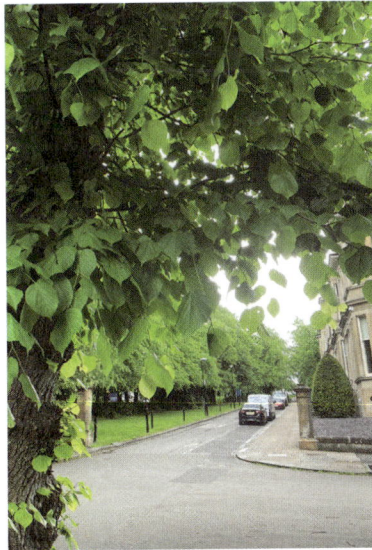

Thursday, 2nd of June

To Clair

I have LOADS of time for a coffee. Chemo is at 3pm. Thanks!

To Clair

We're walking the dogs round the terraces and will come by you at half ten. X

To Susan

Just arrived for it… A wee word with the cannula gods would be appreciated.

To Susan

The waiting room is freezing, so a nice warm basin will be required!

To Ronnie

It was the nurse who did my very first chemo and she got the cannula in in one. She's also the person I spoke to on Sunday on the helpline. x

To Clair

First go! To answer your cannula question

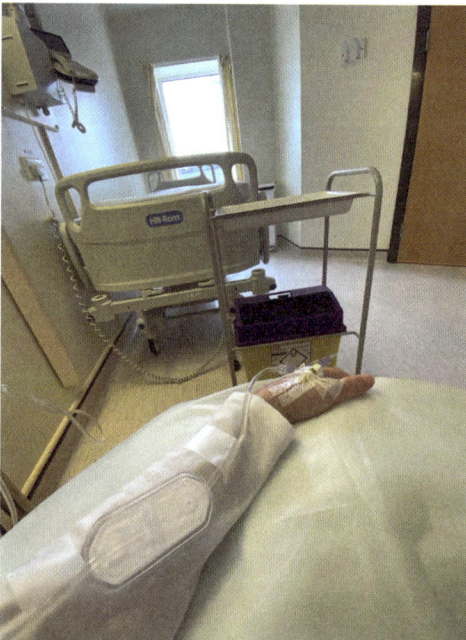

To Ronnie

I might walk home. I feel like I need the fresh air. If you wanted to walk to meet me, that would be nice. Maybe bring Fergus…?

It's lovely to be able to walk home from the Beatson after chemo. Great to be close enough and well enough. #WalkingTherapy

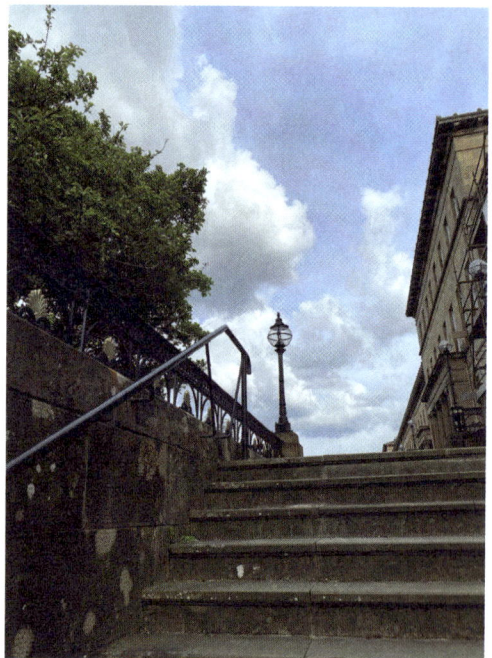

Saturday, 4th of June

To Clair

I really lost the head game with chemo this time. Thanks for being there. X

Sunday, 5th of June

Happy 85th birthday to my dad! The sun always shines on his birthday. #HappyBirthdayJoe

Monday, 6th of June

To Kate

It'll be lovely to have you at Connect Fest. If you have any time for a wee Zoom practice, I'd love that, too. X

To Kate

Hi Kate,

I've attached my presentation and your version of the script. Each time there's a word or phrase (including a title) in BOLD CAPS, you would change the slide (if that's okay!).

G x

To Kate

You are TOTES my Debbie McGee!

Tuesday, 7th of June

I know this is the height of frivolity, but I'm incredibly happy to be back at my lovely hairdresser (in the same chair where she shaved off what was left of my hair last September). And a wee pre-birthday cake! #sillywithhappiness

Sunday, 12th of June

To Clair

We're going to walk the dogs towards you in about ten… xx

Monday, 13th of June

To Ronnie

Have a safe flight. xx

To Kate

I'm having my hair funked up in Uddingston at 11.15, so should be home

157

before 2pm and then have to leave the house at 5pm because the presenters need to be there early, so whenever is good for you in that window would be perfect!

Tuesday, 14th of June

To Kate

I'm home and reading over, if you're free for a practice. My plan for later is to have dinner at four (my guts are not doing well thanks to the chemo, and I need to eat then take anti-nausea or the evening will be off before it starts) and then I'm going to leave here at 5 to walk to the CCA. Presenters have to be there for 5.45. x

To Kate

Thanks for all your help! You were the best!

Wednesday, 15th of June

What a great celebration of works in progress at Connect Fest last night. Such a diverse range of fantastic work and brilliant panelists. Thanks to @ alyssaowrites and to everyone else involved!

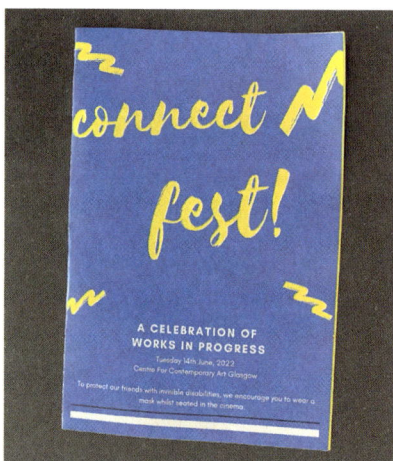

To Johanna

I'm good! (apart from boring side effects) How are you? I was actually off at the CCA last night giving a short presentation on my new project. It was my first real life event since a conference in Kent in February 2020. Fingers crossed I didn't pick anything up!

To Susan

It was good, thanks. I enjoyed being in front of an audience again (little diva that I am) and folks seemed really engaged. I also bumped into my old playwright mentor Peter Arnott and am now having coffee with him in a couple of weeks, so that was nice. AND my hairdresser funked up my hair for the occasion.

Thursday, 16th of June

To Susan

Fergus and I are in the Botanics. I was losing the head game a bit so went for a walk along the Kelvin and ended up on a bench people watching. Or squirrel watching, in Fergus's case.

To Susan

At least I didn't run away from home. I did that the night before chemo two weeks ago. I only got as far as my sister's back garden though.

To Susan

I thought I should go home to the other

dogs. And you're right, try as I might I failed to outrun myself, so I'll get my Dolly wig out and belt out some Jolene. (note to self: must buy a Dolly wig)

✉️

To Alan

Thanks for saying that, Alan. I'd been wanting to ask about booking a place on the Wednesday night summer course, but was thinking you might refer me to the attendance officer!

I'm finding treatment a bit relentless, so need lots of distractions. Today I've been editing my homework piece to entertain myself.

I hope you've had a good week.

Gillian

🐦 **Monday, 20th of June**

What a beautiful morning to walk to the Beatson for a heart scan. #Glasgow #WalkingTherapy #FocusingOnNoticing

🐦 **Tuesday, 21st of June**

At my GP surgery waiting to be called for pre-chemo bloods. It doesn't seem like three weeks since the last time. #TimeFlies

🐦 **Thursday, 23rd of June**

Galvanising myself with a coffee and some thoughts about my new project, Artefacts of Illness. #chemoday #medhums #morningcoffee

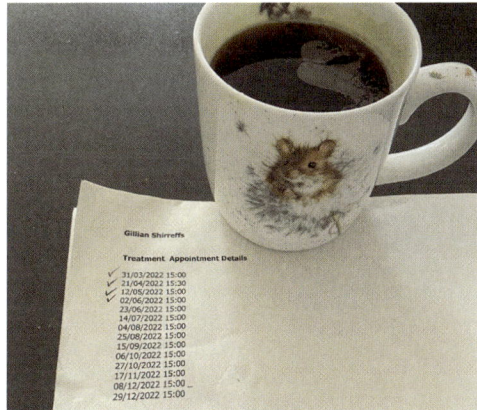

💬

To Johanna

I'm waiting to be called. It's very busy today.

💬

To Johanna

Dose reduction this time. I'm doing well (I think), but mention has been made of my deranged liver function.

🟢

To Ronnie

The infusion started at 3.50, so should end about 5.20. I think a lift would be good today.

🟢

To Ronnie

Cannula in first go.

To Ronnie

The saline is finished. Just waiting on someone to come and disconnect me.

To Angela

Hi Angela,

That's me just home (it was very busy there today). I've opened the box of anti-nausea tablets and there's only 20 of them, so a ten-day supply. Last cycle I had to keep taking them for two weeks, so I wonder if I could have enough in case that happens again this cycle. Hopefully it won't with the dose reduction though.

Many thanks,

Gillian

Sunday, 26th of June

To Karen

I have a question… are you here the week of 11th July…? Ronnie has been asked to go to the US and it's chemo week. If you're here, would you be able to drop me and pick me up from the Beatson on the 14th, if it's raining. The last time he was away there were no parking spaces, and I had to ask a man if I could have his space so that I wasn't late (I probably told you that already). It was pretty stressful. xx

Wednesday, 29th of June

To Jen

A beautiful evening on Loch Lomond. Can't wait until you're here again. x

July 2022

Et voilà… I have a hairstyle (and eyebrows). #milestones

Monday, 4th of July

To Laura

I have another six months of the antibody/chemo treatment. I do have good days, so I'm doing fine. xxx

Friday, 8th of July

To Karen

I still have some abdominal pain but it's not quite as bad. I took an omeprazole this morning, so maybe that's helping… Are you having a good day? X

Saturday, 9th of July

To Clair

I hope you have a lovely day! I'm wearing a chemo through the night purchase that is actually a success. The one and only. Floaty blue dress for a floaty blue-sky day. xx

Sunday, 10th of July

To Karen

You're off the hook for Thursday. Ronnie's trip has been cancelled. He needs to be away another chemo week now (cycle 8) and has to be in Romania on 18/7 for the week. I'm relieved not to be on my own. I hate chemo week (said the broken record). xx

To Karen

Thanks for the coffee and garden chat this morning. It was lovely. I was just out the front dead heading and found my sunglasses… in a flowerpot! X

Wednesday, 13th of July

It's 300 days since I started treatment for breast cancer. And 300 days later, people are still reaching out, giving support and sending cards that arrive out of the blue from the other side of the ocean. #Day300 #Kindness #ItTakesAVillage #ChemoWeek

Thursday, 14th of July

A coffee and a deep breath to start the day. Cycle 5 wasn't brilliant, but I had a good pre-chemo appointment yesterday and am hopeful that the changes to my 'takeaway' drugs make a difference in Cycle 6. #ChemoDay #TDM1 #Cycle6of14

To Karen

Still waiting to be called. I just overheard mention of being short staffed and run ragged…

To Susan

I was up in the 4th floor overflow area and the staff were brilliant: professional, friendly, engaged. And cannula in one!

Friday, 15th of July

To Georgi

Thank you for the good vibes, Georgi. They must have worked. I was upstairs in the overflow area on the 4th floor and the care was kind and thoughtful.

A bit washed out today, but only 8 more chemo days between now and 29th December.

I hope you have a lovely restful weekend.

G xx

Saturday, 16th of July

To Clair

I'm heading round to Penny Black. Do you need anything… a wee card… a wee pencil…? xx

To Clair

A pencil, it is!

To Molly Jo

I spoke to a radiotherapy consultant who said what I'm describing in terms of sensation/pain is something called cording that can happen after surgery, radiotherapy or both. It's caused by scar tissue forming.

Tuesday, 19th of July

To Libbe

Hi Libbe,

Thanks for all of the wonderful cards that arrived last Wednesday on what was Day 300 since I started treatment (Ronnie's engineer brain seems to always know these numbers and he'd pointed it out earlier that day). Well, what a brilliant surprise! I love that the wonderful wombats took such time and care to send birthday wishes and happiness across the ocean. I can only wonder at what adventures my envelope of joy had on the way here, but I'm so glad it arrived when it did. It was the perfect way to bring good cheer on the day before chemo number 6 of 14 (of my post-surgical treatment).

I have 8 more sessions of TDM1 (chemo/antibody treatment), which is being referred to as my 'insurance policy'. The chemo before surgery did most of the heavy lifting in terms of treatment, followed by the surgeries and radiotherapy, so I'm definitely on the downward slope now. I have some side effects from the TDM1, but it's nothing like the previous chemo (thank goodness!) and I even have hair now (crazy short curly hair) and eyebrows and eyelashes. It's amazing the difference some of those superficial things can make.

I'm due to finish treatment on December 29th, so am hopeful to have a Neenah trip at some point in 2023. I miss my Fox Valley friends and have been very aware of the prayers and support from you all, so would love to come and say thank you in person.

Sending love and best wishes from Scotland!

Gillian x

Wednesday, 20th of July

1 year ago today, drying myself after a shower, I noticed a lump in my right breast. The cancer had already spread to the sentinel lymph node. PLEASE check yourself regularly. #BreastCancerAwareness #HER2+

To Susan

An odd anniversary… It's a year today since I noticed the pesky lump… and thank goodness I did!

To Clair

I might have had a wee glass or two tonight. It's a year today (I realised). By date not day. It felt a bit much. I was such a wee innocent back then.

📱 Monday, 25th of July

To Clair

In case you needed to know this today… the skinny headband is the new pinafore…

To Clair

In more hair news… I'm out with Fergus. It's windy. I can feel the wind in my hair…

📱 Tuesday, 26th of July

To Ronnie

Hope the next flight is on time! X

To Ronnie

Love you, too. xx

To Ronnie

I'm having some of your delicious lentil soup for lunch. xx

📱 Wednesday, 27th of July

To Ronnie

Beautiful pic! That's my kind of view. xx

To Ronnie

I miss being on holiday (which I know you're not). x

To Ronnie

Miss you. Kiss you. xx

📱 Thursday, 28th of July

To Ronnie

Are you on your way…?

To Ronnie

Will you make your connection? x

🐦 Sunday, 31st of July

Lovely morning walk to distract myself from being on the cusp of chemo week. Made a bee-eautiful friend. #FocusingOnNoticing #NatureIsNurture

165

August 2022

Back at my GP surgery for pre-chemo bloods. Chemo week seems to roll around so quickly... #timeflies

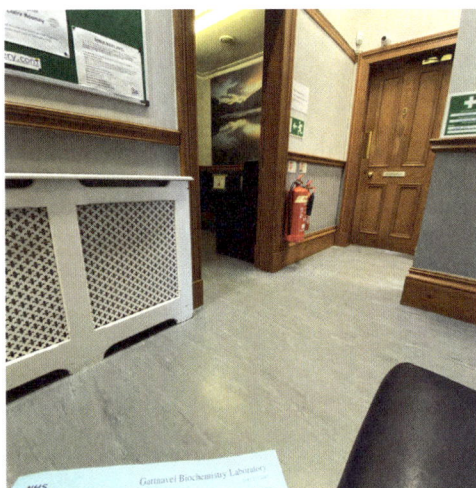

Wednesday, 3rd of August

To Alan

Hi Alan,

I'm afraid I've ended up out trying to walk off the pre-chemo anxiety that's hit me like a brick tonight. I can't face going home yet, so I'm afraid I'm going to keep walking and will miss tonight's class.

Sorry!

Gillian

Thursday, 4th of August

Today is chemo day. It's number 7 of 14 of the post-surgical antibody/chemo treatment. I'm grateful that after today I'll be halfway through (the infusions), but why is it that I'm getting more and more anxious about walking through the hospital door...? #chemoday #breathe

To Ronnie

I'm downstairs in the main area. The man in the next chair in the 'chemo corridor' just went up to the desk to say he'd been waiting since 1pm…

To Karen

It's a bit like being picked for Scottish country dancing…

To Karen

Was taken into Area 4 about 15 minutes ago by a lovely nurse. Cannula in and infusion started. X

Thanks to @KeeperOfPybus for his brilliant, "intensive care". It feels very appropriate to be reading it during chemo with such lines as, "The windows are tinted so there's no view in. People shouldn't look into cancer wards. They might not like what they see." #amreading

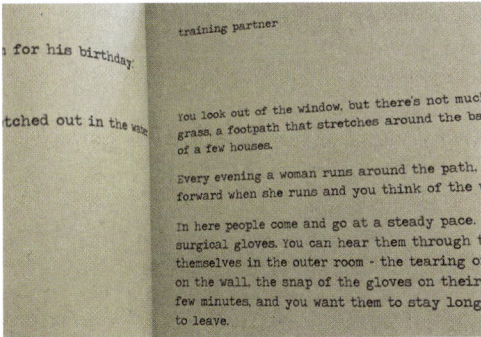

To Ronnie

I'd like to walk home. I think I'll be done about 6.20pm. x

Friday, 5th of August

To Clair

American guests are here. Negative PCRs.

Saturday, 6th of August

To Clair

We're heading off on our evening walk, if you're free and fancy it. xx

Tuesday, 9th of August

Heading off to a wedding in Ireland. First time away since moving back from the US in September 2019. A beautiful day for a crossing.

Wednesday, 10th of August

To Clair

I hope Fergus is behaving. I have a wee F-shaped hole in my heart. xx

To Karen

It took us over 12 hours with a wee mistake that involved getting closer to Dublin (and Dublin's traffic), but we got here and it's lovely. The weather is scorchio, though, so we're heading out to the coast for a breeze. Hamish and Daisy are with the parentals and Clair is helping out by taking Fergus on a long walk at night and having him for sleepovers. xx

One year ago today (after noticing a lump a couple of weeks earlier), I had a mammogram then a biopsy and was told, 'There's something in your breast that shouldn't be there.' Today I had a lovely walk along a beautiful beach.

To Clair

Did Fergus sleep/behave last night…?
Have you any socks left…? xx

To Clair

I hope your week is going well. Thanks for all your help with Mr Fergus! X

Friday, 12th of August

Another beautiful day in Cork. It was even a bit hot for me, so our morning walk was a wooded one. #Ireland #AmWalking #FocusingOnNoticing

Sunday, 14th of August

We've had a brilliant last day in Ireland. We were here for the wedding of a couple who are as beautiful on the inside as they are on the outside. And what a stunning setting. The best break I could have had from treatment. #Ireland

Wednesday, 17th of August

To Angela

Hi Angela,

I hope you're well.

I wanted to ask you about something odd. After getting up this morning I noticed that my right breast looked red and felt hot to the touch (there was a marked difference in colour and temperature between it and my left breast). It's not so noticeable now: it might just be very slightly redder and very slightly warmer, but there was an appreciable difference first thing this morning.

I just thought I would mention it and ask if this is something that can happen…? And, if so, why?

Many thanks,

Gillian

To Alan

Hi Alan,

I'm the worst pupil, ever. I'm not feeling great today, so will have to miss tonight. I missed last week because we went to Ireland for a wedding (we got the ferry and did almost everything outside, to try to stay safe). We travelled home on Monday. I seem to have taken too much out of myself as I now feel pretty awful.

Sorry!

Gillian

To Anna

Hi Anna,

The Beatson helpline asked me to contact you about some changes in my right breast.

To give you the background (see also the emails below), when I woke up this morning my right breast was hot and red. This settled down, but I sent Angela an email just in case it was something I should mention to her. Later in the morning I was aware of heat and discomfort in the breast so contacted the helpline in case this was a sign of infection.

The helpline phoned my GP surgery who arranged an appointment for 4.15pm today. I was examined by two different doctors as the breast was tender, appeared swollen and is dusky in colour. The GP phoned the helpline, who contacted my oncology team, who suggested it sounded more like something I should speak to you about.

The GP has done bloods and I've been asked to phone the helpline again if I notice that I have a temperature / if there are any further changes.

Many thanks,

Gillian

📞 **Thursday, 18th of August**

To Clair

Hospital phoned. I've to go and see the surgical nurse at 2pm. I'm walking the dogs towards you just now. xx

📞 **Sunday, 21st of August**

To Clair

Hey! I'm free falling in a funk… fancy a walk…? xx

💬 **Monday, 22nd of August**

To Johanna

I hope your week has started well. It was lovely to see you yesterday. I have a quick question… I'm having my 1st anniversary mammogram at 11am tomorrow. The "area" is still a bit tender, so I'm thinking it's going to be quite painful. I don't normally take pain meds if I can help it, but would it make sense to take something tomorrow morning before I go to Gartnavel…?

To Johanna

Thanks! And this rain IS miserable. It's ruining my Princess Di hair!

To Ronnie

I'm still up, if you're able to call. xx

Tuesday, 23rd of August

At my GP waiting to be called for pre-chemo bloods. #TimeFlies

To literary agent

Thanks, Sarah. I appreciate the update.

I was thinking of tweeting this the other day... The advice when out on submission is to write another book. Instead, I got cancer.

It's not exactly in keeping with my upbeat brand, however, so I didn't.

I am sad about Brodie, but I understand. And I do want to write another novel because I loved writing Brodie. I just need to figure out how to get my mangled brain where it needs to be to get going.

Gillian x

To Clair

Thank you! I tried the hospital car park. No joy, so I drove down by Cafe Source 2 and got a spot on Devonshire Terrace. I've just knocked back an ibuprofen and about to head to the hospital. xx

A bit of a medical day for me... now at the hospital for my 1st anniversary appointment. I'm not sure what it involves (the letter gives nothing away). I think I remember being told I'd have a mammogram (but am in the wrong waiting room, so am a bit confused). #HospitalAnxiety

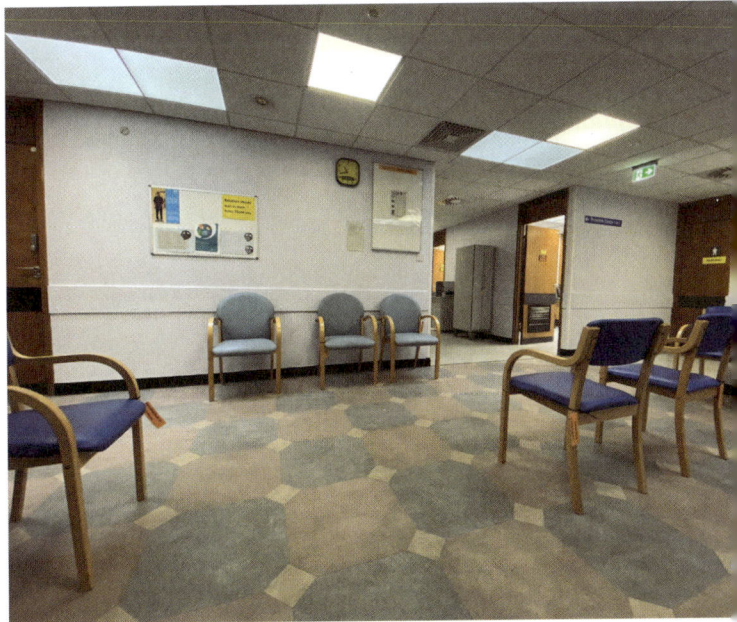

To Clair

Done. No mammogram. It'll happen within the next 8 weeks. Just an examination and a chat. xx

To Johanna

So… turns out I misunderstood… my 1st anniversary appointment was a chat and an examination. The Clinical Nurse Specialist will now organise my mammogram, which will happen in the next 8 weeks. I took an ibuprofen, so I'll need to fall over now to get some use out of it.

To Johanna

She said everything seemed fine. And there was a trainee there who used the phrase, "such a neat, wee scar'. The Clinical Nurse Specialist seemed nonplussed about last week's bright red breast. She just nodded and attributed it to the radiotherapy. xx

Wednesday, 24th of August

To Clair

I've decided I'm going to learn to knit and you're the first person I'm going to knit for. (I wish that didn't sound so much like a threat)

Thursday, 25th of August

To Karen

Thanks. I've been sent up the stairs to B9. Clair and Fergus walked me here. Thanks for offering to come over. Clair is going to walk me back and then probably we'll sit out for a bit, so I should be good. I was taken straight away today! xx

To Clair

The infusion is already up and running! I'll text when I'm done and meet you halfway. xx

To Clair

Two nurses complimented my daisy necklace. xx

To Clair

That's me walking out now. xx

Saw these beauties on my walk home from the Beatson. #FocusingOnNoticing #NatureIsNurture #AmWalking

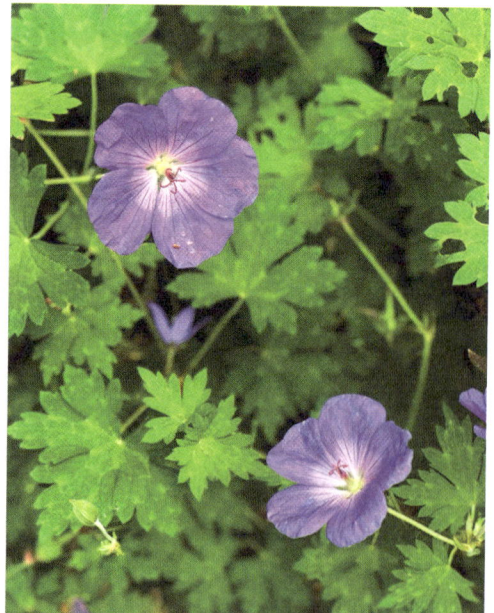

Friday, 26th of August

To Clair

Thanks. I'm good. Very glad it's today and not yesterday. Thank you for making yesterday so much better than it would have been. xxx

Saturday, 27th of August

To Karen

What a beautiful day! If you're about in the garden at all this afternoon, I could pop over, if it would be okay… x

Sunday, 28th of August

To Clair

I was a bit ropey this morning, but a wee Daisy dog walk helped. xx

To Clair

I need to shop. Or eat a tin of tuna. Again.

Wednesday, 31st of August

I'm trying to manage some year-since-diagnosis anxiety that seems to have hit me like a train. I promise there will be writing, but there will also be knitting. Thanks @ekreeder for the encouragement and @theyarncake for the advice and supplies. #newknitter

September 2022

Saturday, 3rd of September

I'm just about through my first ball of wool so will now have to wait for a visit from my mum so she can show me how to transition to the next one without just tying a big knot mid-row. #amknitting #knittingtherapy

Wednesday, 7th of September

To Clair

I'm just about to cast off your scarf… It's perfectly imperfect.

Last week I decided to knit for the 1st time since primary school. I needed salve for the mind and thought knitting might be just the thing. Today I have a scarf (in lovely wool from @theyarncake). It could be neater, but I loved knitting it. #distractiontechnique

Friday, 9th of September

It's our 22nd anniversary, so we went down to the loch side to look for wonky heart-shaped stones to add to our collection. A couple of dolphins kindly put on a show for us. #NatureIsNurture #LochLong

To Karen

We saw dolphins! They must have known that it's our anniversary.

To Karen

There was a wee splash of something, too…

Tuesday, 13th of September

I've just had my pre-chemo bloods done at my GP. The person who does it is brilliant. It's clear she cares and she always does it so well. #carefulandkindcare

Thursday, 15th of September

It's treatment day again, so there will be coffee, deep breaths, and distractions until my appointment at 3pm. Today is 9/14 of the post-surgical chemo and 17/22 overall. (the cup is sneakily covering up my CHI number)

To Ronnie

Thank you for making me feel better about the awfulness of going through this. xx

To Karen

Cannula in two.

To Susan

My current view…

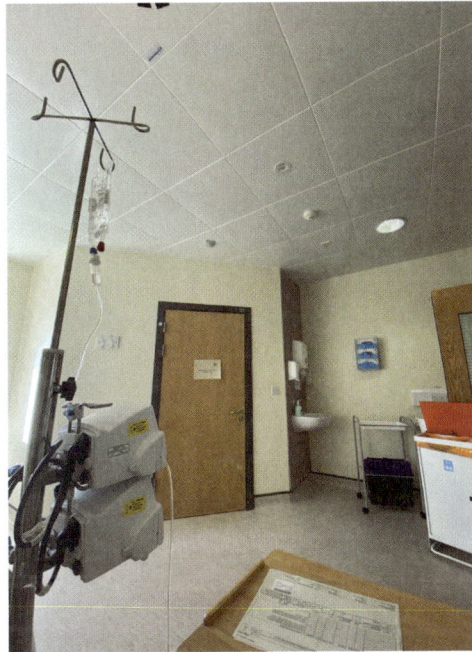

To Susan

It took a couple of goes to get the cannula in and there was a lot of blood… so I don't have a pillow under my hand (as usually happens) because they couldn't scrub the blood out of it and there didn't seem to be another one available…

Friday, 16th of September

I started #breastcancer treatment a year ago. It feels like a day to reflect on the love and support I've received, often just a small, unexpected gesture of care (sometimes a knitted hat!). Thank you to everyone who has reached out to help me through this difficult season.

Saturday, 17th of September

To Kirsten

Just wanted to send you love and say thanks for the help, support and care you've given me on this journey. Yesterday was one year since I started chemo. I also had my first post-surgery mammogram yesterday, which actually was nowhere near as bad as I feared thanks to taking a pain killer half an hour before. Anyway, all of this has got me thinking about the people who were there for me, especially at the most difficult time during the chemo at the beginning. The current chemo isn't fun but it's so much more manageable than the pre-surgical stuff. All this to say, I wanted you to know how much I appreciate your acts of kindness. Sending much love to you and Scout. xx

Sunday, 18th of September

To Libbe

It's so nice to hear from you, Libbe! What a whirlwind of a summer you had!

I have fourteen post-surgical chemo/antibody treatments that happen on a three-weekly cycle. I started at the end of March and am due to finish with them at the end of December (the 29th), if everything goes to the current plan.

It's been a hard year of treatment, but I've also been very aware of the love and support of family and friends, which has allowed me to get through it.

I'm really looking forward to being able to visit Neenah again so that I can say thank you in person.

In terms of what I'm occupying my days with... I've taken up knitting. I'm not great at it, but it seems to be helping with anxiety. I'm almost finished my second scarf in three weeks. I'm also writing a little fiction, but only a very little. It seems I don't have the necessary concentration at the moment. The dogs are also a good distraction. They need to be walked and played with regardless of what else is going on!

Sending love to you, Luke, and the wonderful wombats.

Gillian x

Monday, 19th of September

To Laura

It's definitely autumn weather here. Low 60s and showery. I think we might be over in Florida in February (all going well) and my friend Clair is thinking she might join us. It's a while away, but it's nice to have something to look forward to after treatment. xx

Tuesday, 20th of September

To Misti

Thanks, Misti. I love the random thoughts approach to email writing.

Random thoughts...

I'm rubbish at staying in touch.

It's so good to know you were here, somewhere, on this continent and that it was awesome.

So happy to hear you'll be back and very much looking forward to hosting you in Scotland when you are.

I hate chemo week.

This isn't chemo week.

I can't wait to be done with chemo.

I have anxiety about so many things now, all, I presume, founded upon the anxiety caused by a cancer diagnosis and cancer treatment.

I'm knitting now.

The knitting helps the anxiety.

I'm rubbish at knitting.

I hope the novel is going again.

Page 260... that's brilliant!

I would LOVE to Zoom.

Gillian

Friday, 23rd of September

To Laura

Flights are booked. In St Pete from 16th to 25th. During my last five chemo infusions I'll just walk along Beach Drive with you in my mind.

To Laura

My friend Clair will be there the whole time. You'll love her. We've been friends since school. She's been brilliant and has definitely helped get me through this. xx

Monday, 26th of September

I had a ball of wool left over from scarf number one, so knitted scarf number three with it. It's part of a 5th birthday gift. #amknitting #distractiontechnique

To Karen

It's less than perfect... It's Lynsey's little boy's 5th birthday today, so I knitted it for him with the ball of wool left over from Clair's scarf. By the time I get to yours there will hopefully be fewer 'unique design features'... xx

Wednesday, 28th of September

To Alan

Hi Alan,

I hope you're well.

I wondered if you would be up for a walk any time...? Selfishly, I really enjoyed both the walk and the chat last time, so would love if we could have another one. It's chemo week next week so if you were up for it, the week of the 10th or 17th of October would be great. The week of the 24th is then another chemo week.

Just on the off chance...

Gillian

To Alan

That schedule is crazy and brilliant!

The 17th would be great, but we could also leave it until November, if that would be better. I'm trying to manage chemo by putting nice things in the calendar for non-chemo weeks (to give me something to look forward to when I'm sitting in the big chair with the horrible cannula in my hand), so our walk could be a November thing to look forward to, rather than an October one... whatever would be best for you.

Gillian

To literary agent

Hi Sarah,

Unfortunately, Hamish has a vet appointment tomorrow morning. I could do Wednesday 19th October at 12.30pm, though.

I'm looking forward to catching up. I'm working away on the new novel (in terms of planning and really getting to know place and characters) and it would be great to get your thoughts at this early stage. I'm still not exactly sure about perspective or how to manage the two timelines.

Thanks,

Gillian x

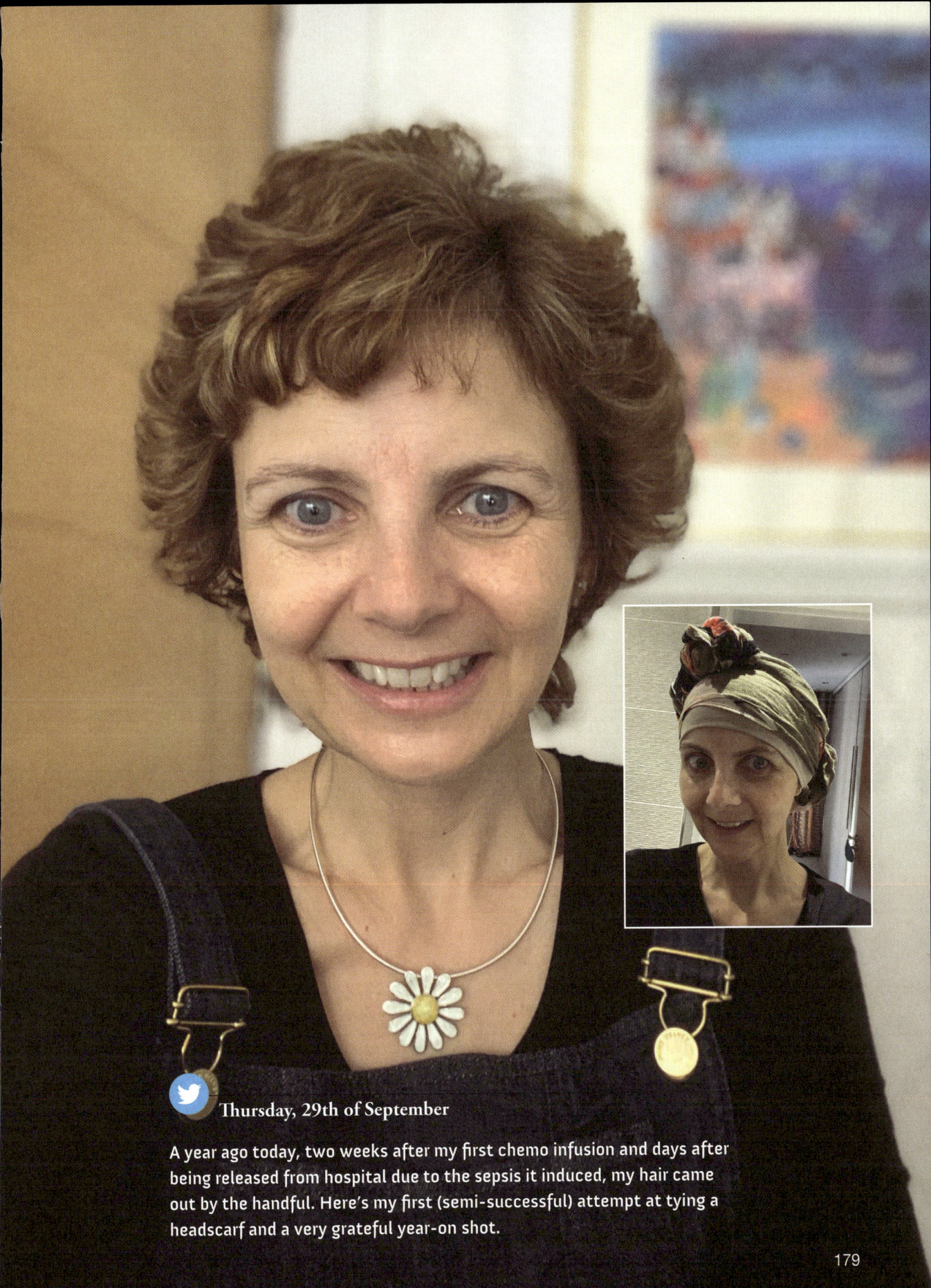

🐦 **Thursday, 29th of September**

A year ago today, two weeks after my first chemo infusion and days after being released from hospital due to the sepsis it induced, my hair came out by the handful. Here's my first (semi-successful) attempt at tying a headscarf and a very grateful year-on shot.

October 2022

Saturday, 1st of October

To Johanna

I'm on scarf four. I did knit one for a five-year-old's birthday though and the one I'm finishing is for a two-year-old. Next, it's a mother daughter matching scarf combo that Ronnie's taking to the States in about three weeks, so I'll need to get my skates on! xx

Just finished scarf four. It's a gift for a toddler. The neater edge is thanks to @ ekreeder and the great advice about slipping a stitch at the start of each row. #amknitting #distractiontechnique

Tuesday, 4th of October

At my GP waiting to be called for pre-chemo bloods. That was a quick three weeks! #timeflies

To Johanna

I still haven't heard about the mammogram. I have my pre-chemo appointment tomorrow so was planning to ask about it then. On Friday it'll be three weeks since I had it. I'm presuming that no news is good news. My hand was badly bruised and swollen after the last chemo and is still a little bruised, so I'm hoping that doesn't signify anything about my platelets (and that it won't cause a problem on Thursday). I've been putting arnica on multiple times a day so am hoping it'll be away by then. xx

To Johanna

They're only supposed to use the left hand because of the lymph nodes being removed from the right side… I'm lavishing it in arnica. Thank goodness the rain stopped. Fergus was VERY unhappy! xx

Wednesday, 5th of October

Waiting for my bloods yesterday, a GP walked by and said, 'Hello, Gillian,' in

a tone that suggested she was smiling behind her mask. It's a busy place and I've only met her once before, but she noticed me, remembered my name, and took the time to say hello. #carefulandkindcare

Thursday, 6th of October

It's treatment day again (10/14 or 18/22 if you add in pre-surgical chemo). My knitting will be coming with me for some waiting room therapy. #scarfnumberfive #amknitting

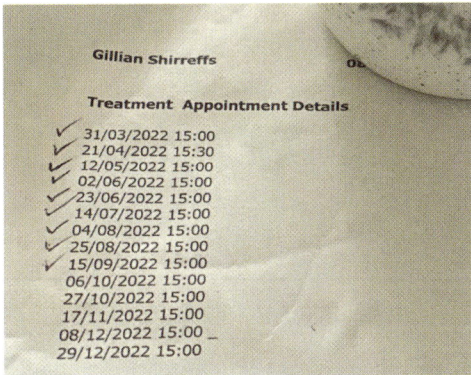

Gillian Shirreffs

Treatment Appointment Details

✓ 31/03/2022 15:00
✓ 21/04/2022 15:30
✓ 12/05/2022 15:00
✓ 02/06/2022 15:00
✓ 23/06/2022 15:00
✓ 14/07/2022 15:00
✓ 04/08/2022 15:00
✓ 25/08/2022 15:00
✓ 15/09/2022 15:00
06/10/2022 15:00
27/10/2022 15:00
17/11/2022 15:00
08/12/2022 15:00
29/12/2022 15:00

Friday, 7th of October

I received this letter today. Phew! And I've discovered that a strip of anti nausea pills are just the right size to redact an address. #scanxiety #goodnews

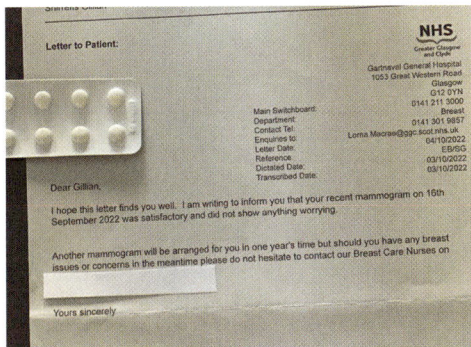

Saturday, 8th of October

It's so nice to get a card out of the blue. These two just arrived from Wisconsin. I'm grateful to our friends over there for their thoughtfulness and care. And even though I'm a Glasgow girl through and through, I feel homesick for WI. #Thankful #GoPackGo

Sunday, 9th of October

To Stephanie

Thanks for asking, but sadly nothing happened with Brodie. Did I ever give you a PDF? (I can't remember - cancer treatment will do that). If not, I'll send one. How are you?

To Stephanie

I can email it. My agent got some really good feedback (beautiful writing etc.), but no one wanted to take a chance on it. Oh, well.

181

To Katie

Aargh! I'm SO sorry. I've become really rubbish at correspondence. If I don't do a thing immediately... aargh!

Treatment is ongoing and it has been taking a toll both physically and mentally. Hence the knitting. And walking. I still find it to be the most useful thing I can do (on dry days; the knitting takes up the slack when it's raining). I would love to go for a walk sometime when you have time and it's not raining. Maybe a Zoom coffee/tea at some point in the meantime....?

I hope everything is good with you. I would love to hear how you are.

Gillian x

✉

To Alan

I'm doing okay but struggling a bit with the head game of it all. It seemed easier when I was sicker, and it was obvious I was having treatment to save my life. I now just want it to be over and I still have three months to go. I'm good at distracting myself though, which helps a lot. I've been taking my knitting to appointments to help manage the desire to just run away.

I'm looking forward to our walk.

Gillian

P.S. On a completely different note... just out of sheer nosiness... is my short story (Daggers) in this anthology or the next...?

✉ **Monday, 17th of October**

To Alan

I love that a woman was knitting before the Dylan concert started and I'm thrilled my wee story will be in this anthology. It's a real boost to think something I've written will be in such a brilliant publication. Even better for me, I wrote it in the nine-day limbo between biopsy and diagnosis when I desperately needed something else to focus on.

Hope you have a great time in London.

Gillian

🐦

I was enjoying #CreativeConversations with the brilliant @passingplace when I saw Fergus chasing this tiny creature around the kitchen. I intervened and relocated the little one to the hedgerow my sister has been cultivating at the back of her garden. #UnexpectedGuest

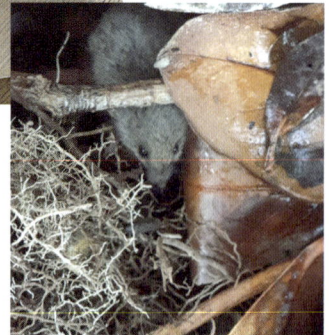

Tuesday, 18th of October

To Victor

Hi Victor,

I hope you're well.

I've had an idea for a way that I can write about my experience of breast cancer, and I wonder if you would be able to help… It's called Sixteen Scarves and involves me knitting a total of 16 scarves by the end of treatment (13.5 weeks and 9.5 scarves to go). By the end I will have had 16 months of treatment, so that maps to the number of scarves. I've been knitting the scarves as gifts for people who have been part of this experience and I'm hoping that each person might be kind enough to write some sort of response. By doing so, I hope that the project might capture not just my experience of the last 16 months but also that of those who have supported me as friend, neighbour, family member, patient.

My question is, would you be willing to let me knit you a scarf (I'm no expert) and then write something in response…? Perhaps about the concept of waiting in healthcare…?

Please don't worry if you'd rather not participate (or have enough scarves already!).

Gillian

Monday, 24th of October

I'm starting scarf eight today. It's going to be three colours… Ponder, Harmony, and Calm. It's for the lovely @ekreeder who knitted me a beautiful hat last year to keep my hairless head warm. #AmKnitting #SixteenScarves

Tuesday, 25th of October

To Clair

Let me know if you fancy a Fergus walk later… x

Waiting to be called for my pre-chemo bloods. #timeflies #cycle11of14

Wednesday, 26th of October

Walking back from my pre-chemo appointment in the beautiful post-rain sunshine. #FocusingOnNoticing #AutumnSunshine #Glasgow

Waiting to be called for treatment 11 of 14 (or 19 of 22 if you count the pre-surgical chemo). #AmKnitting #DistractionTechnique

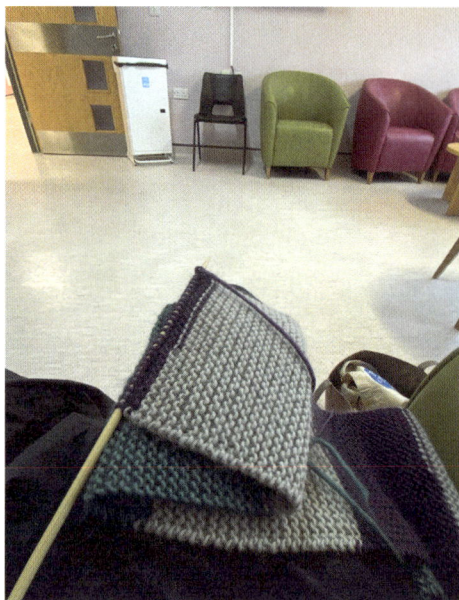

To Ruth

Look what arrived! I told Hamish it was from EK and he wagged his tail and gave it a big sniff! xx

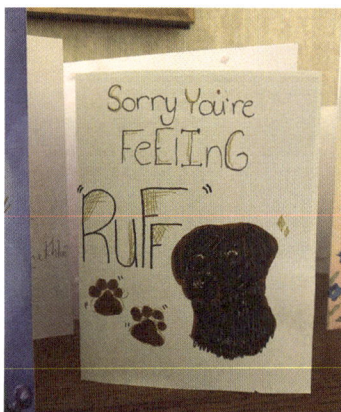

Scarf number eight. I learned a lot about knitting with multiple colours. My report card would definitely say 'could do better'. But it was knitted with love and as much care as I could give. #AmKnitting #GettingThroughTreatment

November 2022

Tuesday, 1st of November

To Victor

Ah! I didn't explain very well... I will knit you a scarf (you're number 11 on the list), send it across the Atlantic and then, inspired by the wonderfulness of it, you'll very kindly write a response to it (about anything you like but I'm guessing it'll be about careful and kind care... and maybe something about waiting).

I'd like to knit together (see what I did there) the words of family, friends, friends who are clinicians, clinicians who are not yet friends, with my own, as I hope this will offer insight into what it is to experience illness, and the giving and receiving of care.

G

Thursday, 3rd of November

I love @thiwurd writing classes. We were given a homework task with the prompt 'in disguise', which got me thinking about hair loss and cancer treatment, so I wrote a story. It was critiqued last night and I got lots of helpful feedback. #WritingCommunity #WritingFictionAsTherapy

Grace

The weight loss was unintentional.

That can happen, her oncologist explained. It's your body fighting the cancer.

It's often the first sign, someone else had said.

Then there was her hair. She'd always kept it long and people were forever complimenting her. Amazed at how thick it was. How shiny. She'd tease her hairdresser that she was going to charge him commission. If I had a pound for every time I've given out your number, Frankie Munro, she would say, I'd be rich.

She read that it wasn't so traumatic if there less of it to fall out, so a couple of weeks before treatment, she booked an appointment. Between them, they decided on a pixie cut. Her chemo hairdo, she called it.

People liked the elfin look. Said it showed off her eyes. Those cheek bones of hers.

Two weeks after the first infusion, it began to happen.

Her hair came out in handfuls.

Once it started, there was something addictive about pulling it out. Only a few strands at a time. At first. She tried to stop herself, but her fingers kept finding their way back to her scalp. Like a ragged tooth your tongue can't quite leave alone.

She brought the small bin from the bathroom into the kitchen. Sat it next to where her laptop was plugged in. Filled it. Emptied it. Filled it again. Every time she put her hand to her head, another wee fistful.

That only lasted a day and then her scalp got painful. She tried to explain it to Frankie on the phone. Told him it was like when you had a tight ponytail in.

That way, she said, when you take the bobble out and the bit of scalp next to where it's been is excruciating. Like that. Except all over.

They'd talked about this already. When she was in that last time. She'd told him about her pal whose cousin had been through it. According to the pal, when your scalp starts to hurt, you need to get someone to shave off whatever hair is left, to stop it hurting.

Frankie didn't miss a beat. Told her to come to the salon just after closing. He'd make sure the others got off sharp.

It was obvious he'd done it before. The way he acted as if it was normal. Chatting away as he changed the attachment on the razor. Removing the remaining hair, one slice at a time. Not everyone could have pulled it off, the nonchalance.

He stood back to admire his handiwork.

Wow, he said. What a beautiful head you've got.

She stared at herself in the mirror. Pointed to a thin indentation that ran the length of her skull.

Except for that, she said. I must have been dropped on my head as a baby.

She laughed then. But it was most likely the shock.

People called her a star. Said she fair suited a hat.

Her favourite hat was the one her wee brother bought her. It was the same grey blue as her eyes and was filled with a thick, soft fleece that gave her head some of its old height, its old heft.

Someone said it was good she was going through treatment at this time of year. Wouldn't it be so much worse, they declared, if it was the height of summer. At least everyone is wearing hats just now.

She smiled and nodded.

Later, when she was in the bath, she replayed the conversation and thought about other ways she could have responded. Maybe mentioning things that were worse. Like sepsis. Or death.

She began to spend hours scouring the internet. Looking at wigs. Imagining herself as a blonde, or a red head. She bought four in different lengths and colours but she only ever wore one of them outside. The honey caramel bob with apricot spice highlights. And she didn't do it often. Feeling like too much of a fraud.

For the most part, the wigs sat untouched in the spare room.

She visited them sometimes, though. Twirled around in each one, going from shortest to longest. Then placed them carefully back on their stands.

Her eyelashes began to fall out almost two months after the first infusion. A few days after that, her eyebrows started to vanish. As though someone was erasing them at night while she was asleep.

Even though there had been no good reason to think it, the idea she wouldn't lose them had inched into her head and the notion had taken root: that she might be the exception. Perhaps this false sense of security was because so much time had passed since her hair came out. And they'd still been there. Stubborn like her.

After they were away, she mentioned to her big sister that losing them was worse than the hair. Laura explained it was because your eyebrows give shape to your face; your eyelashes frame your eyes.

Maybe so, she'd said.

But she knew that wasn't it. There was something else. Something about the waxy uniformity of her face. She would catch it looking at her when she walked by reflective surfaces: staring out from glass doors and car windows.

She'd heard stories about people whose hair never grew back, and she'd told herself that would be okay. If it happened. That she would cope. But then, a fortnight after pre-surgical chemo was done, a dark bristle began to jut through her scalp, prickly to the touch, and she knew she'd been lying to herself.

After five months there was a load of it. Only a centimetre or two in length but thick, like before. And curly. She joked that she looked like Laura's toy poodle, Dougal, after his worst ever haircut.

By this point, the hat had been discarded. It was May, so she knew it would draw more attention than just brazening it out. And she felt much better in herself. The worst of the chemo was behind her as was surgery and the fifteen sessions of radiotherapy. Just nine months of the targeted immunotherapy to go: chemo-lite, as no one called it.

The first time someone didn't recognise her, she almost said something. Words formed in her mouth. Anne. Hello. But no sound came out. Anne was a neighbour. Not someone close. And she might just have been distracted. Running late for something.

Although, even if Anne had been in a rush, it would only have taken a second to smile back. She wondered if it had been intentional: that she'd somehow offended Anne and had been ignored as a punishment.

But it kept happening.

Donna from the Tuesday night quiz. Paula from the gym. Mr Strachan, her old driving instructor. Her pal Julie from that evening class she used to go to.

Julie had walked right past her on the Great Western Road, without so much as a glimmer of recognition. Then there was Andy from work. He was in the post office in the next queue. She lifted her hand in a half wave. And nothing. Not a flicker. Granted it was busy and she'd been off her work for ten months, but she'd sat in the next cubicle to him for years. They must have eaten lunch together a million times.

It was like a strange new skin had been stretched over her.

If she was honest, by this point it had become a bit of a game.

She would go about her business in broad daylight and count the number of people she knew who didn't recognise her. She bought a notebook and pencil to keep record. When she'd get home, she would jot down names, dates, and where it happened.

By the end of the summer, she was convinced she had a superpower.

Then one afternoon she ducked into a shop on Queen Margaret Drive. To shelter from the rain. And she heard a voice.

Hello, Grace. It's lovely to see you.

THE END

Later published in Issue 82 of *The Interpreter's House*

Scarf number nine. I knitted this one for the oncology pharmacist I see once a cycle. She exemplifies careful and kind care. #AmKnitting #GettingThroughTreatmemt

To Ronnie

Thank you for these beauties! They might be the prettiest yet. xx

Wednesday, 9th of November

To Alan

Hi Alan,

I'm afraid I'm not going to make it tonight. I'm sorry to miss the class.

I also have a question. I'm turning my scarf knitting into a project exploring my experience of cancer. I'm knitting 16 to match the 16 months of treatment and I'm asking the folks I knit them for to give some sort of creative response to their scarf / receiving the scarf as a way to represent the importance of community. I'd love to knit one for you as part of it because having a place I've been able to go as a reader / writer as opposed to a cancer patient has been really important to me (even if the treatment has meant I haven't been as often as I wanted).

If you don't fancy being part of it (which I'd completely understand), don't worry! I'll knit you a scarf regardless (just not one of the initial 16).

All the best,

Gillian

To Alan

I'm so pleased! Thank you. If you let me know what colour (or colours), I'll make yours number 12 (I'm on number 10 just now).

Gillian

Thursday, 10th of November

I finished scarf 10 today. My work rate isn't as impressive as it might seem as I ran out of wool for scarf 9 (on my big needles) so started scarf 10 (on my small needles) and kept knitting them turn about. This scarf is for my mum, who has been amazing. #HookedOnKnitting

Friday, 11th of November

Waiting to be called for my echocardiogram. #waiting

My latest scarf is for the brilliant and revolutionary @vmontori. He wanted it in @patientrev orange, so I shouldn't fall asleep knitting it. And doesn't the @Beatson_Charity tote make a brilliant knitting bag... #AmKnitting #GettingThroughTreatment

Monday, 14th of November

Chemo week is not my favourite week, but I finished my latest scarf today, so that's good. It'll be winging its way to @vmontori very soon. #AmKnitting #GettingThroughTreatment

Tuesday, 15th of November

At my GP surgery waiting to be called for my pre-chemo bloods. #timeflies #cycle12of14

191

Wednesday, 16th of November

What a beautiful, chilly morning to walk to my pre-chemo appointment at the Beatson. #WalkingTherapy #Glasgow

Thursday, 17th of November

Waiting to be called for TDM1 treatment 12 (of 14). #AmKnitting #DistractionTechnique

Listening to the brilliant Dance Move by @WednesdayErskin is helping get me through chemo today. Such a great collection of short stories.

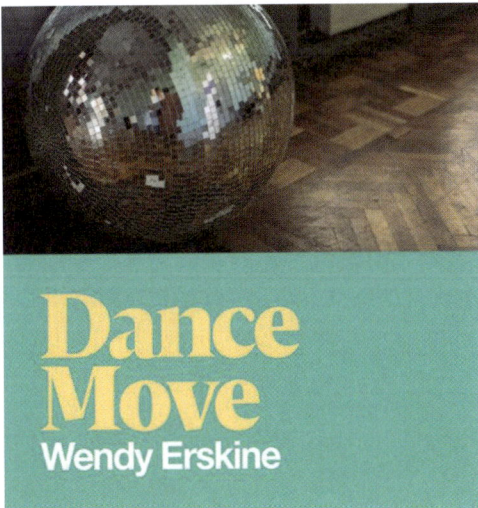

Dance Move
Wendy Erskine

To Clair

I had lovely Annabel One and cannula in one. It took a lot longer because of the hydrocortisone infusion and then they wanted to leave it half an hour so that it was working. I still felt pretty yucky with the TDM1 infusion.

Sunday, 20th of November

I'm thrilled to have a story in this beautiful anthology. I wrote it in the gap between biopsy and diagnosis as a distraction from life - it's a quietly dark piece about a village's annual whist competition. Why not grab a ticket for this brilliant event! #WritingCommunity

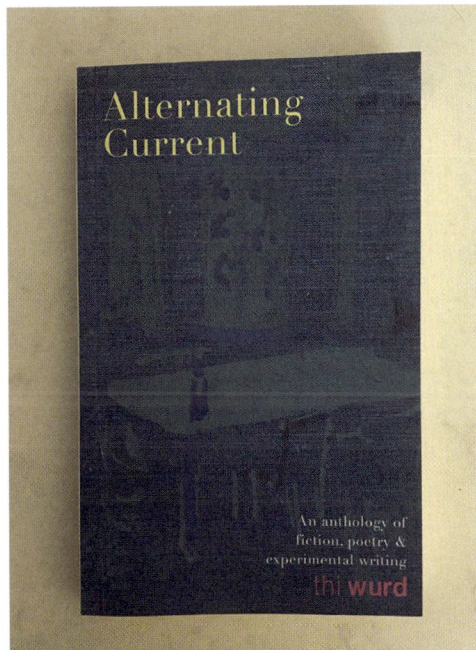

Alternating Current

An anthology of fiction, poetry & experimental writing

thi wurd

Wednesday, 23rd of November

My latest scarf is for @thiwurd as thanks for the fantastic classes where I've been able to feel like a reader and a writer, not a cancer patient. The teal (ish) colour is a tiny homage to the brilliant new anthology. #SixteenScarves #WritingCommunity

I've been doing some prep for a virtual WIP event next week, so have been attempting to get my artefacts of illness into some semblance of order, including the 64 hospital letters I've received since July 2021. #TalkingObjects

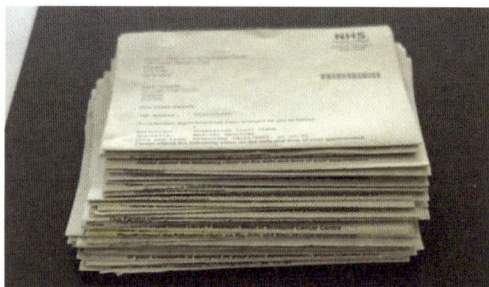

And here's what I've been knitting on my fat needles for the last week or so. This one is for my sister who's been an incredible support. Thanks for all the pan drops @ewoksrock! #SixteenScarves #SixteenMonthsOfTreatment #DistractionTechnique

To Angela

Hi Angela,

I was asked to email you with a couple of questions about my next treatment by the nurses on B9. Alice had added a bolus of hydrocortisone but there was nothing on the script about whether or not they should wait after it. In the absence of any instructions, they waited 30 minutes before starting my TDM1 infusion.

I was asked to email you to find out what is supposed to happen (I don't have an email address for Alice) as they presumed I'll be getting the hydrocortisone from now on. Also, if they do have to wait the 30 minutes, they asked if it would be better if my appointment was moved earlier because I kept the staff late last time. My appointments are always at 3pm and the saline flush wasn't through until 6.15pm.

I should have emailed earlier. Sorry! It went out of my head after the infusion.

My next treatment is next Thursday

Many thanks,

Gillian

To Susan

The name of your wool is Wisdom. It seems very apt. I've been getting West Yorkshire Spinners wool because they give a portion of the profit on each ball to a mental health charity. Their wools don't have a colour, just a name. Also, I know I should probably be saying yarn instead of wool.

December 2022

Friday, 2nd of December

To Angela

Thanks for getting back to me, Angela. Hopefully they won't have to wait, so they don't need to change my appointment time. I'm worried that it would push back my dates (and you know how much I want to finish on the 29th!).

I'd be very happy to knit you a scarf, if you wanted. I'm very much an amateur knitter though, so there are always a few wee minor flaws (unique design features). I'm doing it as part of a medical humanities project exploring the experience of breast cancer. I'm partly doing it as a way to say thank you to those who've supported me but also because I'd love to include the voices of other people in the project, so I've been asking folks if they'll offer some sort of response to their scarf (I've not really worked that bit of it out yet).

And if you didn't want to be part of the project, I'd still love to knit you a scarf.

Thanks again,

Gillian

I finished another scarf today. It's for one of my neighbours. She's walked with me, talked with me, and before my first surgery (when I was very anxious) made me a lovely gift filled with lavender to help me sleep. #SixteenScarves #SixteenMonthsOfTreatment #GlasgowNeighbours

To Karen

Thanks! I'm feeling well physically, but the chemo week dread has reared its ugly head. x

Sunday, 4th of December

To Susan

I'm glad you like the scarf! Thank you for helping get me through this. Your help has been so important. I still have the lavender pouch you gave me before my first surgery. I keep it next to my pillow, like a talisman.

To Johanna

I'm good, thanks. Knitting my latest scarf - a chunky olive green one (so a wee bit Christmassy). Penultimate chemo on Thursday. xx

195

✉ Monday, 5th of December

To Paul

Thanks, Paul! I appreciate you asking Lauren. My only other question is what colour she would like. I've been using wool that supports a mental health charity (they donate a portion of each sale), so if she could choose a colour she likes, that would be brilliant. The link is to their super chunky range, which should keep her nice and warm.

Many thanks,

Gillian

🐦

Between the cold weather and trying to manage the anxiety of treatment week, this is my fastest scarf ever. Let's hope it doesn't have too many 'unique design features'! It's for the wonderful @KateReidGlasgow who has been a great friend and pick-me-up. #SixteenScarves #Kindness

🐦 Tuesday, 6th of December

Waiting to be called for my pre-chemo bloods. Enjoying the smiley snowman. #Waiting #Timeflies #Cycle13of14

✉ Wednesday, 7th of December

To Alan

Hi Alan,

Apologies. I'm not going to make tonight's class. My mum and dad are moving into a bungalow this week and we have them staying with us during it (you can probably imagine what it's like packing up a house that's been lived in for over 50 years). And it's also treatment week this week, just to complicate matters.

I hope it's another great class. I'm sorry to be missing it.

Gillian

🐦 Thursday, 8th of December

It's treatment day again. It'll be my 13th infusion of TDM1 (of 14). It's also a year to the day since my final infusion of pre-surgical chemo. I'm walking with a friend at noon. There will also be knitting. #WalkingTherapy #Cycle13

✉

To Johanna

Still in the chair. Half an hour to go. Cannula in two. xx

To Johanna

It's okay. It's the second last one. Thanks for checking in. You're always so good. xx

Sunday, 11th of December

To Stephanie

It was SO lovely to see you all on Facetime! I love the Wisconsin Brodie Book Group!

Tuesday, 13th of December

I finished my latest scarf today, which will soon be on its way to my brilliant pal Georgi. We had a writing retreat just before chemo began, which was a much needed distraction. I'm also grateful for our shared writing space. #SixteenScarves #SixteenMonthsOfTreatment

Wednesday, 14th of December

To Ronnie

Two things I might forget to tell you… there's an orange light on my dashboard that I think might be an early warning for the oil and the heating control in our room needs new batteries (has died). xx

Sunday, 18th of December

To Clair

Hope you had a lovely time! I'm heading over to the parents' house soon, but I fancy doing a wee bit of a Byres Road shop later in the afternoon, if you're free/up for it. xxx

Wednesday, 21st of December

To Laura

Hi! Sorry for the delay! My parents are moving house (to a bungalow as the stairs have become too difficult) and have been staying with us for the last two weeks while we do some work to the new house. I hope everything is going well with you. xxx

Sunday, 25th of December

To Clair

Merry Christmas!

To Clair

FaceTime coffee sounds great! I'll be in my Christmas pjs. xx

To Clair

We have neither placemats nor napkins… so it's Irish linen all the way!

Tuesday, 27th of December

I finished my latest scarf last week but only made the tassels for it today. It's for the @Beatson_Charity telephone befriender who called every week during my first few months of treatment. Such a brilliant service. #Kindness #SixteenScarves #SixteenMonthsOfTreatment

Wednesday, 28th of December

My GP was closed yesterday so I'm at the Beatson first thing to have my pre-chemo bloods done. I'll be back later this morning for my pre-chemo appointment. #Cycle14of14

Thursday, 29th of December

I have treatment 14 of 14 this afternoon (or 22 of 22 if you count the pre-surgery chemo). I'd love to go for a long walk to help manage the pre-treatment nerves but it's pouring, so thank goodness for knitting. #TreatmentDay #GlasgowWeather #KnittingTherapy #AndBreathe

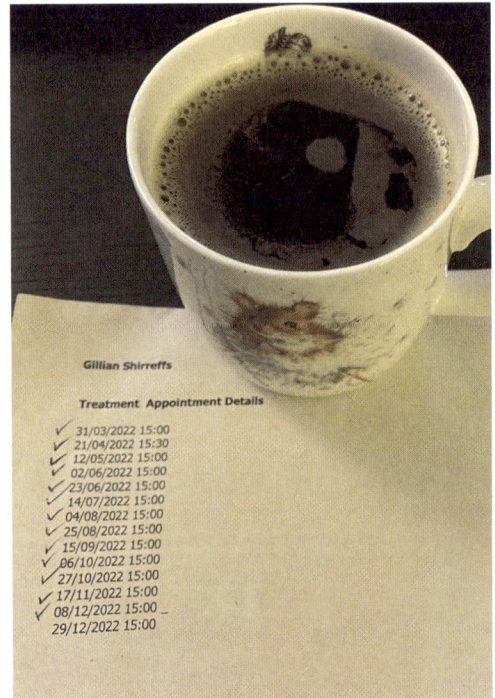

To Susan

I have my final fill up at the poison palace today. At some point I'd like your take on how I talk about finishing / being finished treatment. I find myself saying… my last treatment, fingers crossed… because I don't want to jinx things, but maybe I'm inviting things by saying it… and maybe it doesn't matter. But words matter. And you are good at this. xx

To Susan

You have no idea how much you helped me. And maybe it felt little to you. But I was flailing, and you gave me solid ground.

To Susan

Cannula in two thanks to the nurse who poo pooed the idea I might have tricky veins. Thankfully she got someone else to do the second attempt.

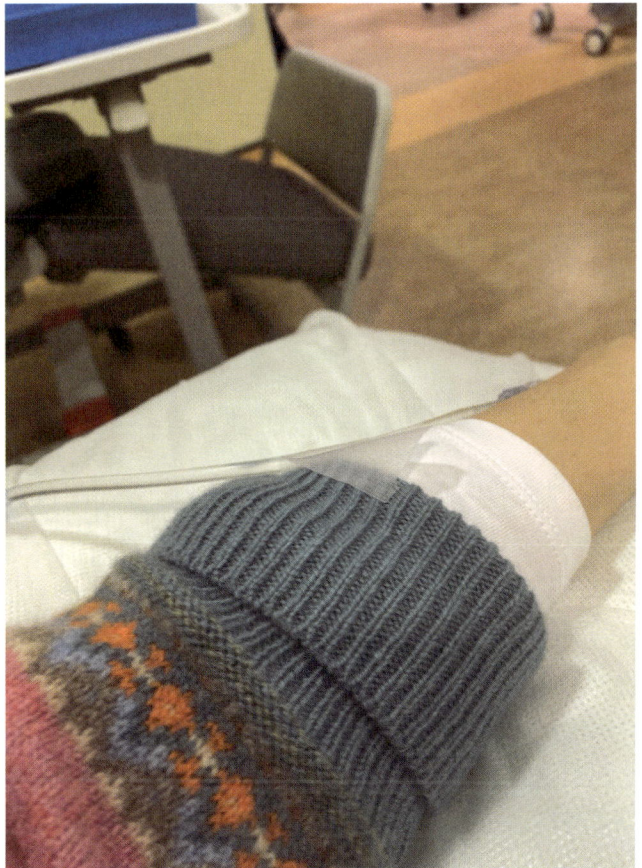

To Cousins

Less than an hour to go of my last treatment. I'll be very happy to be back home tonight. xx

To Johanna

Almost done… 30 minutes to go… Thank you for thinking about me. You're the best. xx

To Johanna

Thanks! It's a Christmas cardigan from Ronnie. Chemo chic.

To Susan

The time is DRAGGING. I've never known it to crawl so slowly. I tried listening to a book. I tried playing words games. I'm now just watching people and drumming my fingers.

To Johanna

Ronnie's already in the car park and apparently the dinner is ready. He's definitely a keeper.

Gillian Shirreffs

Treatment Appointment Details

✓ 31/03/2022 15:00
✓ 21/04/2022 15:30
✓ 12/05/2022 15:00
✓ 02/06/2022 15:00
✓ 23/06/2022 15:00
✓ 14/07/2022 15:00
✓ 04/08/2022 15:00
✓ 25/08/2022 15:00
✓ 15/09/2022 15:00
✓ 06/10/2022 15:00
✓ 27/10/2022 15:00
✓ 17/11/2022 15:00
✓ 08/12/2022 15:00
✓ 29/12/2022 15:00

The list is ticked. Thanks to everyone who has supported me since I was diagnosed 18 months ago and through 16 months of treatment (22 infusions, 2 surgeries, 15 sessions of radiotherapy). For every text, word of encouragement, card, and thoughtful gift. #Kindness #Community

January 2023

Sunday, 1st of January 2023

To Clair

Happy New Year!

To Clair

Likewise! 2023 is going to be fab!

To Clair

Although… I did give up my cool for you… which means I love you the most.

To Susan

I'm here for the good times and the love. Wishing you and yours the same and a big dollop of anything else Pablo fancies.

To Jenny

And a Happy New Year to the best roomie, ever! And I'll take that bloody awesome 2023! xx

To Jen

Thanks! Wishing you a wonderful 2023! Can't wait to see you in Feb.

To Cousins

Happy New Year! All best wishes for 2023. xx

Monday, 2nd of January

To Victor

Thank you, Victor. I cried on the first read; smiled on the second.

There is truth in it. And experience. And hope. And humour.

And now I want to write an essay on waiting.

But I'll wait. Just a little longer.

Gillian

Monday, 9th of January

To Karen

Just back at the car after walking from Gartnavel. Bloods done in the surgical ward by a nurse who remembered me (more likely my odd name) from the surgeries I had last year. X

Tuesday, 10th of January

To Laura

Yes! We'll be there on Friday February 17 and I know we'll enjoy our adventure with you. xxx

To Laura

We fly out 6 weeks after infusion 22 and they count them in three weekly cycles, so I should have had three weeks to recover.

Friday, 20th of January

To Misti

Helloooo!

Aaaargh. Almost on a daily basis I think - must write to Misti. And then I don't. There are a lot of things I want to do that slip by me each day. I'm tired and flat and in something of a fog. And the days pass. And I don't do the things I want to do in them.

Although, I have become a bit of an obsessional knitter. So I do that. No thinking is involved and I think (see what I did there) that is the trick. My brain has grown lazy.

I also watch a lot of nonsense on my laptop (whilst I knit). Detective dramas / police procedurals - from all times and places and some of which I watched 10, 20 or 30 years ago. Chewing gum for the eyes.

How are you? How's the family?

Can we Zoom soon? I still haven't figured out life post-treatment. I have a post-chemo appointment with my oncologist next Wednesday, so I'm telling myself I'll do it after that. Let's see... Regardless, I'm free for a Zoom with you.

Gillian x

Monday, 23rd of January

To Jen

We fly on the Monday. Glasgow - London, London - Tampa. Then drive down to Naples, so I'm presuming we won't be there until late on the Monday…

To Jen

I'm feeling a bit anxious about seeing people who I haven't seen since before all of this happened (when I still had all my lovely long hair). And I didn't have the best social skills to start with!

Tuesday, 24th of January

To Johanna

We just dropped a couple of bottles of water round to Clair. Do you need any? xx

To Johanna

Ronnie managed to get 12 x 1.5L bottles, so I suppose it depends how long this goes on… I have my post-chemo appointment with Dr McPherson tomorrow, so let's hope I'm not too smelly!

To Johanna

Thank you! Although hopefully we won't need it by then! I think they've been working on the water main since about 4pm. xx

My post-chemo appointment is tomorrow. I'm going laden with scarves (well three). One for my oncologist, one for my oncology nurse and one for the chemo nurse I saw most often. I'm sure I'll seem a complete looney-tune for saying thank you in this way. #Gratitude #KnittingTherapy

Wednesday, 25th of January

To Johanna

Thank you! It's great the water is back on. I can go to the appointment freshly showered. I hope you have a good day. xx

Friday, 27th of January

To Beatson Cancer Charity

Hi,

I'm interested in self-referring to the Fear of Recurrence group programme. I was diagnosed with HER2+ breast cancer in August 2021 and have just completed sixteen months of treatment. I had my post-chemo meeting with Dr Kerr this week.

During one of my pre-chemo appointments, Alice Brooke suggested I might find this programme helpful once I'd finished treatment, so I thought I would email to enquire.

With best regards,

Gillian

February 2023

Wednesday, 1st of February

I finally knitted Ronnie a scarf (it's his birthday today). I can't even imagine how difficult the last 18 months have been for him. I'm grateful for every walk in the rain, bowl of soup, thoughtful card, word of encouragement, hand hold.

Wednesday, 8th of February

To Jen

We'll be late on Monday night. Likely after 10pm. We're heading to St Pete on the Thursday. Hopefully we'll get some time together. xx

To Jen

We should be in Neenah the week of May 13th. I'm looking forward to that too!

Wednesday, 8th of February

To Georgi

Dearest pen pal,

Sorry for not replying sooner! I was so pleased to get your email. I've been starting an email to you (in my head) for weeks now.

I'm not what I was. I don't suppose the person who goes into this thing is ever the same person who emerges post-treatment, which is a challenge because I don't know how to be anyone else.

Ronnie said the other day that I'd lost my spirit, and it made him sad. And maybe that's a better description. I'm a spiritless shell of my former self.

The post-treatment appointment has left me less good (which wasn't very good to start with) than I had been. My odds haven't changed (and they're very decent), but he said something along the lines of...

... for someone with your type of breast cancer who's had the treatment you've had, it's likely you'll not be bothered by this cancer again. But there are no guarantees. And with your type of breast cancer, if it does come back, it usually does so quickly. Within the first couple of years.

And somehow, even though the odds are unchanged, the speed of the (less than likely) return felt like a punch in the stomach.

I responded with anxiety and after a few days a flat quietness came over me. And that's where I am now. Flat and quiet. And sad. With a big side helping of buck-yourself-up-you-stupid-cow.

But enough about that.

As for the scarf, I'm so pleased you like it. That makes me happy. I did try to knit friendship and care into it. I can't even remember what I was thinking I hoped people might do. I've had an essay from Victor and a poem from Susan the Neighbour but have given no direction to anyone because I find myself directionless. And I can't imagine doing anything on this project (if it will ever be a project) in the near future, so please don't worry about doing anything other than enjoying your scarf. And maybe someday I'll appear in your email with a hope for something as yet unclear.

Take care,

G xx

Friday, 10th of February

To Georgi

Thank you. I like the thought of Gillian-as-Dormouse very much. And it feels like a much better thing on which to ruminate. You DO have all the wisdom.

Sending the best of thoughts to the east.

G xx

Wednesday, 15th of February

To Laura

Hello from Naples! We got here on Monday night after about 23 hours of travel. I haven't felt great, but hopefully I'll be feeling better by the time we head up to St Pete tomorrow. It'll be so nice to see you. xxx

To Laura

I think the journey was just a bit too much for me six weeks post-chemo. And having different food seems to have been a struggle for a system that's been so gently

managed for so long. I'm hoping staying hydrated and taking things easily will help. As will seeing your beautiful face. xx

Thursday, 16th of February

To Laura

I feel I should issue a warning… be prepared for crazy chemo curls. I left my hair to dry on its own yesterday… xx

Sunday, 19th of February

To Karen

Perfect weather… Clair's in full sun… I'm under an umbrella. X

To Karen

Another beautiful day in paradise… xx

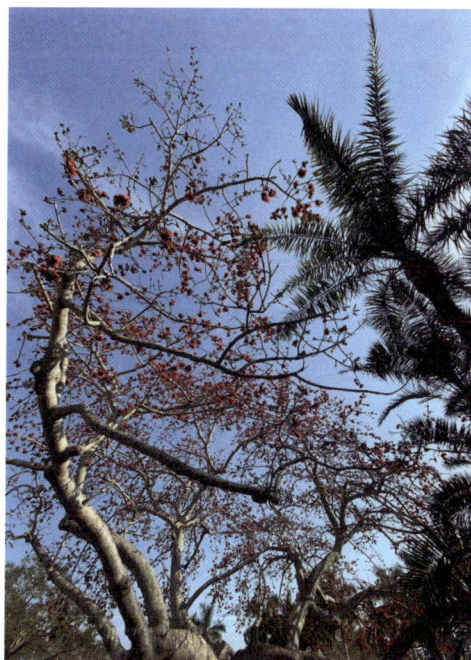

To Johanna

Clair and I are sitting in the avant-garden at the Salvador Dali Museum in St Pete. xx

📱 **Saturday, 25th of February**

To Laura

All checked in and through security. Thank you SO much for taking us to the airport and for EVERYTHING. xxx

To Laura

SO nice to see your lovely son!!! We were at the gate, and he just walked by! xxx

✉️ **Tuesday, 28th of February**

To Anna

Hi Anna,

I'd appreciate if I could speak to you about something.

For the past month or so my lower ribs on the right-hand side have been painful to the touch. I've experienced cording since the summer, which is less noticeable now, so I've been hoping it's related to that. There's now a small part of me though that's getting anxious it's something more sinister, so I thought I should try to speak to you to help put my mind at ease.

Is there a time I could call that would be convenient for you?

With many thanks,

Gillian

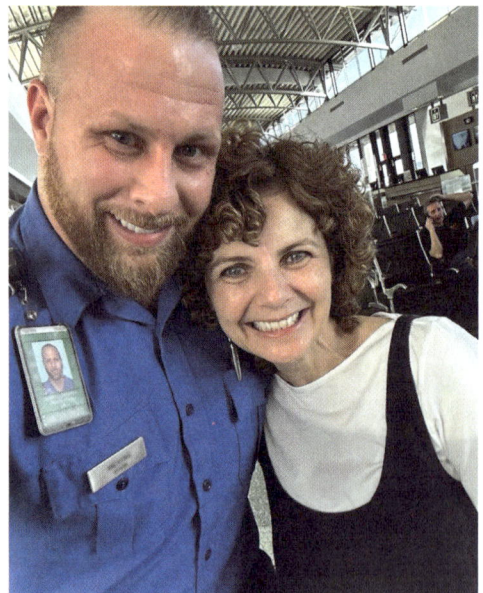

March 2023

Friday, 3rd of March

Learning to embrace the #ChemoCurls.
And just grateful to have hair
(and eyelashes and eyebrows).
#whatadifferenceayearmakes

Wednesday, 8th of March

To Johanna

I got a call from the nurse this afternoon. She said it was most likely something muscular but that she would make an appointment for someone to see me in a couple of weeks. I think it would be good to have someone put my mind at ease.

Thursday, 9th of March

To Anna

Hi Anna,

Thank you so much for phoning me yesterday. I really appreciate you organising an appointment for someone to have a look at my ribs.

I had a GP friend over tonight and she suggested I send you a photo of the lower rib area because I've noticed that there is something there that you can see (although the photos aren't great). It's a sort of puckering both on the ribs and below them.

Thanks again for your help,

Gillian

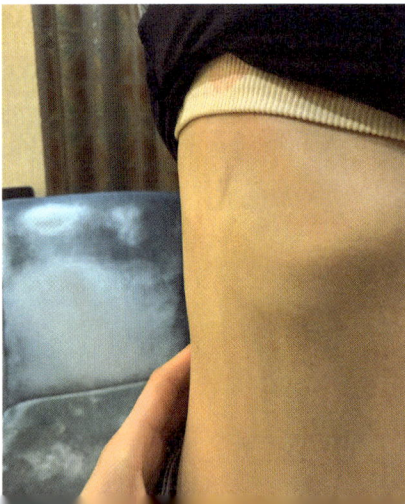

Saturday, 11th of March

To Clair

I'm not feeling brilliant. Very dickie tummy for two days. I think I might phone the GP for an appointment next week because this has been on and off for three weeks or so… it's maybe a post chemo thing. I weighed myself yesterday (which I hadn't done for a couple of months) and I'm down about six pounds (or more). xx

Wednesday, 19th of March

To Morgan

Dearest Morgan,

Wishing you and your lovely family a wonderful St Patrick's Day (a little late - sorry)! I hope you're having a lovely weekend.

I finished 16 months of treatment at the end of December. I very much appreciate the fact that you were praying for me when I was going through it all. Knowing of the love and care I was getting from around the world, made an incredible difference to me.

I have now gone from being bald to having a big mop of curly hair. It was the pre-surgical chemo that made it fall out; the treatment I had after surgery didn't affect it, so it's been growing like a weed for just over a year. A very curly weed!

We're planning to be in Neenah in May (13th to 20th), so hopefully we might see you around!

Gillian xx

Tuesday, 28th of March

To Johanna

I was at Gartnavel today. I saw a lovely doctor who spoke to me, examined me, and then went to speak to Mr Walker, who came along to see me. He was brilliant. He took time to explain about what would have happened to the area post surgery/radiotherapy and that it was now more vulnerable to injury/pain. He was very reassuring and said because the pain had now resolved there was no need for a bone scan. (I'm not sure if I told you but I had acupuncture – I sometimes go for the nerve pain in my hands and feet - and I told the acupuncturist about the rib pain, which he then treated and within a couple of days it was gone!) Mr Walker also said the bowel changes/weight loss weren't a red flag for him and said to go to my GP about it. I am VERY relieved. The other doctor then said that everything felt good and normal when she examined the breast/lymph node area. She also said the puckering on the ribs and below them was linked to treatment and wouldn't be seen if I wasn't so slim. Phew! Thank you for always being there as a listening ear! I appreciate it so much. xx

Thursday, 30th of March

To Georgi

Hi Georgi,

I hope spring is starting to spring in the east. Today, despite a little rain earlier, has felt mild and good.

I'm sorry to have been silent for so long. It doesn't mean I haven't thought about you and wondered how you are and hoped that things are well and the universe is being kind.

It's three months since I finished treatment, and I have no idea where the time has gone. In that time, I've managed to go to Florida and have a health scare. I'm not even sure if I told you I was tagging along on a Ronnie work trip mid-February. I think I was anxious about the mechanics of it, so chose not to dwell on it beforehand.

Turns out it was very ambitious to cross the Atlantic barely six weeks after finishing chemo. Who'd have thunk?

In addition, two months ago my body chose to throw in some ongoing rib pain, bowel changes (more?!), and weight loss, which took my mind back into dark corners. Thankfully, my surgeon (who saw me yesterday) is calm, relaxed, and certain it's all treatment related. Phew!

I hope things are gentle and restful with you.

G xx

April 2023

Sunday, 2nd of April

To Misti

Misti!

I'm so sorry to have been radio silent. Florida was lovely but exhausting (and too hot).

I had a bit of a health scare, but my surgeon is happy, and I trust him. I'm planning and plotting a ridiculously uncommercial novel about some animals who solve crime but never get any credit.

I hope things are good with you.

G x

My chemo curls are currently helping me channel 1980s knitwear catalogue. #embracingthecurls

Saturday, 8th of April

To Laura

Thank you! Happy Easter to you and all the family! Two of our little Easter bunnies

Tuesday, 11th of April

To Misti

I'm doing okay, just trying to figure out how to get back into a writing routine. I want to sit down and do it, but it seems I get to the end of each day (which have been filled with filler-type things - and important things like helping parents and looking after dogs) and I haven't written a word. It's very annoying. I did write something for a project (WAY over the deadline, but still in time to be allowed to participate), which I'll send a link to when it goes live (it's a website with work about a nearby ruin of a Victorian asylum, which also happens to be the site of my cancer hospital and the general hospital where I was diagnosed / had the surgeries - they were built in its extensive grounds).

G x

To Stephanie

I hope you're well. I wrote something and thought I'd send it along because you're always so kind about reading my writing…

Gartnavel Ghosts

What follows is a working out.

A back and forth.

A negotiation of place and time.

But first, a potted history. It's the summer of 1991. A 21-year-old girl is invited to attend an interview at Gartnavel Royal. She gets the job. It's the summer of 2021. A 51-year-old woman is invited to attend an appointment at Gartnavel General. She gets cancer.

Clearly, the cancer was already there. Growing. Like the fear in her belly. But it wasn't there until the examination followed by the mammogram followed by the ultrasound followed by the biopsy followed by the appointment with the breast surgeon who has in his possession the pathology report containing the results of the biopsy, confirming she has breast cancer.

More accurately, the results of three biopsies: tissue was taken from two sites in her breast and one site, a lymph node, under her arm. Two of the biopsies show cancerous cells (one site in her breast and the lymph node in her armpit). The third biopsy shows pre-cancerous cells (in the other site in her breast).

More accurately, in my breast.

In my armpit.

June 1991

I sit down on a chair in an empty corridor and wait for my name to be called.

I've just turned 21 and I'm nervous.

I suspect family connections have secured the interview (I'm the daughter of two nurses, one of whom is a friend of someone *higher up*). I turn this over in my mind and hope it won't count against me with the *not so high up* person who is about to stumble over the pronunciation of my ridiculous surname; that instead my unbridled enthusiasm coupled with the fact I'm hardworking and studying for a degree in English Language, will go in my favour.

My previous jobs have been seasonal and mainly involved dishes – the washing of them – and I've typically been referred to as 'the student'.

Why bother learning someone's name if they'll be gone in a matter of weeks?

I feel in my bones that this job, if I get it, will be different.

It will mark a transition.

August 2021

I indicate and make a left turn off Great Western Road.

I'm reminded of the butterflies I felt in my stomach when a vehicle in which I was a passenger made this same turn thirty years earlier.

The car park is busy.

A space finally opens. It's tight but I manoeuvre into it.

Forward and back; forward and back.

I take a breath.

Check my appearance in the rear-view mirror.

And step into August sunshine.

As I approach the entrance of Gartnavel General, I see it not just through the eyes of the 51-year-old woman I've become, but also through those of my younger self.

The front door slides open, and we walk in, together.

I locate the waiting area and check in.

The man through the glass smiles and indicates I should take a seat.

It's early.

My appointment has been made for just before the breast clinic begins, so I have my choice of chairs. Despite this, I choose the one nearest to him.

When my name is called, a name I opted to keep despite the married alternative being so much easier to say, I'm aware of my younger self, standing, too.

After the doctor examines me, she draws a circle on my right breast in black pen.

I assume this is not good.

I'm told to go to radiology where, she explains, I'll have a mammogram.

I follow her directions, aware of little other than the anxiety that has taken root in my chest, a tightness underneath my ribs. Significance surrounds me: in the walls that form an honour guard as I walk to my next destination; in the new waiting area with its Covid information and carefully spaced seats; in the sound of my name being mispronounced once more.

I know, without being told, that a change has taken place.

The idea that it will be fine, that I will leave unscathed, has vanished.

June 1991

The project team onto which I've been hired is new.

Brand new.

Our mission is to equip both inpatients and outpatients with useful life skills.

My role in all of this is to teach adult literacy. Thanks to a budget overspill, funding has been made available for a three-month post (a perfect way to spend my last long university summer holiday: earning whilst learning to teach). Thankfully, I won't be alone in this endeavour: my role will sit alongside a permanent post, which has been filled by someone much older and wiser. A colleague who will become a coffee-buddy, a lunchtime friend.

On my first day of work, the former ward in which we're to be housed is in a state of flux. Beds and privacy curtains are being replaced by desks and chairs; side rooms are being transformed into teaching spaces.

The first order of business is a crash course in Adult Basic Education. I approach it in the manner of a teacher's pet. I complete the course and receive a certificate which, a year later, will share box space with my degree scroll.

Once certified I meet my first student, Alec – not his real name.

Alec looks older than my dad. I realise that this could make our teacher/student relationship difficult. His openness, though, is humbling. It becomes clear that he wants me to teach him how to read and write, and this desire is greater than any discomfort he might feel about my lack of age and life experience.

In our first lesson, I start at what I think is the beginning.

I awkwardly reintroduce Alec to the letters of the alphabet.

What develops is a conversation. About life. Its complexities.

I'm taught just how fortunate I am.

August 2021

I meet my oncologist for the first time on Wednesday the 25th of August. I'll later learn that pre-chemo appointments always happen on a Wednesday, at least the twenty-two that are in my future do.

Dr Kerr – not his real name – is based at the Beatson West of Scotland Cancer Centre. This is a building that didn't exist in 1991. It's in what was lawned gardens, from memory, and sits in front of the Maggie's Centre, another new kid on the block.

Thanks to the *Writing the Asylum* project, I've seen old photographs of the Gartnavel campus, showing a farm on this site. A farm which was attached to what was then The Glasgow Royal Lunatic Asylum. I presume its purpose was to provide sustenance for both the body and the soul.

As a structure, the Beatson looks good: it has modern lines and is unobtrusive in the landscape. It gives, at least to me, a sense that excellent medicine takes place inside. And there's something calming about it: light colours and a nice amount of glass. If a building can instil confidence, this one does.

In terms of location, it's close to the train station – a train station I often used as a girl, commuting to and from my job at Gartnavel Royal – so I likely walked over the ground on which it was built many times never imagining that someday a hospital would spring from the soil under my feet. A hospital that would send me a letter inviting me to attend an appointment with an oncologist.

An oncologist I never wanted to meet, but who is everything you could want in one: an expert in his field; a clinician who listens; a consultant who thinks out loud and changes his mind, right there in front of you, as he tries to ensure he balances each and every variable to make certain he provides the right treatment for you (in this case, me).

June 1991

I quickly learn to tailor my lessons to suit the interests and motivations of my students.

For instance, Alec – still not his real name – wants to be able to read the newspaper.

Despite spells as an inpatient, he's managed to hold down the same job for years and takes a newspaper to work every day. He tells me he pretends to read it at lunchtime, whilst eating his sandwiches.

Once we've worked on what are deemed to be the fundamentals, our time together is spent poring over words and sentences cut from the pages of the Daily Record, his paper of choice.

I find out a fair deal about football during the hours we spend together. In particular, the machinations of two local clubs. None of which I commit to memory.

I tend to go for a walk during my lunch break. The pleasant weather draws me out into the garden grounds.

One of my colleagues is a horticultural tutor. I like to skirt the periphery of the small groups he teaches. There's a clink to their rakes and trowels I enjoy and I'm sure I can smell the warmth of the soil as they turn it over.

In the shadow of the old asylum, I sometimes let my mind wander, imagining the stories of this place: the footsteps that went before.

I never think about those that will come after.

September 2021

My first infusion of chemotherapy is arranged for the 9th of September, our 21st wedding anniversary.

Keen as I am to get started, I'm relieved when the date is changed to the 16th.

In truth, I'm not keen, but it's what I tell people.

I still haven't figured out my relationship to the cancer in my body. I'm scared of it and what it will do to me, but the means of its destruction are frightening, too.

Poison. Cut. Burn.

It's not the more common of the breast cancers: my hormones are not involved; some other action is at play.

The word aggressive has been used.

My lay person understanding is that it grows and multiplies more quickly.

Is skilled at spreading.

It's probably best, I realise, that we get straight on with its annihilation.

But keen is not what I feel.

Due to its aggressive nature chemotherapy comes before surgery.

Or maybe it's because the cancer has already exited the breast.

I don't exactly understand why and I'm not sure it's been explained.

But there is a reason.

One that doesn't bode as well as if it were otherwise.

That's the sense I have been given.

September 1991

A nip enters the air.

Autumn arrives with the turning of the leaves: the year ages in shades of orange and yellow; green gives way to gold.

My final year at university is looming and my three-month contract is about to end.

Or so I think.

I'm called in to see my boss.

She has a proposition.

There's some money available for a part-time position.

Just one day a week.

Would I be interested?

Of course.

Of course, I would.

September 2021

The first infusion introduces me to 'the chemo corridor' and 'the big chemo chair'.

I believe these are just my terms, but they could be part of a shared consciousness.

It also introduces me to canulation.

My hands are soaked in hot soapy water to make the veins easier to see.

To work with.

On this occasion my right hand is chosen.

It has good veins, I'm told.

Thankfully, the nurse manages to canulate in one.

This will not always be the case, but I don't know that yet.

I also don't know that in 60 hours, or so, I'll spike a temperature.

That when I phone the Beatson helpline I'll be told to go to the Queen Elizabeth.

[In this time of Covid, the Beatson will have no truck with anyone spiking a temp.]

I don't know about the seven hours I'll sit in an overflowing waiting room.

Waiting to be seen.

Or the sepsis that is waiting for me.

The masks and gowns; the isolation room; the IV drip of antibiotics.

The days and nights I'll spend perilously unwell.

Or that when I return to the Beatson for my second infusion, I'll be rail thin and bald.

Apt to cry easily.

A ghost of my former self.

October 1991

It's a challenge, but I'm just about able to juggle my work at Gartnavel with senior honours English Language and my role as Vice President in charge of Welfare on the Student Representative Council. It mainly involves prioritising Gartnavel and the SRC over lectures, tutorials, and library time.

I tell myself it will be fine.

My Gartnavel students have been reduced to a handful, one of whom is Alec.

Both he and I are pleased that we're still working together. With some urgency, we focus on writing now, along with the paragraphs he's reading from the Daily Record. I suggest we use lists and letters as a way to practice words and sentences.

We start simply with the sorts of lists he can take to the supermarket and build up to letters to an invented pen pal, who is interested in football.

Alec's progress suggests to me that he was more able than either of us realised.

Perhaps it was partly an issue of confidence.

Or maybe, during his short, disrupted education, he had assimilated more than he was aware and just needed someone to spend time with him, helping him unlock things he already knew. Someone who would focus solely on him.

December 2021

My final cycle of pre-surgical chemo takes place on the 9th of December.

At least, we're hopeful this will be the last cycle. I've had three more emergency hospital admissions due to treatment-related infections – all of which have been quite grim – and my understanding is that it would be helpful to move me onto the surgical stage, even if it means more chemo afterwards.

There's to be an MRI first, which is scheduled for December the 22nd.

Before it happens, I'll have had another emergency hospital admission.

A gift from that last chemo session, which has a wallop in the tail.

Terrible as chemo has been – and it has been the most awful thing I've ever experienced – I'm more frightened of surgery.

My one previous experience of it didn't go well.

In the May of 2001, a minor day surgery morphed into something much worse. Something that put certain of my organs under strain, in particular my kidneys and pancreas. And involved a week in hospital on a drip.

No one ever discovered what had caused my body to react in that way.

There was talk that it might have been a reaction to the anaesthetic.

December 1991

Gartnavel's landscape has changed again.

November's gusts have stripped away the leaves.

The predominant palette is mud brown.

We've moved out of our home in the West House having been relocated to a wooden and glass building that sits in the grounds below.

I'm reminded of being a little girl at St Machan's Primary School.

My Primary Two and Primary Three were spent in 'the huts'.

Our new arrangement feels remarkably similar, down to the displays of work we've affixed to the walls. To make the place more cheerful, more inviting.

But it has the same temporary feel.

No one says this.

We all agree it's good that our skills centre has a dedicated place.

A 'non-hospital' space.

Encircled by nature.

Amidst grounds that shelter birds and rabbits and foxes in wintry thickets.

January 2022

The night of my first surgery for breast cancer is spent in Ward 4A of Gartnavel General.

I don't sleep.

Presumably, this is as a result of the aftereffects of the various drugs I've been given and the excitement I feel that the operation is over. And I've survived, my terror of the anaesthetic having come to naught.

The sun rises late and lazily; the slow January dawn reveals the view from the window opposite: Gartnavel Royal.

As I study its dark form, I'm struck by the thought that this building, this ruin of a place I once knew – in which I walked and talked and taught and grew – had been there throughout this thing that other people call a journey.

Watching.

It was, after all, the original inhabitant of this site; within its grounds these other hospital buildings were brought to life.

Its empty windows have kept silent vigil.

It was there, just steps away, during that initial examination and the biopsy that followed. Its towers and buttresses offered strength and solace during chemotherapy and now, here it stands, my morning companion.

In my reverie I am transported back.

Not to the mid-1800s of its birth, but to my own youth.

To the girl I was when I first walked up its sweeping driveway and stepped inside.

March 1992

It's cold and wet, but swathes of crocuses have begun to replace the snowdrops of winter.

Colour is returning to Gartnavel.

Finals are almost upon me.

The last day we all knew was coming, has arrived.

There's coffee and cake.

And laughter.

Alec has written me a thank you card.

It feels like a greater achievement than anything I'll ever do academically.

March 2023

I could never have imagined that this is how I would return to Gartnavel.

Regardless, its grounds and its buildings hold a special place for me.

It ushered in my adulthood; gave me my first 'proper job'; instilled my love of teaching; was a place of growth, of blossoming.

And yet, the hardest moments of my life have happened in this place.

It's where I was told there was "something" in my breast "that shouldn't be there".

And that the surgeon hadn't got clean margins.

That there hadn't been a complete response to the pre-surgical chemo.

It's where I had two surgeries.

15 sessions of radiotherapy.

22 infusions of chemotherapy.

It was in the shadow of the asylum, that we experienced it together.

The girl I was. The woman she's become.

I've comforted her; held her hand.

She's reminded me that this is a season, and seasons pass.

Commentary

This commentary reflects on the difficulties I encountered when trying to write *Gartnavel Ghosts* and explores the ways in which Gartnavel itself helped me to overcome them.

I was excited to be part of *Writing the Asylum*. A brilliant project. An important one. I approached the patient record I was sent as a researcher, a reader, a writer. But I was also in the midst of cancer treatment, and I just couldn't connect.

I therefore went in search of something that would inspire. I dug through records. Looked at myriad photographs. Immersed myself in an archive that is fascinating.

Yet I was left cold.

The problem, clearly, was with me.

This realisation led me to start from first principles: my own experience of Gartnavel and its ghosts. I started the piece many times. Over and over. It was a formless thing just outside of my reach. Nothing would come. And what did was turgid, so I classed it as nothing. It wasn't the writing I expect of myself.

After over a year, I wrote the reflection that follows. It became the key to unlocking *Gartnavel Ghosts*. I offer it to you now as a representation of what it has been like, for me, as a writer who was diagnosed with breast cancer, to try to write again.

A Reflection

I've found it difficult to write about Gartnavel. I've found it difficult to write. I hadn't expected to. Because writing is what I do. It comes as naturally as brushing my teeth. As easy-breezy as drinking that first coffee in the morning. Or it did. Before cancer.

Cancer is the thing that gave me the second half of my Gartnavel story. Cancer is also the thing that has made me 'not a writer'. Who'd have thought? I get a creative writing doctorate, and, in short order, I lose the ability to write. To think in the way a writer thinks. To think. About something other than cancer.

It feels like there isn't a place for me. Not anymore. And yet this is a project about place. A special place. Gartnavel. And I've fitted there twice. *1991. Gartnavel Royal. I get my first proper job. 2021. Gartnavel General. I'm told there's something in my breast that shouldn't be there.* The euphemism isn't mine. It's borrowed from my breast nurse (not her actual title).

I feel like I no longer fit. In places. With people. I don't fit into me. The shape has changed. The shape inside. The shape inside the bit that other people see. The shape inside my skin. Inside my bones. Let's say, for talking's sake, my inside shape used to be a large parallelogram. Maybe now it's a small kite. No room for writing. Or for thinking the thoughts that precipitate writing. But fear still fits. And it's taking up more room. As is the awareness of mortality. My own mortality. Anticipatory grief. The fear of missing out. The fear of being missing. From lives. From places.

The frame has also changed. There's less of it. Less fat. Less muscle. Not so much hair. And what there is of the hair is strange. A stranger to me. It's curly. In an old lady perm from some point in the 1980s way. An old lady perm from some point in the 1980s that the old lady forgot to tend. I was bald. For a bit. That was worse. But not as bad as the moments before surgery. Or than chemotherapy. Or sepsis. Or waiting for the effects of radiotherapy to bloom.

Which brings me back to Gartnavel. The way it blooms. Less tended than it once was. Yet its beauty undiminished. Grass and flowers and trees. Wilful in their survival. Their roots deep and intertwined. They gird themselves in fallow times. Flourish when the season allows. Ever beneath the steadfast watch of the asylum. Under its protection.

And I realise that I, too, have been planted in this place.

So many of us have.

I am surrounded by those who came before.

Those who have walked with me.

And those who don't yet know their path will bring them here.

To find healing amongst Gartnavel ghosts.

Monday, 17th of April

To Ronnie

A man stopped in a minibus full of OAPs to say what a beauty of a dog Hamish is. I said he was ten and a half and the man said: NO. That dog looks like a show dog. xx

To Ronnie

I had brushed him earlier…

Wednesday, 19th of April

To Alan

Thanks, Alan. I've been meaning to get in touch with you.

It seems it's not that easy to get over a cancer diagnosis and sixteen months of treatment, either in body or mind. All of which is to say, that I've struggled. I thought I would get back to doing the things I like to do and seeing the people I like spending time with, but neither has happened. I'm starting a Fear of Recurrence course through the Beatson Cancer Charity in May and I'm hoping that it, and the passage of time, will help.

I hope it's a great night on Friday. I know it will be.

Take care,

Gillian

Friday, 21st of April

I was telling Ronnie about a memory I have from my 4th emergency admission (5 weeks into chemo). He told me he'd taken a photo of me that night. Given my research interests, he thought I might want it someday. So here's July 2021, before I found the lump, and October 2021. #breastcancer

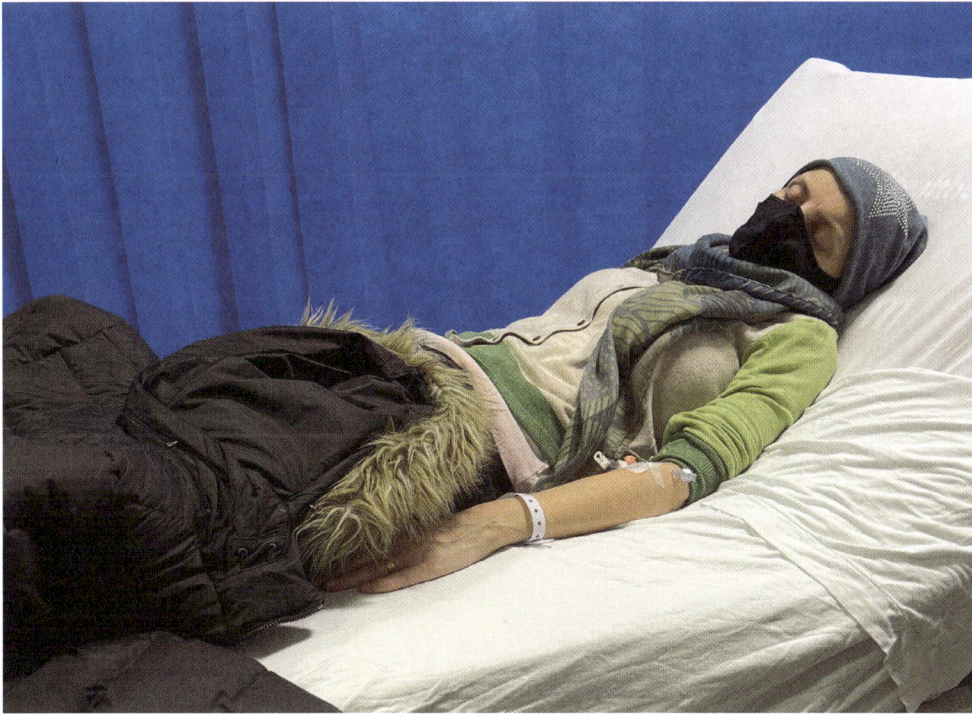

Sunday, 23rd of April

Cancer removed my filter and left me with a big dose of tardiness... is something I said this morning. Ronnie replied that it would make a good title for a book. #breastcancer #unrelateddaisy

Tuesday, 25th of April

To Michael

Hi Michael,

Thank you so much for your understanding when I had to step down from the rota and for your prayers.

I finished treatment three months ago and feel ready to go back on the rota, if there's a need for another reader. We're away from May 13th - 21st, but other than that, I would be available to read at the Sunday night Mass.

With kind regards,

Gillian

When I write about illness now it's mainly about my experience of #BreastCancer so for #MSAwarenessWeek I thought I'd post a link to a piece I wrote a few years ago on life with #MultipleSclerosis. #WritingAsTherapy

MS ALPHABET

A is for Autoimmune

Coughs and sneezes spread diseases, or, in my case, cause my immune system to go haywire. This makes teaching difficult. Teenagers are great but they often cough and sneeze and their pesky germs rarely see the inside of a handkerchief.

B is for Bladder

Mine has learned to lie. It tells me it's full when it's not. A lot. I clamber back into bed after a bogus call of nature and it starts to whisper. I need to go. You've just been. I need to go. You don't. *I NEED* to go! You don't. *I REALLY NEED TO GO!* You really don't. *I REALLY NEED TO GO!!* Maybe you do. And I clamber back out of bed.

B is also for Bowel

But I don't know you well enough.

C is for Claustrophobia

I'm a bit on the claustrophobic side. Five minutes into my first MRI, I learn this. Over the next eight years I have four more trips inside the noisy white tube (don't think coffin, don't think coffin). After number five, I decide there won't be a number six.

D is for Dogs

I discover that dogs are indifferent to a diagnosis of multiple sclerosis. I live with two. It seems I still sound like the same human. I still look like the same human. I still smell like the same human (except for the faint whiff of antiseptic that sometimes clings to my hair). They're not sad. They're not anxious. They're not awkward. They don't feel sorry for me. Whenever they see me they wag their tails in delight.

E is for Elephant

One is waiting for me when I come home from the hospital that first time. It has taken up residence on an invisible floral sofa in the centre of the living room. When my remission is in full swing, it follows me out into the world.

F is for Fatigue

I learn first-hand that fatigue is one of the most common symptoms of multiple sclerosis. I begin to use the word sickie-tired to distinguish this form of tiredness from its more humdrum cousin, normal-tired. *Sickie-tired: a sudden dizzying swirl of nausea and exhaustion.*

G is for Gabapentin

Gabapentin does nothing for me. That's not strictly true. It makes me feel drunk. However, what it's supposed to do is decrease my neuropathic pain. It doesn't do that.

H is for Hands

My first relapse starts in my toes, as do all of my future relapses bar one. As the symptoms work their way up my body, day on day, I start to repeat, in my head: *as long as it doesn't affect my hands.* Over and over: *As long as it doesn't affect my hands.* The disease is deaf to my mantra. By day six, my hands are affected. They feel as though they've been transformed into gigantic baseball mitts. Gigantic baseball mitts lined with tiny pieces of broken glass.

I is for Ice

It flows through the veins in my feet. This can be a sign of imminent relapse. But often it just means I'm cold.

J is for Jam Jars

Labels are for jam jars, apparently. I'm told this. It doesn't matter that the person who declares it is someone I like. Someone I respect. I'm offended. It suggests I have a label. It suggests I'm being defined by it. I learn I can be quite touchy.

K is for Knitting

My hands are clenched for almost a year. I do it as a way to minimise sensation: the tighter the fist, the duller the sense of broken glass. I only allow my hands to un-fist when I have things to do that require fingers: typing, eating poached eggs, opening drawers, getting dressed, drinking coffee, writing on the whiteboard, signing my name, feeding dogs, getting undressed. I decide I want to take up knitting. As a hobby. I become obsessed with the notion that one day my hands won't feel like shard encrusted baseball mitts. Instead, my fingers will make knitting needles clack at their command. This remission reaches my wrists in month ten. By month eleven, my hands are fine. The notion to knit passes.

L is for Lumber Puncture

I rank things. I always have. Seasons (autumn, spring, summer, winter); colours (purple, yellow, green); dead pets (Tasha, Hobbes, Calvin, Sooty). It's an affliction. I discover that my number one most despised medical procedure is not, in fact, a lumbar puncture. Given the unlikely game show dilemma of… Which one will you choose? A lumbar puncture or an MRI? You have only thirty seconds to decide… To the sound of a big clock ticking down, I'd yell, 'I'll have the lumbar puncture, please, Bob!'

M is for Michelin Man suit

During one relapse my body feels like it's been swallowed by a Michelin Man suit. The feeling lasts for months. Even when my Michelin Man suit begins to deflate, if I exert myself, or take a bath, the suit balloons to full size. I imagine an MS fairy hanging out with my stalker elephant. If she catches me climbing a staircase or going for a walk, she whips out her little foot pump and I am Michelin woman once more.

N is for Numbers

The MS Society estimate that there are over **130,000** people with multiple sclerosis in the UK and nearly **7,000** people are diagnosed each year. By this estimate **19** people are diagnosed with MS each day.

O is for Object

At times, I feel like one. It happens when someone, too busy to look up, tells me to take a seat. It happens when someone, too tired to talk, wheels me from this place to that place. It happens when someone, too distracted to notice I'm terrified of needles, inserts one into my arm.

P is for Pregabalin

Pregabalin is another drug that's prescribed for neuropathic pain. I find it more effective than gabapentin. I stop taking it because of the side effects - dizziness, mild nausea, brain fog. When I do, I discover the neuropathic pain it's been dulling for almost two years, is just as dull without it. I'm reminded that my body is clever. My body repairs the damage.

Q is for Questions

I'm asked surprisingly few. I'm sure it's not that my friends and family members are uninterested. I'm suspicious they're interrogating Google instead.

R is for Relapse

There's a moment when you realise it's happening. You're watching *Vera*. At the advert break you get up to make yourself a cup of tea. You notice your feet are cold. You can't feel the floor. Or. You're marking *Macbeth* essays. You notice your toes have become ice. You get up from your desk. You can't feel the floor. You steel yourself for what's to come.

S is for Scotland

Scotland is the MS capital of the world. Perhaps that's why when I'm first diagnosed everyone I come into contact with tells me they know someone who has it. Or that they at least know someone who knows someone who has it. *The mum of one of the wee girls in Cara's class has a sister with it. / I bumped into Dave the other day and one of his pals was diagnosed with it last year. / My auntie's neighbour's cousin has it.* I start to think it's possible that everyone in Scotland does actually know someone with MS. Or they at least know someone who knows someone who has MS. I find myself wondering what the government is doing about it.

T is for Three

This is the number of days my body is able to tolerate high dose corticosteroids. The standard treatment for a moderate to severe relapse is 500 milligrams of prednisone for three to five days. I once manage four days. The experience teaches me that three is the magic number.

U is for Ultrasound

When I compile my *tolerable-medical-procedures-that-are-done-to-me* ranking, ultrasound goes straight in at Number One. Even when an impossibly full bladder is stipulated as a prerequisite, having an ultrasound is top of the pops.

V is for Vienna

My husband's job takes us to Austria for twelve months. We're living in Vienna when I have my eighth relapse. I spend five days in the care of Krankenhaus Barmherzige Brüder – The Brothers of Mercy Hospital – in the city's Leopoldstat district. There are actual Brothers of Mercy in the hospital. They wear brown robes and shuffle through the day ward of the neurology department distributing hot drinks. On my first morning, one of them brings me a coffee. His eyes don't meet mine, but he radiates reverence rather than reserve. That same day I make a trip to the canteen and discover they offer a fine selection of beer and wine. Austria steals the top spot in my *best-hospital-experiences-by-country* ranking.

W is for Writing

Writing helps me manage neuropathic pain. When my brain is fully engaged in the challenge of writing and rewriting sentence upon sentence, it's too busy to pay attention to anything else. People who know about pain management tell me this is called distraction technique.

X is for X-ray

It may be surprising that having an x-ray didn't make the top spot in my *tolerable-medical-procedures-that-are-done-to-me* chart (bearing in mind this procedure doesn't involve anyone actually touching you). However, when you factor in frequent exposure to radiation and my worry-wart nature, you might understand why it's only ever made it to Number Three in the rankings.

Y is for Yikes

During one particular relapse my right hand decides to spasm intermittently and without warning. It's a Friday night. My husband and I are having a meal in a small restaurant near our home. The table is dressed in white linen and has a single yellow rose as a centrepiece. I'm enjoying a glass of white wine. It leaps from my hand and smashes against the wall.

Z is for Zap

Lhermitte's Sign is often associated with multiple sclerosis. When a person experiencing Lhermitte's Sign tilts his or her head forwards, a sensation similar to that of an electrical current will travel down the spine and into the limbs. In addition to cold feet, this symptom often informs me that a new relapse has begun; I tip my head to look at my keyboard and an electric shock runs down my spine. Zap.

May 2023

📱 Monday, 1st of May

To Johanna

4pm is great! Glasgow is our oyster… wherever you fancy…? I'm so out of touch with the world of being out and about… xx

✉️ Wednesday, 3rd of May

To Tony

Hi Tony,

I hope your week is going well so far.

Are you still okay to meet up at Cafe Gandolfi today?

I'm planning on heading there for 12.30pm, but just thought I'd better check it's still okay for you.

Thanks!

Gillian

✉️

To Stephen

Hi Stephen,

Thanks for getting in touch! A coffee and a chat would be great. How about the coffee shop attached to Roots and Fruits…? Let me know when would be good for you…

Thanks again,

Gillian

✉️ Saturday, 6th of May

To Stephen

Hi Stephen,

I maybe should have mentioned that I'm away in Wisconsin 13th - 21st of May, so if you do have time next week it would be great. I could do Monday afternoon or Thursday afternoon, if either works.

Otherwise, I could do something the week of the 22nd of May. Either the afternoon of Mon 22nd or after 2pm on Thurs 24th.

Let me know if any of those days/times would work for you.

Many thanks,

Gillian

📱 Sunday, 7th of May

To Johanna

Thoughts are being thought… and a wee Brodie meeting on Monday. In our coffee shop (now that I know and love it).

✉️

To Tony

Hi Tony,

Thanks for putting me in touch with Stephen. I'm meeting him for a chat /

coffee at 2pm today.

I'll let you know how I get on.

Take care,

Gillian

To Stephen

Hi Stephen,

It was great to meet you both today.

As discussed, I've attached a copy of Brodie.

Please let me know if there's anything else you need from me just now.

With many thanks,

Gillian

To Alan

Hi Alan,

I'd love to go for a walk on Wednesday, but I'll be in Wisconsin. It's a work trip for Ronnie and I'm tagging along. We made the arrangements last year when I was still in treatment to give me something to look forward to. I'm not looking forward to the journey though, but I'm excited to see friends I haven't seen since we left in 2019. I've also got a real soft spot for the wee community we used to live in. We've booked an airbnb a couple of streets over from our old house.

If you've got any time for a walk at the end of May / beginning of June, that would be great.

I hope the classes are going well!

All the best,

Gillian

To Stephanie

Currently waiting for our luggage at Appleton airport. Excited to be here after a very long journey.

📱

To Johanna

We finally got to our airbnb in our old neighbourhood and friends had left a welcome basket on the front porch. And this morning the back garden was awash with gorgeous creatures - chipmunks, a baby rabbit, and all manner of birds including a male and female cardinal bird. xx

To Clair

I hope your week is going well. I've had

two and three social things on every day so am completely whacked... at Kari's for coffee this morning, then Pilates (in real life), then dropping off a gift for Molly Jo's baby, then out to dinner with our old next-door neighbours. Tomorrow, I have coffee in the morning with Gitte and then after Ronnie finishes work, we're off up north to stay with Angelo and Jen. We're there until Saturday morning when we then start the LONG journey home. xx

✉ Friday, 19th of May

To Stephen

Hi Stephen,

I hope you've had a good week. While Ronnie's been busy working, I've been catching up with Wisconsin friends and neighbours, which is lovely, but the jet lag has definitely been a killer.

I had the call with Sarah on Monday and she's agreed to release me from my contractual obligations regarding Brodie, but said she would still like to represent future work.

Looking forward to having lunch on the 28th.

All the best,

Gillian

✉ Wednesday, 24th of May

To Beatson Cancer Charity

Hi,

I finished treatment for breast cancer in December 2022. I was supported by the Beatson Cancer Charity throughout my sixteen months of treatment (telephone befriending, wig service, general care and support) and I'd be delighted to help out with the Lived Experience Group in any way that I can.

With best wishes,

Gillian

📞 Saturday, 27th of May

To Stephanie

We'd be delighted for you to stay at ours, which would be close for everything you're doing when you're here!

To Stephanie

Brilliant! Let's have a Facetime when you have time.

To Stephanie

I have a lunch at 1pm, but I should definitely be back by then. The lunch is with a Glasgow publisher to talk about Brodie...

✉ Monday, 29th of May

To Georgi

Dear Georgi,

Sending all best wishes for this sunny Bank Holiday Monday.

Times I've thought about you recently...

driving around the Castle Policies in Bothwell near where Abby and Not Victoria hoodwinked a policeman

anytime I encountered a news item about the snooker

when I read about the sad death of George Logan / Dr Evadne Hinge other assorted times with no apparent trigger when my dear pen pal came to mind

I hope you are well and that this supposed-to-be-sunny week is a lovely one for you.

G xx

🐦

I'm pleased to be five months post-treatment but it's also come with some difficulties so I'm grateful for the incredible @Beatson_Charity and their six-part Fear of Recurrence programme that I started last week. And for the example of my hardy spring pansies. #breastcancer

📞 **Tuesday, 30th of May**

To Stephen

I've got my Wisconsin friend here doing her filming next Monday and Tuesday and I'm tagging along. Would any time on Wednesday or Friday work? (Thursday's my birthday)

🐦 **Wednesday, 31st of May**

I know I'm learning to embrace the #chemocurls, but I was at the hairdresser today (she's only allowed to cut a skliff off it) and I asked her to dry it straight... #feelslikeme #rubbishatselfies #darkcirclesarein

June 2023

To Stephen

Thank you, Stephen! I can't wait to have a look. I'm heading off to a Beatson Cancer Charity Fear of Recurrence course in Elderslie this morning (week two of six and they've told us this is the most emotionally challenging week...). I'll be able to have a look later today.

Many thanks,

Gillian

🐦

At the @Beatson_Charity Fear of Recurrence programme today we were told to go off and be kind to ourselves, so Fergus and I have headed to the Botanics. #WalkingTherapy #DogTherapy #FocusingOnNoticing

✉

To Stephen

Thanks, Stephen. It's brilliant to see Brodie taking shape! I love the idea of the flower motif.

There are a couple of things I have questions about because this is new to me, but hopefully we can talk about them when we catch up on Zoom next week.

Thanks again!

Gillian

🟢 **Sunday, 4th of June**

To Clair

We've got Stephanie and Andy arriving at 1.30pm, so there has been much tidying and cleaning. xx

Monday, 5th of June

To Clair

Thanks! I'll pass the birthday wishes on to Joe Cool. Dropping the folks off at a fancy dancy studio and then heading over to see him. Hope your day goes well! xx

To Stephanie

Fergus and I are in the Botanics. Andy walked with us along the river and kept going when we crossed the bridge to come in here.

To literary agent

Thanks, Sarah. I very much wish that we could have done this together. I'm grateful for your support and belief in Brodie.

Please accept this email as acknowledgement of the termination of our representation agreement.

With all best wishes and hopes that we can work together in the future.

Thanks again,

Gillian

 Thursday, 8th of June

To Stephen

Thank you, Stephen!

Best birthday present, ever.

Gillian

To Stephen

Hi Stephen,

Thanks for all the emails! I'm just in from the Beatson Fear of Recurrence course in Elderslie and yesterday I was out doing family stuff all afternoon / evening. We're heading into town for some birthday shopping now, so I'll get my Brodie head back on tomorrow.

I can't tell you what a brilliant present it was though, to wake up to your email and see Brodie looking like the Brodie of my imagination. Thank you!

Gillian

What a lovely day to celebrate another birl around the sun.

Wednesday, 14th of June

Our sweet boy. Hamish.
August 2012 - June 2023.

To Clair

We just walked down to the river and back. It's been a hard day. Fergus and I will be going for another mental health walk later, if you're around and want to join us. xx

Friday, 16th of June

To Clair

I'd love that, but I need to be at the Beatson for a meeting at 11.30am. Do you fancy coming round here for a coffee just now…? It's lovely out the back… xx

To Clair

Can you bring your own milk?!

Saturday, 17th of June

To Stephen

Hi Stephen,

I met with the Regional Fundraising Manager for the Beatson Cancer Charity (Charlene) yesterday and one of her colleagues. It was a lovely meeting.

I spent about an hour with them talking about my experience of both the Beatson hospital and Beatson Cancer Charity and how important the careful and kind care I received from both had been to me and still is.

They seemed delighted I'm dedicating Brodie to the Beatson and donating the author proceeds to the charity and are keen to support where they can.

I hope you have a good weekend.

Gillian

Wednesday, 21st of June

To Zoe

Hi Zoe,

I hope your summer is going well.

I'm really excited to be able to tell you that I have some good news about Brodie. It has a publisher now (something I didn't think would ever happen). It's Stephen Cameron (Into Books). I'm incredibly happy and I think Stephen is the right person for Brodie, and for me.

It isn't public yet, but it'll be published in September (eek!) and Stephen has started planning the promotion. He really likes the early reader quote you gave me and would like to use it. Would that be okay?

Something I'd decided (when I didn't think it would ever be a reality) was that if Brodie ever got published, I'd give anything I made from it as a donation to the Beatson charity. Stephen is very supportive of this, and they seem thrilled (even though I've explained it's not likely to be much!). I just really want to give back to them as I got such incredible care during my treatment.

Thanks again for your kindness and support over the years. I appreciate it more than you know.

Gillian

Thursday, 22nd of June

To Zoe

Thanks, Zoe! And your email has made mine. :-)

A coffee would be lovely! I'm around all summer. It's great not to be in treatment now, but I've been left with some trauma from it all, which I'm managing my way through. Doing lovely things certainly helps.

Thanks again!

Gillian

✉ **Friday, 23rd of June**

To Stephen

Hi Stephen,

I've had a think about excerpts that might work for the filming next week. Where I wasn't sure, I've given a couple of options for the character in question.

If you get a chance, let me know if these will work or if I should look for others.

Many thanks!

Gillian

✉ **Tuesday, 27th of June**

To Olga

Hi Olga,

I hope things are well with you.

I'm excited to be able to tell you that I have some good news about Brodie. It has a publisher (something I didn't think would ever happen). It's a Glasgow-based publisher, Stephen Cameron (Into Books). I'm very happy and I think Stephen is the right person for Brodie, and for me.

It isn't public yet, but it'll be published in September (eek!) and Stephen has started planning the promotion. He likes the early

reader quote you gave me and would like to use it, if you would be comfortable with that. Would that be okay?

Also, thank you for always reaching out and offering me words of kindness and encouragement during treatment. It made a difference and I'll always be grateful.

With best wishes,

Gillian

✉ **Wednesday, 28th of June**

To Stephen

Thanks again for today, Stephen!

Also, I got a lovely email from Louise Welsh this afternoon. She said it would be a privilege to grace such an excellent and original novel.

Very best,

Gillian

📞 **Thursday, 29th of June**

To Clair

I've just forwarded you the teaser… It's very exciting… xx

Friday, 30th of June

To Georgi

Thank you, Georgi. We'd known for months that it would eventually happen. Hamish had a mass on his liver and couldn't get treatment because of kidney issues, so he was having palliative medication/care. We did our very best to keep him happy and comfortable. He was still wagging that big tail of his until the end.

In Brodie news (who ever thought I would have Brodie news?! Not me!). A Glasgow-based publisher (Stephen Cameron at Into Books) is going to publish it! He swore me to secrecy because he wants to own all the communication/promotion stuff, but he's putting out the teaser this afternoon, so I wanted to tell you before it's on social media. As you can imagine, I'm like a small child - clapping my hands and saying yay a lot. It's been nice to have something go in the right direction. It feels like it's been a long time.

Sending the best of wishes.

G xx

🐦

Thrilled to be able to share this! I'm so grateful to @intocreative for believing in BRODIE and in me. And for the epic trailer (I'm really embracing the chemo curls now!). And I'm so happy to try to give back to the amazing @Beatson_Charity for all their incredible support.

> **into** **Into Creative**
> @intocreative
>
> 💥 BIG NEWS 💥
> Into Books are proud to be publishers of @SunshineScot's debut novel, 'BRODIE'
> Publ: Sept 2023.
> The novel & writer's story will blow you away!
> Gillian has committed to giving every penny she makes on the book to @Beatson_Charity
> Cover reveal July! Epic trailer.. 😊

📞

Elizabeth and Kate

It's official… Brodie is being published in September (eek!) by Into Books. There's a trailer on Twitter and everything! Thanks for all your help, support, and belief.

Elizabeth and Kate

Me, too! I think it's hysterical he used the outtakes. He said they captured me much better.

July 2023

Saturday, 1st of July

To Heather Suttie

Hi Heather,

Stephen gave me your email address. Thank you for getting in touch with him. I'd love to speak to you about Brodie.

With kind regards,

Gillian

To Cousins

Thanks, Marie! The publication date is 8/9/23. The cover reveal will happen in a couple of weeks. I've seen an early version and I love it. xx

To Misti

Thanks, Misti! I'm glad you're starting to feel better.

I'm not sure if you've seen my Twitter... and I'm not sure if you know that I now have a publisher for Brodie. A small Scottish independent who are brilliant.

Here's the teaser he did to announce that Brodie will be out in September.

G x

Wednesday, 5th of July

To Ronnie

I hope you have a safe flight. xx

To Ronnie

Love you. xx

Saturday, 8th of July

To Tony

Hi Tony,

Thanks for the help with Brodie! It's much appreciated.

Monday is great. Where / when do you fancy...?

Gillian

Tuesday, 11th of July

To Linsey

Hi Linsey,

Thanks for having me in today. It was lovely to see you again!

Apologies that I wasn't more mentally prepared. I can't believe I don't have my 'how would you briefly describe Brodie to someone in the pub' answer down pat! I'll make sure I have in the future though, so thank you for asking me!

Very best,

Gillian

Walking that old familiar path again, but this time not to the Beatson. I'm headed to a recording studio a stone's throw away to start recording the audiobook of BRODIE. #Excited #Grateful #ALittleBitTerrified

Audiobooks helped get me through chemo (and steroid-filled sleepless nights) thanks to brilliant books by @OlgaWojtas, @CJessCooke, @WednesdayErskin, @truesarahsmith, @rachelle_ata and @passingplace so having BRODIE in this form is important to me. #grateful #debut

Tuesday, 18th of July

To Stephanie

I finished the audiobook recording today! 36 chapters in 15 hours. The penultimate thing I read was the acknowledgment page… xx

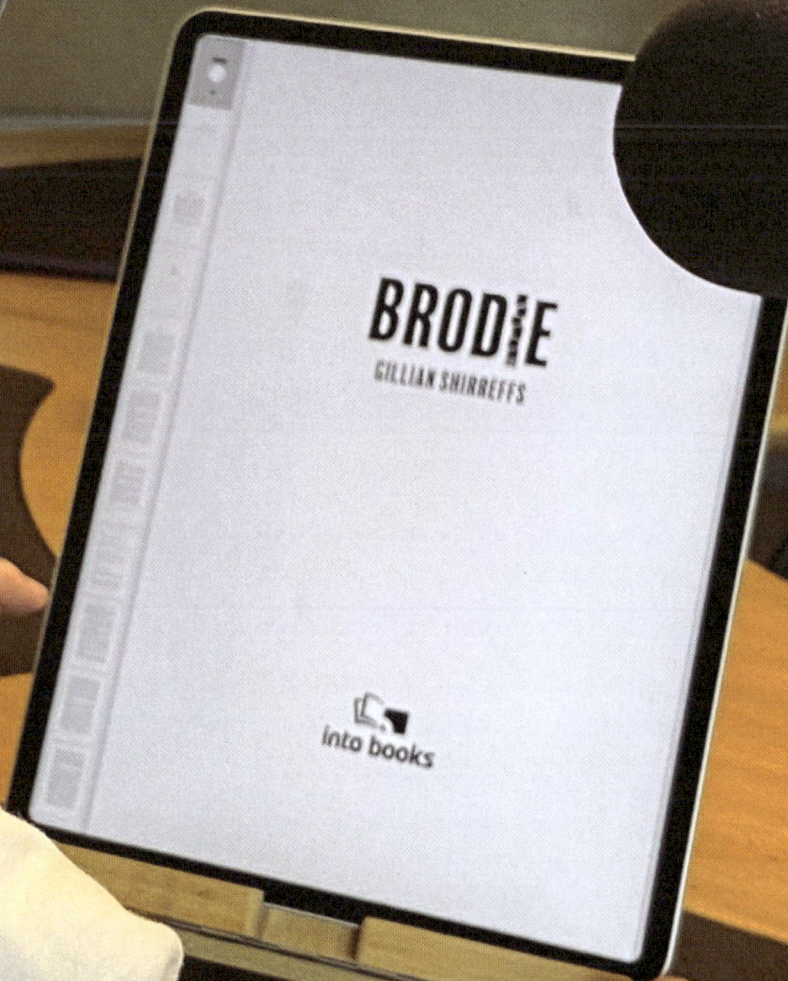

Thursday, 20th of July

Two years ago today I noticed a lump in my breast. If I'd been examining myself regularly, I might well have found it before the cancer spread to the sentinel lymph node. Please watch @Liz_ORiordan's video and mark a date on the calendar to examine yourself monthly. #breastcancer

Saturday, 22nd of July

To Jen

You are MORE than welcome to stay with us! We love our Ninivaggi time. It's up to you though. We understand if you want your own space. Looking forward to seeing you!

To Jen

Honestly, you're such easy guests and we'd love to have you and Ronnie was thinking he'd take some time off, if Angelo is taking any while he's here.

To Jen

Does Bella know which Halls of Residence she's in yet…?

Tuesday, 25th of July

To Alan

Hi Alan,

No sooner had I declared I was going to self-publish, than Brodie got a publisher. I should have tried that trick two years ago! Not only that, I really like Stephen and think he's the perfect fit.

He'd asked me to keep it quiet until he put out the teaser announcing it, which meant even though I was itching to tell you at the Saturday class, I couldn't.

Thanks for all your help and support over the years. If Brodie has any good sentences in it, they're down to you.

All the best,

Gillian

Saturday, 29th of July

To Sandra

Hi Sandra,

I hope you're having a good summer.

I'm six months post-treatment and starting to get back to a normal life.

I'm not sure if you've noticed on Twitter but Brodie is going to be published (something I didn't think would ever happen). I'm so happy about it. It's Glasgow publisher, Into Books, and Stephen feels like a really good fit.

He's putting together an information sheet and would like to include your quote, so I wanted to check if that would be okay with you.

I've attached the cover reveal he just did. I cried when I saw it.

Thanks again for your support and encouragement.

Gillian

✉ **Sunday, 30th of July**

To Sandra

Thank you so much, Sandra. I really appreciate the support.

I'd decided during treatment that if Brodie ever did get published, I'd donate any money from it to the Beatson, so that makes it feel even better that it's actually happening. It's really nice to be able to use my work to say thank you.

Very best,

Gillian x

✉

To Olga

I'm sorry you won't be able to make it, Olga, but I look forward to meeting up in real life. And I love the idea of Brodie being held hostage.

See you soon-ish!

Gillian x

✉ **Monday, 31st of July**

To Linsey

Thanks, Linsey. I'm glad she's happy with the interview.

I feel like I'm pretty bad at this stuff. My pre-cancer brain was definitely sharper!

🐦

I've been talking about my experience of breast cancer and the amazing care and support I've received from @Beatson_ Charity. #Grateful CarefulAndKindCare

August 2023

✉ **Tuesday, 1st of August**

To Linsey

Thank you, Linsey! I'll get the Glasgow Times for my parents. They're in their 80s and will be delighted!

Gillian x

To Cousins

It looks like I'm in the Glasgow Times…! Page two, apparently. xx

---

To Stephanie

Your photo of me is being used in the press… I hope you don't mind!

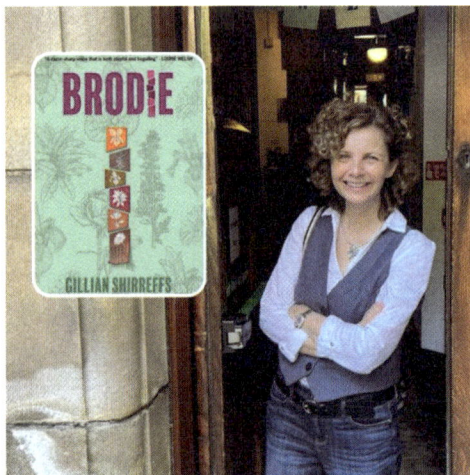

🐦

Grateful to have the chance to speak about the wonderful services of @Beatson_Charity and grateful to my amazing publisher @intocreative for making it all happen!

To Johanna

There's been a bit of Brodie publicity because the Beatson Cancer Charity put out a press release yesterday and a wee video interview on their socials…

Glasgow author to donate profits of first book to Beatson Cancer Charity

planetradio.co.uk

To Stephanie

I can't wait to see you in September!

I take my parents rolls and a paper every day. Today my 86-year-old dad was delighted when he opened it and saw this. #JustAWeeGirlFaeCampsie

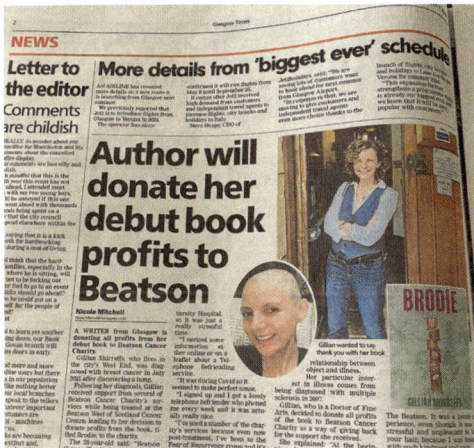

NEWS

Letter to the editor
Comments are childish

More details from 'biggest ever' schedule

Author will donate her debut book profits to Beatson

Nicole Mitchell

Wednesday, 2nd of August

To Cousins

Ronnie just got a call from a colleague to say his wife heard me on the Radio Clyde news this morning (they recorded me on Monday). I'm scared to listen in case i sound like a complete looney tune!

Elizabeth and Kate

I'm really hoping you can both come along to the launch. The details haven't been finalised yet, but we now know it'll be the evening of the 7th of September in Oran Mor. The super supervisors back together!

Monday, 7th of August

To Stephen

Clare English said yes! She's flying back from holiday on the 6th.

To Zoe

Hi Zoe,

I hope your summer is going well.

Brodie's book launch is going to be on Thursday 7th September from 6pm until 10pm upstairs in Oran Mor. It's going to double as a fundraiser for Beatson Cancer Charity, which I'm just as excited about.

The music isn't quite pinned down yet, but it looks like there will be an acoustic set by two of the Bluebells and some music by Cory Chisel (a brilliant American musician I know) and BrownBear (the amazing singer Matt Hickman). Clare English has kindly said she'll MC the night. In the near future Clare and I hope to be doing some collaborative work around illness, patient-centred care, and creativity.

I hope it's not inappropriate ask, but we're going to have a couple of non-Brodie readings, and I'd love it if you did one of them. Please don't worry if that won't work for you, I just thought I'd ask in the spirit of shy bairns get nowt.

Very best,

Gillian x

✉ **Tuesday, 8th of August**

To Zoe

That's amazing. Thank you so much, Zoe!

I want it to be a fantastic night, which means it should be a celebration of so much more than me and Brodie. In eleven days, it'll be two years since I was diagnosed with breast cancer. I went through a dark time, even before I started my treatment, which then turned out to be an endurance course. I know there are no guarantees, so I want to do lovely things with lovely people for as long as I can, which will hopefully be for a very long time to come.

I'm really excited that I can give back to the Beatson. There were many times when I was sitting in the 'chemo corridor' or 'the big chemo chair' or I was lying in a hospital bed in the QUEH that I couldn't see beyond the next hour or the next five minutes, so to think I'm now able to plan an event that will allow me to give something back makes me really happy. And I'm so delighted that you'll be part of it.

Gillian x

🐦 **Wednesday, 9th of August**

NEVER did I think my bald head would be on the front cover of the Kirky Herald. Ah well, the amazing @Beatson_Charity is worth it.

📞 **Thursday, 10th of August**

To Clair

Bella has been allocated Murano Village. I looked at the map. There's a footbridge to Maryhill Road.

To Clair

That's good to know. It's also great that she's so close to us.

📞

To Jen

I'm not sure if you've looked at it on a map, but she pretty much has to walk by our house on the way to and from Uni, so lots of opportunity to drop in for food, drink, or puppy snuggles. I told Clair and she said all the kids she knows who lived there loved it.

📞 **Friday, 11th of August**

To Stephanie

Stephen has ordered Brodie wrapping paper with the idea that if someone wants to buy a book as a gift, I can sign it and then we wrap it for them. How are your wrapping skills…?

📞

To Stephen

Brilliant about the Westender (except if they hate Brodie). And in more happy dance news Matt said yes to saying he'll be there. He said he'll liaise with you about format.

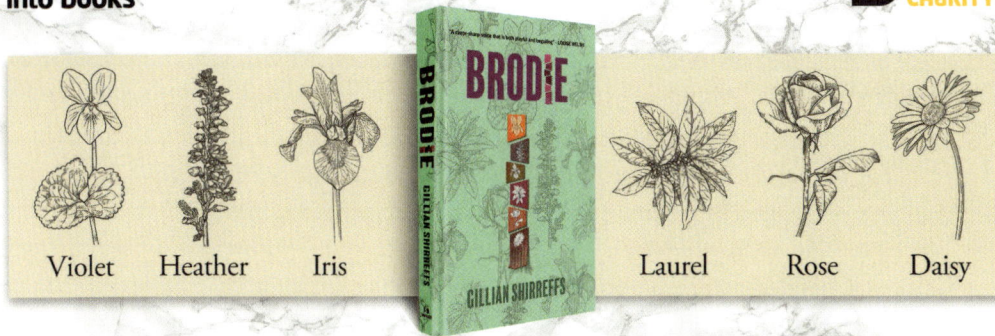

into books

IN AID OF BEATSON CANCER CHARITY

Violet   Heather   Iris   Laurel   Rose   Daisy

BRODIE

GILLIAN SHIRREFFS

To see ourselves as Brodie sees us...

Book launch. Òran Mór - Thursday 7 September 6pm (Finger buffet included)

I'm excited for Brodie's book launch and grateful to the brilliant people who've agreed to be involved. It'll be an opportunity to fundraise for the amazing @Beatson_Charity, which makes me so happy. #Brodie #Debut

Tuesday, 15th of August

To Action on Sectarianism

Hi,

I wonder if you can help me. My novel, Brodie, is being published next month and I begin the acknowledgements by thanking the teachers who encouraged and inspired me. I mention three by name, one of whom is (as I knew him) Mr Gallagher, who taught me English at St Ninian's High School in the 1980s.

I was hoping to invite those three teachers to the book launch, so was trying to track them down. Unfortunately, when searching for Mr Gallagher, I was sad to read the piece on your website from June 2019 about the Hugh Gallagher Award because I think it might be my Mr Gallagher.

If it is, I'd like to somehow get a copy of my book to his family, just to let them know how fondly he's remembered by a pupil he taught over 30 years ago.

If you can help me in this regard, I would appreciate it very much.

With thanks and best wishes,

Gillian

✉ **Wednesday, 16th of August**

To Alan

Hi Alan,

I hope your week is going well. It sounds like the classes are as great as ever.

I'd love if you're able to come along to the book launch on the 7th of September. There's a very short guest list that I've put your name on, but I completely understand if you're not able to make it. I just wanted to let you know that you've been very important to me as a teacher and whether you're there or not, it's something I'll be mentioning.

All the best,

Gillian

📞

To Clair

Fergus looked up at me with big eyes and asked me to ask his Auntie Clair if there was any chance we could go on a Botanics dog walk tonight… xx

✉

To Charlene

Hi Charlene,

It was lovely to see you today!

I was over at my parents' house this evening and they asked if they could pay for eight tickets for Beatson/clinical folk, which they've now purchased.

I'm very happy for you to give these to folks as you see fit and if there are any others, numbers permitting, I can add more tickets to accommodate.

I'd love if you invited my clinical team, in case any of them are able to make it.

With many thanks,

Gillian

🐦 **Tuesday, 22nd of August**

I just had a phlebotomy appointment in a bloods clinic that happened to be in the ward where I spent the night after both #breastcancer surgeries. It was for an unrelated, run-of-the-mill thing, so I thought it wouldn't be difficult. I was wrong. #AndBreathe #DrinkingCoffeeNow

Wednesday, 23rd of August

To Stephanie

Look what I have in my sticky paws... Stephen gave me some boxes so that I could sign the pre-ordered copies...

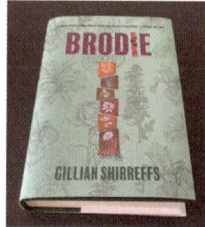

Friday, 25th of August

To Heather Suttie

Thanks so much for today, Heather. I really enjoyed talking with you and I will take your very good advice... always expect empathy.

I'm not sure if you're free on Thursday 7th of September, but if you are, I'd love if you came along to Brodie's book launch / our Beatson fundraiser in Oran Mor. We have a small guest list that I've put your name on, just in case. It's from 6pm until 10pm, but you could drop in at any point.

Thanks again!

Gillian

To Stephen

I was at Go Radio earlier recording a podcast with Heather Suttie, so your ears might have been burning... She's brilliant. I really enjoyed talking with her. I've just sent her an email saying she's on the guest list for the launch, if she can come along. Her podcast is called The Book Alchemist.

Sunday, 27th of August

To Stephen

Hi Stephen,

I hope you've had a good weekend. I've signed three boxes of books. I plan to keep going and get through the rest of the pre-orders by mid-week.

Thanks!

Gillian

To Stephen

I love signing books!

Wednesday, 30th of August

To Clare English

Hi Clare,

Thanks again for yesterday! I'm SO happy you're the MC.

I got an email from Charlene (Beatson Regional Fundraising Manager) to say that it will be their CEO, Martin Cawley, who'll be coming along to say a few words.

Gillian x

Thursday, 31st of August

To Stephen

I phoned Janice's producer after I sent the email and had a really nice conversation with her.

September 2023

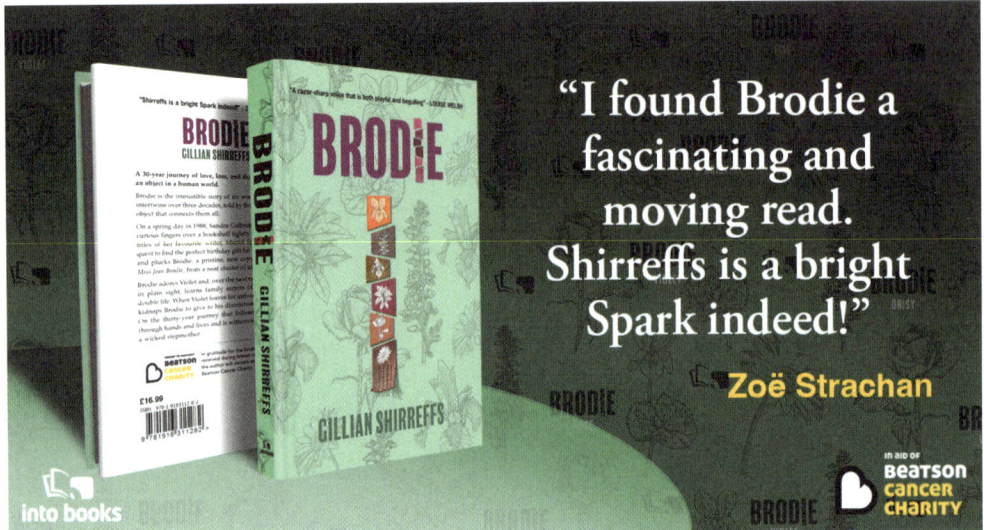

Friday, 1st of September

I'm so excited we're now in the month Brodie will be published. The last two Septembers I was in active treatment for breast cancer (my 1st chemo was Sept 2021; my 15th was Sept 2022). It feels great to have things like book launch and publication day in my calendar instead!

Saturday, 2nd of September

To Johanna

Thank you! I know Brodie's a wee bit heavy but if it makes it to Marrakesh, I'd LOVE a photo of my book on such an amazing adventure!! Did you open both copies…? I wrote a little something in the front of one of them… xxx

Sunday, 3rd of September

Delighted to be on the Afternoon Show tomorrow talking about #Brodie and @Beatson_Charity with the amazing @JaniceForsyth (also very nervous!).

BBC Radio Scotland - The Afternoon Show, 40 years of Taggart on TV, S...

bbc.co.uk

Monday, 4th of September

To Stephen

Brilliant! A BBC person just phoned to check I was still coming… while I was buying my mum and dad's paper and rolls…

To Clair

I'm on at 3.40pm. Just a wee bit terrified. xx

Thanks so much to the brilliant and very lovely @JaniceForsyth for having me on today. I loved speaking to you about Brodie (in real life). If anyone wants a listen, I'm on chatting about Brodie and the incredible @Beatson_Charity

To Misti

Launch Thursday! Official Publication Day Friday!

Here's a link to me on the radio… I'm at 2 hours and 11 minutes… x

Tuesday, 5th of September

To Jacqui

Thank you so much for my beautiful waistcoat. I love the flowers! That was incredibly thoughtful of you.

Looking forward to seeing you on Thursday!

Gillian xx

Wednesday, 6th of September

I'm so excited that Brodie has made it to Lochgoilhead and Marrakesh! #Brodie #BrodieInTheWild

Lochgoilhead

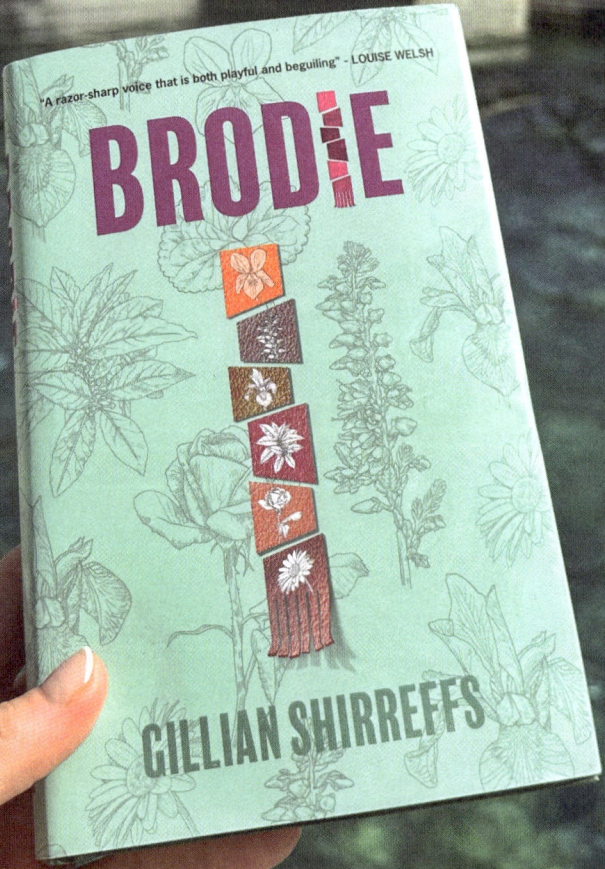

"A razor-sharp voice that is both playful and beguiling" - LOUISE WELSH

BRODIE

GILLIAN SHIRREFFS

Marrakesh!

✉️

Thursday, 7th of September

To Charlene

That's brilliant! I'm so glad Alice the Pharmacist will be there. Ronnie and I called her the "game changer" because after she got involved with me, every time my body decided it didn't like something, she figured out what to do.

I'm so pleased you'll all be there. I really want this to be a celebration of the brilliant work you do as much as anything else.

Gillian x

📞

To Stephen

Thank you SO much! I love my flowers and the beautiful Brodie paper! Please say thanks to Jan, too.

📞

Friday, 8th of September

To Stephen

EX-HAUSTED. Thank you so much for everything. You and Jan have been incredible and I'm very grateful.

To Stephen

I'm going to try to respond to the social media stuff after I've worked through the emails, texts and WhatsApps.

To Stephen

Brilliant! You deserve all the best writers to be queuing up to get in that boat! But don't forget me and my next one… please!

🐦

One of my favourite photos from last night. Me and my wee cousin. It's taken decades (and some chemo for me), but we now have the same hair. #CampsieCousins

Saturday, 9th of September

To Johanna

The launch was lovely and a bit overwhelming. xx

To Johanna

My surgeon and my nurses were there, which was very kind of them! xx

Thursday, 14th of September

To Charlene

Hi Charlene,

It's taken a week but I'm getting there. I've finally written a 'to do' list, so things must be back to normal.

Thanks again for all your help. If you ever need me to do anything, please just ask. I clearly love talking about what a wonderful charity Beatson Cancer Charity is!

Gillian x

Friday, 15th of September

To Zoe

Hi Zoe,

I hope you've had a good week.

Stephen would like to video an interview of me talking about Brodie in Caledonia Books. I'd love if you would be able to be the interviewer, if that's something you would be okay doing...? The owner has said we could do any Sunday from the 24th of September.

Very best,

Gillian x

I started chemo on the 16th of Sept 2021 (the first of 22 infusions that would be in my future). Today I am incredibly grateful to be two years on and walking along the lochside. Also very happy that Brodie is hanging out with me in beautiful Cove. #LochLong #Brodie

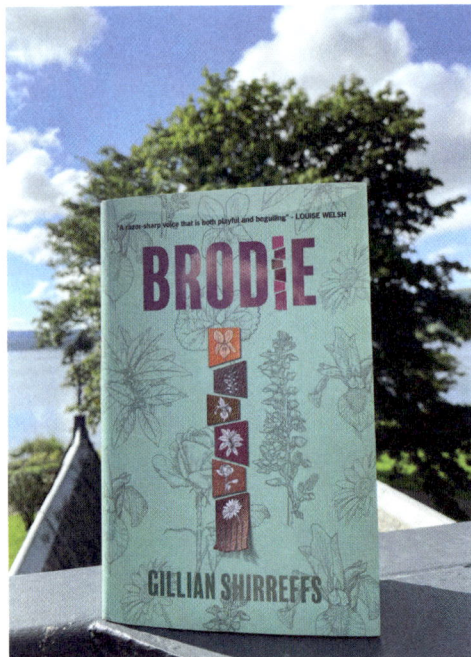

256